P9-CSG-396

Acclaim for Ethan Casey's previous book,
Alive and Well in Pakistan: A Human Journey in a Dangerous Time (2004)

"The author's real journey is a search for common humanity."
—*The Daily Telegraph*

"Casey plunges into Pakistan like a knife, unearthing and unraveling the often unexplainable and unpredictable contradictions of a country on the edge. Pakistan just happens to be one of the most complex and difficult countries to describe, but Casey does a magnificent job. Casey's prose sings, and his portraits are master class. A conjuror of images and sensations in an unpredictable land."
—Ahmed Rashid, author of *Taliban* and *Descent into Chaos*

"A delightfully penetrating read ... Casey brilliantly depicts the events and scenario in Kashmir in the 90s. ... He deftly weaves the dissonant perspectives and poisonous vocabularies partisans bring to matters of dispute in the subcontinent along with the simple voices and ideas and emotions of the common people."
—*The Tribune* (Chandigarh, India)

"*Alive and Well in Pakistan* is distinguished by its author's quest for honesty. Ethan Casey stubbornly refuses to embrace the grand theories of others or to indulge his own preconceptions. Instead, he gives us the insights of a singular, clear-eyed, and humane traveler. The result is an intelligent and compelling book."
—Mohsin Hamid, author of *Moth Smoke* and *The Reluctant Fundamentalist*

"Wonderful. What an incredible journey, a model of travel writing. So worldly yet personal. Given our current involvement in the region, it should be read by everyone."
—Edwidge Danticat, author of *Brother, I'm Dying*

"*Alive and Well in Pakistan* serves us well in rescuing the very ordinariness of life in Pakistan from the sensationalism and scare-mongering of self-interested pundits, the media, and even politicians."
—Munis D. Faruqi, *Harvard International Review*

MR. MACM DONATION 3/6/12

OVERTAKEN BY EVENTS

A Pakistan Road Trip

ETHAN CASEY

To Steve Rumsheep, fellow friend of Pakistan — *Ethan Casey, June 2010*

Valley Community Library
739 River Street
Peckville, PA 18452-2313

BLUE EAR BOOKS

First published in 2010 by
Blue Ear Books
P.O. Box 85315
Seattle, WA 98145-1315
USA
www.blueearbooks.com
info@blueearbooks.com

© Ethan Casey, Blue Ear Books
www.aliveandwellinpakistan.com

The right of Ethan Casey to be identified as the author of the work has been asserted by
him in accordance with the Copyright, Designs and Patents Act of 1988.

All rights reserved. No part of this publication may be reproduced, stored in a retrieval
system, or transmitted in any form or by any means, electronic, mechanical, photocopy-
ing, recording or otherwise, without prior written permission of the publisher.

ISBN: 978-0-9844063-0-2

Credits:
Book Design and Composition:
    Barbara Ann Swanson, Pica^2 Graphics, Colorado Springs, CO, www.pica2graphics.com
Cover Design:
    Jason Kopec, jkopec@ikgd.biz and www.ikgd.biz
Photographer:
    Pete Sabo, Seattle, WA, www.petesabophotography.com; pete@petesabophotography.com
Printer:
    Scott Morris, Morris Printing Services, Arkansas City, KS, www.morrisprint.com
Project Manager and Copyeditor:
    Sharon Green, Panache Editorial, Inc. Colorado Springs, CO, panache2004@msn.com
Website (www.aliveandwellinpakistan.com):
    Imran Arshad, while working as Senior Software Engineer for Zoniversal
    (www.zoniversal.com), Lahore, Pakistan. imran.arshad01@gmail.com

CONTENTS

Heading Home 1

Chapter 1   A New Narrative 3
Chapter 2   A Little Bit All Over The Place 57
Chapter 3   The Guy Who Kept Coming Back. 98
Chapter 4   Grand Trunk Road Trip 186
Chapter 5   Different Worlds. 229

Online Resources, Further Reading, Acknowledgments. . . 275
Map 279

Nothing is settled in Pakistan. ... Because the plot has yet to be resolved, the audience stays interested. Every small event may hold the key to the denouement.

Emma Duncan, *Breaking the Curfew*

He would always be one for whom the return was as important as the voyage out.

Ursula Le Guin, *The Dispossessed*

HEADING HOME

Zaka Shafiq was kind enough to drive us to the airport in Karachi. Zaka was a friend of a friend, a well-groomed, mild-mannered young business guy, still learning something I had never yet learned: how to look comfortable in a suit. At the tail-end of an exhausting six weeks, en route to the airport for our flight home, Pete and I had just squeezed in one last conversation, with a famously intense and prickly education reformer named Sami Mustafa.

"My objective in life is to be able to ask intelligent questions," Sami Mustafa had said. "And I will leave you with that advice. You will have achieved a lot, if you could only ask intelligent questions. Historically we're not asking the right questions."

We were impressed. "I only got one word: accountability," said Pete in the car. "And I see it here."

"Pakistanis like to argue," I observed to Zaka. "It's one of the things they do for fun."

"That's what makes this guy different," he said. "He'll argue with you, but then he'll go and crack a few knuckles too. He's blunt but effective, and that's what matters."

Zaka asked about the book I would be writing. I didn't want to think about it yet. I was heading back to my comfy little bike-friendly Seattle lifestyle, and I needed simply to be at home for a while. Spring was coming, there was gardening to be done, baseball was about to start. I wasn't yet ready for the writing. I knew already that it was bound to turn out like the trip itself: too much to try to squeeze in, too little time, too many distractions and commitments, too quickly overtaken by events.

I told Zaka what I had in mind.

"It'll be out of date by the time it's published," he said.

"If you write a book like that right," I said, "then the future events should echo back. I'd like people to be able to read it years from now and say, 'He saw that coming.' I also want it to be about the personality of this country."

"Oh dear," Zaka said.

CHAPTER 1

A NEW NARRATIVE

When history happens in a place you know personally, it messes with your head. I visited Haiti for the first of many times in 1982, as a teenager; when the crisis over Aristide and the Haitian boat people hijacked the world's front pages during the excruciating early months of the Clinton administration, I endured an agony of helplessness far away, in Bangkok. The place name Guantanamo Bay took on personal meaning for me then, as the place the U.S. Coast Guard took Haitians they intercepted fleeing to Florida. When the semi-revolution came to Kathmandu in 1990, it hit home because I had lived there as a student in the mid-1980s.

Those early experiences reinforced a predilection for taking history personally. Much water had yet to flow beneath the bridge in Haiti and Nepal, and in other places I traveled inflicting experience on myself: Burma, Cambodia, Zimbabwe, Detroit. During the later Bush years, I returned full circle and saw truths I had learned elsewhere at play in my own country. You keep going back to places where you've experienced history because you feel that, somehow, there's sense to be made of it. But when a place has been your home and something terrible happens there in your absence—well, it hits home.

So the feeling was familiar when Kurien walked into his flat in Mumbai and told Pete and me about the attack on the Sri Lankan cricket team in Lahore.

* * *

I had arrived sixteen years earlier in Bangkok seeking adventure, only to find myself stuck in an office job. I had not come to Asia to sit in an air-conditioned building copyediting other writers. So I quit the *Bangkok Post* newspaper and flew to Delhi. Like anyone, I could list proximate reasons for my life's turning points, but that would be beside the point. One thing I can say is that my choices reflect a willful streak. "Why do you always have to do things the hard way?" my father once lamented in exasperation, and I've always wondered at the answer to that.

It was all his fault, actually. "I didn't go as far afield as you guys did," he confessed to me once. "But I did feel the need to get out of town." He had gotten the hell out of Dallas at twenty-one because he considered it the sticks. I was even more stubbornly prodigal, and it wasn't until, now in my forties, at a church in suburban Denver where I had just spoken about Pakistan and he took me aside to say he was proud of me, that I felt I had finally accomplished something and earned the right to come home. It was far from the first time he had said those words, and he hadn't laid the burden on me; I had shouldered it willingly. But why?

My obsessive need to travel has been a lifelong search for home. Every other family in Wisconsin was German or Polish and five generations deep. Ours came from elsewhere, and was headed there too. In 1994, elsewhere was India. Leaving Bangkok, I visited what was then still called Bombay and other obligatory places and returned to Kathmandu. But I spent many weeks in Kashmir, at what turned out to be the height of the separatist uprising in the disputed region. It was my thin-skinned provincial's resentment of centers of power and attention that led me there and, eventually, to Pakistan. I didn't see why the presumption should go against the separatist Kashmiris either because they were Muslim or, less explicitly but no less pervasively, because they were weak and remote.

I first went to Pakistan in 1995, because I thought I was writing a book about Kashmir and felt fairness compelled me to see it from the Pakistani point of view. Before I knew it I had been there several times, for weeks each time. I spent a month there early in 1999, when Prime Minister Nawaz Sharif was becoming dangerously isolated and paranoid; I returned in June and July, when the Kargil crisis between Pakistan and India was coming to a head. When the army under General Pervez Musharraf seized power that October, I was unsurprised to the point of being relieved.

In early 2003, a Pakistani friend asked if I knew anyone who might want to spend a semester teaching in Lahore at the new Beaconhouse National University. I was living tenuously in England, bored again, seeking ways of escape from a failing relationship. The World Trade Center had been blown up, Pakistan seemed to have something to do with that, and why wouldn't I want to be there? Everything was said to have changed on September 11, 2001, but that couldn't be entirely true. I jumped at the chance, because it offered an opportunity to live for a sustained period in a society I had known previously only as a foreign news reporter, too briefly each time, at moments deemed newsworthy; because it would allow me to press pause on the hectic itinerant life of a freelance journalist, and to articulate to young students some of what I had learned about international reporting and about the world; and because I could bring my experience of Pakistan full circle, after a decade, by writing a book.

The book I wrote was a first-person travel narrative, not only because that was the kind of book I was able and willing to write, but because it's the kind of book that rarely gets written about Pakistan, and one I felt the country needed and deserved. Even as enraged "beardies" shouted in the streets and politicians alarmed the world with their brinkmanship, what about everything else that was happening in Pakistan? It's impossible to ignore politics when writing about Pakistan; nor is it always necessary to attack the political story head-on. So I made the contrarian decision to write about everything else and to let the politics seep in, as I knew it would.

I had first pitched a book about Pakistan in 1999, before the coup, to the London literary agent Gillon Aitken. "This is a cynical world, the more's the pity," he had responded. "There are very few people in it, outside the subcontinent, who give a damn about Pakistan." In retrospect I wasn't yet ready to write that book—which was just as well, because by 2003 a lot had changed. I arrived in Lahore on September 11 of that year, determined to notice and record whatever happened to happen, and confident that the slice of history I stumbled across would say something true and interesting. I went into the project with no governing theory or agenda, nor did I emerge with one. What I didn't want was to add to the perpetual torrent of mere commentary. I felt the most useful thing I could do was to dip my oar into the rapids of history at a promising-looking spot somewhere along the bank, ride them downstream wherever they might lead, and record whatever I found significant as coherently as I could manage.

I had intended the book as a summing-up (if not a full stop, then at least a semicolon); but since its publication in late 2004 it had been overtaken by events. I had other ambitions and interests, but Pakistan remained stubbornly in the public eye. After thirteen years overseas I came to Seattle, and Pakistani groups around the United States began inviting me to speak at fundraisers for the education and health projects they supported in Pakistan. My involvement with them, and Musharraf's distressing declaration of a state of emergency on November 3, 2007, led to plans to make a documentary film. In the meantime I began speaking to mainstream American audiences, but found myself admitting with chagrin that I had not been to Pakistan in three, four, five years. So here I was now, on my way back again.

As an American writer concerned with Pakistan, I took as my task not only to listen thoughtfully and respectfully to Pakistanis, but to translate or approximate their views in ways that enhance the understanding and enlist the sympathy of Americans. I mean human sympathy, not necessarily political sympathy, although they inevitably dovetail. That was the public aspect of my purpose in writing *Alive and Well in Pakistan*. But, just as I had privileged Pakistan because I believed other writers treated it as a distasteful and rustic sideshow to their pro-India predilections, now I must lean in the other direction. In the fourteen years since I had been to India, it had become a global presence too enormous to disregard. India also had been, very recently, the victim of a sinister and deadly attack launched from Pakistan: the sixty-hour siege of Mumbai that began on November 26, 2008. Now, I needed to listen with attention and sympathy to Indians, to hear what they had to say about Pakistan. And the two countries' connection was intimate to the point of being umbilical. Like it or not, it was wrong to write about one without writing about the other. Mumbai was where this trip needed to begin.

* * *

In the weeks before our arrival I had nailed down as many meetings as I could, knowing full well that planning such a trip fully and firmly was not only a fool's errand but a bad idea. Even an American business trip should be only about half planned, to allow for chance encounters and opportunities, and a six-week journey around the subcontinent is never going to go according to plan. I had many friends and contacts in Pakistan, but in India the trail had gone cold. In Mumbai in particular I knew almost no one. But my dread that we would show up, only to meet no one and learn nothing, was tantamount to a thrill of anticipation. And if we made too many contacts ahead of time, we wouldn't be able to meet them all anyway.

Kurien Abraham was a Syrian Christian from Kerala in South India, an editor at a TV channel specializing in business coverage, an affable bachelor in his early thirties, enjoying what seemed a carefree urban lifestyle out of a sparsely furnished little flat in a five-story building in the Santa Cruz East neighborhood near the airport. He had welcomed us with unceremonious hospitality, happy to share his floor for a week in return for our company. His desk job had rendered him a little pudgy, and his doctor had ordered him to exercise. So most mornings he went out, grumbling cheerfully, to spend an hour at the gym. This morning he returned a few minutes behind us, and we turned on the TV to watch the Breaking News coverage of the Lahore cricket attack.

"Was this an inside job?" asked the Times Now anchor. "This is an attack that raises many more fundamental questions. The most alarming thing about this encounter is that these terrorists were allowed to get away. How did they know in which of three buses the Sri Lankan team was traveling?"

Later we would speak to Pakistanis about what happened that day in Liberty Circle and, by the time we reached Lahore, some time had passed and the shock was wearing off. But our first, vicarious exposure to the incident was a blow.

Phrases assailed us through the screen: *dastardly incident* and *banana republic* and *security lapse of monumental proportions* and *the kind of pathetic security establishment you have in Lahore right now*. The anchor wondered "why the response to this attack has been so slow" and asked again: "Was this an inside job?"

"We have a few straight questions to ask here on Times Now," he said. "How is it that the Sri Lankan team's movement was known? What is presidential level security today in Pakistan? The attackers escaped in separate groups. What we want to ask the authorities in Pakistan is: Have any of these attackers been caught?"

"If there's one channel that wants to bomb Pakistan, it's that channel," Kurien told Pete and me. "It's a war-mongering channel. It's the Fox News of India." Times Now was owned by the Times of India Group and rated number one among news channels. "They're not actually right wing," explained Kurien. "They're very critical of the right-wing parties in India. They're sensational. Anything that

8

sells papers." The anchor we were watching, Arnab Goswami, was the head of Times Now. Kurien's friend Mahrukh worked for him.

On the screen now, Lahore police chief Haji Habibur Rahman was saying that the gunmen had come in an auto rickshaw with rocket launchers and grenades, and that they "looked like well trained." Lahore, said former Pakistan cricketer Zaheer Abbas, "is one of the best-policed cities in that part of the world."

"*Inshallah* the players might survive," said the police chief. God willing.

"He's trying to say the police sacrificed their lives," said Kurien. "In 26/11 they tried to say the same thing, that the police sacrificed their life. All the newspapers came out and said bullshit, the security was lax."

"26/11" was the catchy numerical shorthand that Indians were already using for the three-day siege of Mumbai three months earlier, when terrorists had come by boat from Pakistan, held hundreds hostage at the Taj and Oberoi five-star hotels and the city's main train station, and killed 163 people.

We were learning that, in Lahore, twelve masked gunmen had arrived in auto rickshaws, and firing had come from at least four sites. The terrorists were "running through the streets and firing on unidentified vehicles." It was, said Goswami, "so frighteningly and horrifyingly similar" to 26/11. In both cases the attackers were "back-packed" and "Kalashnikov-wielding." They had shot out the wheels of the Sri Lankan team's bus. "This is a well-planned attack. They tossed a grenade under the bus. It just didn't explode. We could have had a monumental attack. There was a raging gun battle in which the players were trapped. One explosion was heard inside the stadium."

Several loud explosions had been heard nearby. Six players from the Sri Lankan team had been injured, two hospitalized. The batter and off spinner Thilan Samaraweera was said to have been shot in the chest and was being operated on in a hospital somewhere in Lahore.

"It is difficult to see how this tour can go on," declared the Sri Lankan president's office. "An official statement will be forthcoming in the next few hours." The team was being recalled to Colombo immediately.

"They are stable," claimed a Pakistani official. "They are all right. There is no damage to any of our honorable guests."

"Imran Khan says that cricketers and sportsmen are safe in Pakistan," sports correspondent Guru Ezekial told Goswami, naming the Pakistani cricket legend and politician. "I would appreciate it if your channel would get in touch with Mr. Imran Khan."

"This was supposed to be an Indian tour at this point in time," Goswami noted darkly.

"All the parents are worried," said a Sri Lankan sports journalist named Mr. Rodrigo.

"Do you think Pakistan is a safe place to play, even after an incident such as this?" Goswami asked Sanath Jayasuriya, a former captain of the Sri Lankan team.

"Actually, we are shocked," Jayasuriya answered. "We have never gone through this sort of thing before."

("He's one of the most formidable batsmen ever," Kurien told us.)

"We don't have the identity of even one of the people who attacked. And this is Lahore," said Goswami. Meaning this is a major city, not Pakistan's scary hinterlands. "The route was supposed to be sanitized; it wasn't. The bus was supposed to be bulletproof; it wasn't. This was not the Pakistani team; it was the Sri Lankan team."

"This is yet another wake-up call," K.C. Singh, former secretary of India's Ministry of External Affairs, said, pointing out that Shahbaz Sharif, Chief Minister of Pakistan's dominant Punjab province and brother of Nawaz Sharif, had just been forced out of office in a move many saw as orchestrated by President Asif Ali Zardari. The Sharif brothers' Punjab-based Pakistan Muslim League (Nawaz) party, Singh argued, "occupies the main center-right space" in Pakistani politics. "It's a very, very dangerous vacuum that's been created at the center of Pakistani life. I think America needs to stop supporting President Zardari, and stop pushing the Sharif brothers into a corner."

Riffing on that theme, Goswami called Lahore "the epicenter of the political free-for-all in Pakistan right now."

The *coup de grace* was that Pakistan was to have hosted the 2011 Cricket World Cup. "You cannot have that planned in what is obviously a banana republic situation now in Lahore," Goswami declared with finality.

* * *

Pete and I left the apartment after about an hour. "Well," he said in the stairwell, "you signed up for an adventure."

Pete Sabo was a Seattle friend who was proving an ideal travel companion. He was middle-aged, lean and bearded, self-contained and taciturn, not to say curmudgeonly; he had grown up one of ten kids in a Catholic family in a town called Lancaster in the desert in Southern California. He now lived with his cat and poison dart frog in a house in Seattle's Ballard neighborhood, which he owned free and clear because he was frugal and earned good money as a molecular biologist in a lab owned by the University of Washington. He owned a fifteen-year-old Ford pickup truck with a rack for his kayaks, but he commuted by bike. He owned lots of tools, knew how to use them, and shopped at Goodwill. When my fiancee, Jennifer, had lived across the street from him, he had let her use his washer and dryer and she had helped plant and trim his garden. Since we had moved to a different neighborhood, he was our most frequent dinner guest and helped me build a set of raised vegetable beds—or, rather, I helped him build them. His truck was always available to us to haul dirt or furniture, and he donated a day of his life to helping me install insulation in our attic. Jenny and I called him Uncle Pete.

Pete was chronically bored and disgruntled with his job, but whenever he threatened to quit, his boss countered by raising his salary. The understanding they had reached was that Pete took time off without pay, more or less at will, to go on long trips. What bothered him most about the job was that he didn't consider it very useful to humanity or the planet; it bugged him to spend most of his waking hours doing work that, at least in certain moods, he considered pointless. He was a very good amateur photographer and had beautiful pictures from places like Alaska and Costa Rica. Wild places were his element, and his eye sought out animals and landscapes. A couple of years earlier he had spent a month hiking across Madagascar, photographing lemurs. The chaotic, overcrowded subcontinent was not his natural habitat, but he was curious and up for an adventure, and he had volunteered to join me on this six-week trip and to bring along his camera and digital audio recorder.

"Yeah, Ethan and I been zippin' around all over the place in those things," I overheard him telling Jenny on a Skype call a few days after our arrival, meaning auto rickshaws. "Yeah, just like on *Amazing Race*. Gotta go here, gotta go there."

It was with a sick feeling in my gut that I left Kurien's flat. I knew the attack's exact location well. Liberty Circle was a major roundabout along Gulberg Main Boulevard, between the horseshoe-shaped Liberty Market and Gaddafi Stadium, site of major international matches and the national cricket training center. I had thoroughly enjoyed a Pakistan v. South Africa Pepsi Cup one-day match at Gaddafi Stadium in September 2003. I had sat in the cheap seats, ignored advice to hide my nationality, and basked in the hospitality and generous if intrusive friendship of the Pakistani common man. An earnest young teacher named Mohammed Faisal had come that day from his village, with twenty of his friends in the bed of a Toyota pickup, to see his first big-league cricket match, and had attached himself to the only white man in the general enclosure. When I asked if he played cricket back home, he replied: "Very eagerly! In our village, despite not having a good ground, our team is always a winner in internal tournaments, regional tournaments." He had protected me from the importunings of rowdies and apologized for their boorish enthusiasm, and patiently explained the game's finer points. When the match was over, he had put his hand on his heart and made a little speech: "It was you who made our journey memorable. At first I didn't know what you would speak to us. I was a bit shy. But you speak to us very nicely. In my village I have no one I can speak English with."

At Liberty Market, I had browsed at Variety Books and bought cream puffs at Shezan Bakers & Confectioners. "Eat as soon as possible," the clerk advised me. "Cream maybe melt." It was Liberty Market I had gone to early in my five-month stay in Lahore in 2003–04 to regain my bearings after more than four years away, and it was there that the fumes and noise and neon of an Asian rush hour had reactivated my nostalgia and reminded me happily of youthful adventures from Manila to Calcutta to Peshawar and above all Bangkok, a city I had hated for five years but then missed when I moved to an English suburb where nothing much ever happened. Across the street from Liberty Market I had been fitted for a tailor-made suit. The charmingly named Groom & Bride Shop was a landmark on the circle. Just past the roundabout was Askari Bank, where the university had deposited my salary. I had strolled through the market one evening in October 2003 and soaked in the conviviality of *iftar*, the moment when the fast is broken at dusk during Ramadan, as little knots of people sat and ate together on the grass in the glow of the shop signs.

I remembered all of this now, grimly. The image Times Now had played was of those "backpacked," Kalashnikov-wielding terrorists, moving in ominous black-and-white slo-mo through Liberty Circle, incessantly, as if it really were happening over and over again.

In the rickshaw my heart was heavy, because I realized that I had no right to ask Pete to go with me to Pakistan. For me, not going was not an option. During my Bangkok years in the mid-1990s, a journalist friend had said: "All you can really do is be a witness." But does that do any good? It depends on what counts as good. I felt I had to go, to be a witness and to make and feel a human connection, however painful. When I was younger I had traveled recklessly. Now, chastened, I couldn't count on visiting Pakistan again with pleasure or enthusiasm. But I did have to visit again.

It was to attend the mahurat or launching ceremony for a Bollywood film about the Mumbai siege that we had had to tear ourselves away from the cricket attack coverage on Times Now. The function was taking place in a ballroom on the lower level of the Marriott hotel near Juhu Beach, with a generous buffet in the adjoining lobby. The movie's title was *Deshdrohi 2: 26/11 War in Mumbai*. "Maybe you will get to meet some Bollywood stars," said one of the front desk clerks, with a cheery head-wobble. "Get some autographs for me!" said the other.

"It's a thriller," I overheard the director, Sanjay Jha, saying to a cluster of reporters in the milling crowd as we walked in. We had met him a few days earlier at a private home. "It involves lot of people. It's non-linear storytelling. Contemporary subject, terror attack. It just happened in Pakistan. So it's like that."

A young woman asked a question I didn't catch.

"I don't think so," responded Jha. "It's a democratic country. You can make your films on anything that inspires you. It's a piece of fiction."

"Any fear of the bigger context?"

"No, no. I think it's a fearless film. And we're just making it. Thank you."

"It's hard to tell," said Pete. "Are the attractive women just wives of the directors, or are they movie stars?" He wandered off with his camera, while I hovered at the edge of another bunch of reporters surrounding a beautiful young actress in an elegant red gown.

14

"Yeah, very sensitive," she was saying. "My director, Sanjayji, he's researched everything, and I'm going to completely follow him. This film has a fairly good message, that you will come to know when you see the film, and I want to do something for my country, and it's a treat to work with Sanjayji. He's a very passionate director."

I caught Sanjay's eye. He was a likeable, enthusiastic guy with an artsy pony-tail and a big, toothy grin. He greeted me and said: "Now you will wait and watch. Function has not yet begun. And later there are few people I would like you to talk to."

Some more reporters buttonholed him. "Connection is contemporary issues," he told them. "I see a great connection of taking up subject of contemporary issue and trying to portray. The title says it all at the moment. Now we have a big journey ahead."

"Which newspaper?" a small woman holding a microphone asked me.

"I'm writing a book," I said. She smiled.

"You can't think of a film just for controversy," said Sanjay. "It leads to certain kind of journey. There it happens."

"So how much is going to be real?" a reporter asked.

"It is going to be fiction, for sure. Realities will be stylized for sure, but it is going to be based on a lot of facts."

* * *

The man at whose home I had met Sanjay took my elbow and introduced me to Mahesh Bhatt, a senior and controversial Bollywood director, producer, and screenwriter. "People here say he's a pro-Pakistan. Like you," he added with a laugh. I sat on a couch with Bhatt and talked amid the hullabaloo. He was gray-haired and wore a light blue denim shirt with the tail hanging out, and had a hawk nose and a rather severe countenance.

"You have a reputation for being sympathetic to Pakistan," I said.

"Cordial, warm, friendly ties with Pakistan is in the interest of India, and vice versa," he replied.

"Do you feel that your work serves that goal?"

"Well, I think so," he said. "We've begun with that intention, and we've come a long way. We've achieved through the movies the last five years more than our predecessors achieved in the last fifty years. And we did create, through the performing arts, the people-to-people contact which has contributed to at least the atmospherics and created a feeling of well-being—which has evaporated after 26/11, after the attack."

"What do you think is going to be the effect of the events in Lahore today?"

"It will deepen the feeling of despair in Pakistan, and helplessness that the leaders of this region are already engulfed in. Because I don't think anybody has a recipe. That includes the black man in the White House and the leaders of South Asia. I don't think we have a thoughtful leader who can navigate us through this dark night in which we have descended."

"How does an artist like yourself respond to that? Do you have any vision for the kind of film or films that you might make on this kind of subject?"

"If movies and books could change this world, this world would be a paradise. I have no delusion. Cinema has a very limited role to play. But it is a glue to bring people together, to which the demonization which we have done about each other kind of recedes in the background. Because before you assault the so-called enemy state, the nation in which you live makes it a point to structure a persona which makes the person look subhuman. Only then will you give them the kind of approval to badger the daylights out of them, like you did in the United States of America. Prior to the attack in Afghanistan and Iraq, there was a kind of demonizing of people of the region which made the American people look the other way. And then through very clever tools of control, they made sure that the images of the barbarism came back home."

"Do you think that can be changed in America now, under the new administration?"

"I wonder. I don't think even America, in spite of the happy ending that you have superimposed on this tragic situation, is really going to look unflinchingly at what you have done over the last eight years to the world."

"Americans have a habit of superimposing happy endings on any story," I suggested.

"That's what an average man wants. He wants fairy tales to lull him to sleep."

"Do you feel that Obama's election was that?"

"I think that the American dream of a black man in the White House is a yarn that the young people of America made into a concrete reality. That is not to take away the charm and the charisma of the man. He has a charm, he has a charisma. But what is the magic wand that he can flash and resolve the problem? A nation which has supported a war of demonic proportions had it coming. You are the architects of doom of the human race. No power is going to reverse it. What you have started, you cannot reverse now. Even the Second World War was supposed to be a good war. Look what happened: It led to the catastrophe of Nagasaki and Hiroshima. This war was the so-called War against Terror, against those values which you say are barbaric. And repeated through tools of mass distraction, amplifying to the world that your vision is the sanest vision and the most civilized, the most humane vision. How? By censoring? By buying people off? By getting wordsmiths to work on your payroll? Bush's America was far more dangerous than Hitler's Germany."

"In what way?"

"Look at the magnitude of destruction. You've not even begun to finish a body count."

"Do you think there's any potential for American people to face that honestly?"

"I don't think so, as of now. As of now there's a euphoria of getting the slum kids onto the Oscar dais and putting the black man in the White House."

"You're very popular in Pakistan."

"So I hear."

"To what do you attribute that?"

"Movies, my presence as an entertainer. And my movies which have unhesitantly attacked the right-wing Hindu forces. I come from a shared heritage: My father was a Hindu Brahmin, my mother Muslim, brought up in a Christian school. I am a post-independence Indian who was really shaped by those secular values. So for me it's a physical reality, not an ideology which I embrace and put it on center stage to win awards. It's a palpable, physical truth. So Pakistan is something which I've never been phobic about. I have not been scared of the Islamic heritage. It's part of my heritage. I can't blame the whole of myself by denying a part of myself, which both the nations were stupid to do. There's a current of five thousand years which runs through this region, which cannot be divided. You cannot tear apart that similarity by structuring lines and having different currencies, having a different national anthem. We're pathetically similar. And I don't see any attempts of ours succeeding in the direction of getting us to wage war. The father of my nation, Mahatma Gandhi, said one thing very clearly which the nation needs to hear very clearly: the Indian nation and the Congress Party in particular, which makes a living off marketing Gandhi. He said, 'If there is no accord between India and Pakistan, this region will be in the vortex of fire. It'll be a hellhole.'"

"He was prophetic," I said, stating the obvious.

"You have to understand that you have come to that point in history where you cannot hurt the other without hurting yourself. You need a new narrative."

"What's the seed of that new narrative?"

"In the simple, profound truth of the father of the nation, who fell to a right-wing force in my country, 'This region can only be at peace if there is a cordial, warm, friendly relationship between the people of this country—Hindus and Muslims—and between India and Pakistan.'"

"Gandhi's not very popular in Pakistan," I pointed out. "Why is that?"

"Gandhi is not even popular in India. Even the Congress people don't live his creed. In fact, he's a convenient icon to bring out and use as a vote-capturing magnet. You've put a monument up to him at every street corner. But to live Gandhi, you have to understand what he lived and died for. Because he was perceived as being overly sympathetic towards Pakistan, he was shot."

A few days earlier I had met Tushar Gandhi, the Mahatma's great-grandson. I found him an interesting and admirable man in his own right: proud of his great ancestor's legacy, and a spokesman for it, but not smothered or overwhelmed by it. A few weeks earlier he had met Martin Luther King III, who had come to India on the fiftieth anniversary of his father's visit. "It was pretty nostalgic," he told me. "And it was very great for my self-esteem and my pride in my legacy." Plump and jolly and friendly, in shorts and a loose polo shirts and sandals, he wore little round Gandhi glasses, a beard, and long, curly, hippyish hair. If you subtracted a bit from his jowls, I thought there was a resemblance. He demurred and told a self-deprecating story about a visit to a kindergarten, where a youngster had piped up: "Teacher, don't lie. He's a wrestler, he's not Gandhi's great-grandson!"

It was diffidently that I presumed to ask Tushar Gandhi what the Mahatma would have said and done were he alive today, but he answered without hesitation. "He thought there were two great tragedies, and if he had lived he would have loved to address both," he said. "One was the partition of India. He would have loved to dismantle that. Even if not in political or geographical terms, in terms of reestablishing the bonds between the people. He may not have bothered about the borders of the political entities of the two nations. But he would definitely have attempted to create a bond of affection between the two peoples so strong that the borders would have become inconsequential. After having done that, I believe he would have addressed the other crime that has been committed against another set of people. And that is, he would have wanted to intervene in Israel and Palestine. And he would be attempting to have a very serious dialogue with bin Laden. He would also be attempting to be in Swat, trying to reason with the Taliban."

"Having seen the timid people of the political class, and even of my fraternity," Mahesh Bhatt was saying now, "the only way they have succeeded in shielding themselves from the wrath of the fundamentalists is to pretend to be jingoistic towards Pakistan. That kind of tribalism. 'Bring me the head of the other tribe.' Only then will you be looked upon as patriots. That is why peace activists are an absolute minority. Yes, I understand, it's dangerous to be right when most of the people are wrong. But you have to stand up and look at history. People who have spoken of revenge have found themselves comfortable in a lot of crowds. But people who have spoken of peace, whether it was Martin Luther King, Gandhi, Christ ..."

"They were all assassinated," I observed.

"Why? Because they were committed to peace."

"There's been a renaissance in artistic things in Pakistan in recent years," I said. "Maybe not so much film, but certainly music and literature. Do you see that as a source of hope?"

"The creative epicenter is now going to be Pakistan," he said. "Because it's a region which is going through turmoil. The young people are very bright. They have the emotional syntax which is common to this region, and they have an outward gaze, and they are rooted to their soil. And they are repressed. Art really blooms in a repressive regime. And the glib democracy of my nation, all the proclamations that we keep on making that we are a free society, is pale in comparison to the voice of those young people who are really hoping to introduce democracy in their country."

"Did Zia do a lot of damage?" Zia ul Haq, Pakistan's military dictator from 1977 to 1988, cooperated closely with the U.S. war against the Soviet Union in Afghanistan.

"Zia was the face," he said. "And America assisted Zia. So the land of the free and the land of the brave was in cahoots with the demonic Zia."

"Are you prepared to consider filming in Pakistan?"

"Yes. I had structured a plan for them, through which I said that an Indian can go to Switzerland, he can go to Bangkok, he can go to Hong Kong. It's a tragedy that he doesn't go to Lahore or Karachi. When you have the workforce which is like ours, you have a skilled industry there, and cost-wise it's very, very cheap. But these are psychological distances; the distances are in our heart. But I think when you hit the rock bottom, that's when you need to whip up the desire for what is possible, for what we can be."

"You were in Lahore last week. What were you doing there?"

"I was in Lahore, and I was in Islamabad with the peace delegation post-26/11, to find out for ourselves, by ourselves, without the interpretation of the government machinery, which was more interested in keeping their old super-narrative going that all the problems originate from Pakistan, and the media which had joined even more vigorously and more aggressively in marketing that position. What was appalling to me was the English electronic media in particular, which was looked upon as people who will give perspectives in insane times. They joined beating the war drums. So we went to find out for ourselves. We met opinion makers, we met leaders, we met peace activists, and we discovered that it's a nation which is at war with itself. It is a divided house. Civil society is aware of the doom that awaits them. It's kind of inching from Swat; it's on the outskirts of Lahore."

"Well, as of this morning it's not inching anymore," I said. "It's in Lahore."

"They are already rounding up those guys who attacked the Sri Lankan cricket team," he informed me. "In fact, one very responsible journalist, Hamid Mir, very brave individual, when he interviewed me for the Geo this morning, said that this is a repercussion of your brave attempts to talk about peace again. He said, 'Your peace delegation had just come, and this is the aftershocks of your peace attempts.'" Geo is the most prominent of several bold commercial news channels launched in Pakistan during the early years of Musharraf's rule. "The irony is that any attempt of the Pakistani establishment to forge friendly, non-confrontational ties makes India vulnerable to terror attacks. Because it's too obvious: there are forces which do not want this region to be peaceful."

"I'm going to be in Lahore in a couple of weeks. Do you have any advice to me?"

"My advice is stay safe. Because we people almost believe we are invisible people, or we have a bulletproof jacket which protects us. One has been pathological in case of danger. I bet you have that streak."

The ceremony began, with much razzmatazz. "Ladies and gentlemen, I request you make absolute silence," said the emcee. "The moment we've all been waiting for—the *mahurat* of *Deshdrohi 2!*" The emcee stood onstage with a microphone, surrounded by the film's cast, before a huge poster showing the dome of the Taj hotel in flames. "*26/11: War in Mumbai*," he intoned in a dramatic voice. "A film which has heart. A film which is going to have soul." And then, over the prevailing hubbub: "Ladies and gentlemen, will you *please* take your seats! You will have ample opportunities with the celebrities who are here. In the meanwhile, the legendary

22

filmmaker Mr. Mahesh Bhatt will do the honors for the *mahurat* for *Deshdrohi 2.*"

Mahesh Bhatt strolled onstage with one of those striped wooden boards. Looking as though he had done this many times before, he performed the "clapping" and said: "*Deshdrohi 2, mahurat,* all the best." Then actors portraying a policeman and Azam Amir Kasab, the lone accused terrorist to have survived the siege, enacted a scene. "Do you think one Kasab can harm India?" the cop asked the young man sternly in Hindi. "No! Even all of Pakistan put together cannot harm India!" The crowd applauded.

Pete was bemused by the whole thing. "Not my kind of photography," he said when I caught up with him. "This is trash photography. And the pictures aren't gonna look good, because there are so many flashes goin' off."

"But from our point of view, these photos are documentation," I said.

"Yeah," he agreed with a shrug.

Onstage, there was much gushing. "As a filmmaker it's a challenge, it's a very sensitive issue," said Sanjay.

"Yeah, yeah, very excited," said the actor Siddharth Koirala. "I wanted to work with Sanjay." The actor playing Kasab was a Muslim named Aslam Khan. "And I hope that it's going to be only the film shots that will be coming to me," he joked.

"You are part of the Indian fraternity," the emcee assured him. "And you are loyal to it. I can feel that."

"It's enough. It is the high time," declared an intense-looking bald man. I think he was speaking rhetorically to either terrorists or Pakistanis. "You just shut up. This is our time now."

"Are you going to be as glamorous in the film as you are on stage right now?" the emcee asked one of the actresses.

"I think not, because I will be playing a reporter in the film," she answered.

"I play the love interest of one of the soldiers," explained the actress in the red dress.

When the ceremony was over, the mingling began in earnest. I got some food, sat with Pete for a while, then had a long conversation with Sanjay Jha. "When do you expect the film to be out?" I asked him.

"That will happen in October–November," he said.

"That's around the time of the anniversary," I noted. "And how long does it take to make?"

"I will shoot fifty days. I have just made a film called *Mumbai Chaka Chak*, that deals with the cleanliness. That is the story of a sweeper, you know, a road cleaner, and he has a dream to clean the city. He is the most weakest man on the street, cleaning the street."

"That's a great story. Do you worry about the ideological or political dimension, or getting attacked from different sides, when this film comes out?"

"Yes, I do. And let me tell you, I think producers will take mileage. For me it will be not very exciting. Because in this country now, trend has come that anybody wants to take a controversy by creating a subject, or by creating an angle for a film. That is not required to do as a filmmaker. It's a democratic country, we have rights of expression, we can tell a story. I would make an honest film, I would make a political thriller. What is exciting me to do this film is that I'll get to say a story in a genre in which I have not said it before. I have never made a thriller. I have made one comedy, I have made one travelogue, I have made one very stylized realistic film. And now this is a political thriller. And it deals with a reality."

"It's a lot of responsibility," I suggested.

"It's a sensitive issue. What else a filmmaker needs?"

"This is a golden opportunity," I agreed.

"Yes. And if it's a kitsch work, if it's a very popular work, pulp work, then it's a journey for me. I'm definitely achieving some truth. You know? It's some truth I'm exploring."

"People ask me a lot, 'Why Pakistan?'" I confided to him. "Why is it that I've given so much of my attention to Pakistan? And I don't have a good answer. I don't know. And that's part of the truth. I needed to learn things that I could learn in Pakistan."

"But now, all of a sudden, you know what it is meaning!" he said. "Today there was an attack, and that was a very sad attack. While we were talking, after we spoke, that news started flashing. And I was thinking of you. Pakistan is going to be in little troubled water, because now there will be strong reactions. Diplomatically, they will be very weak. They'll have to answer a lot of things. Because it was the Sri Lankan team. It's not an Indian team there."

"It could have been the English team, or the Australian team," I said.

"Or an Indian team. Any team, that's not important. The importance is that they couldn't protect them. The state couldn't protect them."

"This incident actually freaks me out more than anything has," I confessed. "Even the Marriott bombing." I meant the devastating truck bombing of the iconic Marriott Hotel in Islamabad, the previous September. "The Marriott bombing really alarmed me. For several days I was really freaked out by the Marriott bombing."

"But this one is not normal," he said. "Nobody is comfortable with this. In the country there will be a lot of people who will be very ashamed. America, I don't know what they will do. It shows how uncontrolled they are."

"I've had several personal experiences in that market," I told him. "I sat in the general enclosure with the common man. I sat there for eight hours, watching that match. Gaddafi Stadium is part of my world, because I've been there."

"How are you feeling?" he asked. "I mean, it's surrealistic, you know? Similarly, the street story, which I told you, of a guy who sweeps, all the locations which were attacked, I have shot. All the locations. It's there in my film. I know how absurd it was. I was sitting at home and watching. I said, 'What is this?'"

"And how am I going to feel," I wondered aloud, "next time I'm there?"

* * *

I had met Kurien Abraham through my friend Ambreen Ali, who had done an internship in India the previous summer. Ambreen to me represented the best of what the younger generation of Pakistani-Americans could become and achieve, with lessons on both sides of that hyphen. She had grown up in the Bay Area and in Seattle, where her parents still lived. Ambreen had earned a master's degree in journalism at Northwestern University and interned at the *Seattle Post-Intelligencer*, then spent a summer at the AFP wire service in Delhi. She and a few others I knew were venturing beyond the customary confines of the Pakistani community in the United States, which tended to urge its children into safely lucrative careers like medicine. To me Ambreen was not only a Pakistani pioneer, but an American starting a career in journalism at a time when to do that at all, whatever your background, required unusual measures of imagination, courage, and motivation. My own career had begun just before the Internet transformed all media. Surviving that sea change had been disrupting and disorienting to me; my role models and points of reference were all from a past that to members of Ambreen's generation was ancient history. What could it mean to them, for example, to be a foreign correspondent? Ambreen would be among those whose work would redefine what a career in journalism could be.

Her relationship to both countries was ambivalent. "I struggle with this concept of feeling connected to Pakistan," she confessed during a long conversation over lunch a few months before my trip. "But every time I go there, I have a return ticket. I'm an outsider." She had visited Pakistan the previous year but had enjoyed India more. "I'm one of the Pakistanis who got to escape," she said bluntly. "My cousins look at me and say, 'What are you going to do for me?' And the whole country looks at its expatriates that way. There's something about the Pakistani community: It's very capitalist, and I don't know why. There's not a sense of collective responsibility. There's a sense that not all of us can be saved, so it's not worth trying. It's almost better than here, though, where you can drive your SUV on the highway and never know that you've driven past a ghetto. And sometimes I'm sickened by myself and my own desire to realize a world that might never exist."

Ambreen sat on the board of a group called South Asian American Leaders of Tomorrow (SAALT). "There's not a difference between a Pakistani cab driver and an Indian cab driver," she argued. "They're being used by this economy in the same way. But even the word 'South Asian' is very politicized. Nobody calls themselves South Asian unless they're part of that movement to call themselves South Asian. It's a political word. It means, 'Let's forget those national identities.' But there's the mistrust. And the politics back home matter so much."

Although she had grown up in America, she didn't feel fully at home there either. "Many parents bring their kids to a new context and then freak out," she said, "and I'm a product of that. I might become American, God forbid. As an immigrant, I never imagined that there were white Americans that were interested in getting to know their roots. One day I hope that my great-grandkids will have that luxury, of not caring where they came from. I don't have that luxury, having grown up in the '90s and having my early adulthood shaped by 9/11. The president told me that I was either with him or with them." It was after September 11, 2001 that Ambreen began exploring her identity. "I started asking who I was: If I wasn't American, what was I?"

I asked if she was religious.

"No," she said.

"Was that a problem for you within the family or the community?"

"Not anymore. For a long time it was, because I was striving to become more religious. When I was fourteen or fifteen I decided to wear the hijab, I prayed five times a day. I read the Quran, from my own motivation. But over the years I've come to peace with the fact that I'm comfortable with my confusion."

But she knew that within her community, her position was awkward at best. "A lot of Jews I know eat pork," she said, a little defensively. "But they will never not say they're Jewish. Being Muslim is an identity in that way. It's all about trying to ground yourself in something. In some ways, Pakistani Muslims are losing Pakistanis to the Muslim cause. There's a tension between your cultural and religious identities, when you're in this country."

Ambreen and her fiance, Bilaal, were planning their wedding, and she had declined promising job offers in both India and Pakistan to make her first home with him in Washington, DC. She found herself "grappling with what an accident everything is—in my life, and in Pakistani history. It's hard to deal with the world being guided by random chance. I really hope my kids understand what an accident it is that they're American. There's a profound sort of wisdom that comes from understanding what that means. It's a small world, and it's becoming smaller. And I don't want them to get stuck in being provincial."

I was fond and admiring of Ambreen, and she had thrived during her summer in India, so I was eager to meet anyone she recommended. "She loved it here," Kurien told me. "She kept comparing it to Pakistan."

I was interested in Kurien's perspective not only as a journalist and a religious minority, but as a South Indian. He compared India to a very dysfunctional family. "This is not a happy union," he said. "If you go to Tamil Nadu, you'll see it's very remote from Kashmir. Tamils openly say that India was an idea that was forced upon them." In his home state of Kerala, "thirty percent of the population is Muslim.

It's almost equally distributed: Muslims, Christians, and Hindus. Most of the big literary writers are Muslim. So the anti-Muslim feeling isn't there. And you don't suffer because of being a minority."

The prevailing attitude toward Pakistan in South India, he said, was, "'Oh, that's a country that we fought two wars with. And there's a problem in Kashmir.' But it doesn't really affect you. Even in the independence struggle, to a great extent South India was removed. You grew up feeling removed from it. My father never spoke about Pakistan. If there's any feeling against Pakistan in Kerala, it's because a lot of Keralites have worked in the Middle East, and most of the racketeers in the Middle East are Pakistanis. The educated Pakistanis would go to the West; the lower-level labor force goes to the Middle East. My dad really dislikes the Pakistanis, because he had to work with some of them. They're a little arrogant, according to my dad, because they enjoy a little more freedom in the Middle East because they're Muslim.

"Bombay has its own Muslim community," he added. "The issue with Pakistan started with the '93 blasts, when people started listening to the right-wing parties. Otherwise, there wasn't any problem. After '93 they started wearing their identity on their sleeves. If you see them on the street and interacting, you wouldn't know there was a problem. But when you get to an apartment block, there's a little bit of a fear psychosis. And it's not only Hindus. There was a Catholic woman I was supposed to take a house from. And she said, 'I'm willing to let the house to anyone but a Muslim.' And being a journalist, I asked her why. And she said, 'You just never know.'" Kurien seemed pretty comfortable with the state of things, though. "The fact is that this is a free country, and you are never made to feel that you are a minority. I can do anything that anyone else can."

"Do you think this has a lot to do with the fact that Hinduism has a large number of gods?" asked Pete.

"It's not really a religion," said Kurien. "Hindus don't understand Islam; they just don't get it. It's written in the book that you're supposed to go and spread your religion. Hindus just don't get that. They're like, 'Why?' They just don't get theological religions, and they never will. Here the real group that's insecure is not the Christians or the Muslims. It's the Hindus. A Christian or Muslim can walk into any institution and get the same kind of education, with government funding. So there's a feeling that, 'We're being fucked in our own country.'"

"Do you sympathize with that feeling?"

He laughed. "The fact is that I've had it easy," he said.

Kurien had worked in Kashmir for a previous employer. "I wasn't prepared to go to Kashmir," he said. "I just walked into the office and they said, 'Go.' Because things were heating up. I didn't know what to expect."

He was twenty-four at the time, in 2002. "I've covered really bad encounters, and I thought it was too early in my career for me to see such things," he said. "This was my first year, and my Hindi was very bad. I used to get my cameraman to ask them questions." Based initially in Delhi, Kurien had been sent to the lowland city of Jammu for three weeks, then to areas near the Line of Control, the de facto border.

"So why did your editor send you there, if you didn't have any Hindi?"

"I guess he thought it would be easier to control me," he said. "The problem was that I was sent there to get stories about good things that the army was doing. The standard question you're supposed to ask is, 'Why is your life so miserable?' And they're supposed to answer that it's because of Pakistan, because they're shelling. But if you ask them honestly, they'll say it's because of both sides. You can't go on like that. But I've learned that most of reporting is like that: You try to get them to say what you want them to say. Kashmir shapes you in terms of what kind of journalist you want to become. You're forced to say and do things that—either you want to say and do them because you want to get the story, or ..." He left the sentence unfinished. "There were just too many lies to start your career out on. And the army is into all sorts of things. And if you send one negative story, they'll just spike it."

"And if you do that more than once, you get known as a trouble-maker," I agreed.

"Then they'll just send you back. But I wanted to stay there."

Jammu & Kashmir State's capital city, Srinagar, was "quite a surprise for me," Kurien said. "If you ask people in India about Kashmir, nobody would say that it's a nice, well-managed little city. It was a nice place. And you expect all women to be in burqas, and it's not true. I wouldn't mind living there." The locals didn't know what to make of him, though. "Their imagination of India does not stretch beyond the Cow Belt. To them a South Indian is very exotic. The minute you say Abraham, they say Ibrahim, and they assume you just have a strange way of pronouncing it." Indian soldiers, for their part, "don't know what they're doing there. It's a conscious effort to keep North Indians away from Kashmir. All the soldiers are from Southern battalions and from the Northeast. They don't know why they're there. So they take it out on the people."

"Wow, it's just like Vietnam."

"Yeah," he said, maybe not quite getting my allusion. "I didn't speak any Hindi. But I would speak to the soldiers in my language, and they would understand, because they're from the South. For them it's just an irritating posting."

"Would you be willing to speak candidly about it?" I asked.

"Sure." He laughed. "As I said, it's a free country. But you've been to Kashmir?"

"Yeah."

"It's a strange place," said Kurien. "You feel sorry for the army people, and you feel sorry for the Kashmiris. Most of them just want to go to war, to get it over with."

For me the first lure had been a callow reverence for a landscape that a Great Writer had turned into literature. V.S. Naipaul had spent the summer of 1962 in Srinagar, had written his short novel *Mr Stone and the Knights Companion* there, and had sandwiched a vivid depiction of the place and its people between more general musings on India in his classic travel book *An Area of Darkness*. But the uprising that had started in 1989 had led to the Indian Army's siege of the Hazratbal mosque in Srinagar in late 1993, which had scrolled up my screen at the *Bangkok Post* as a news item and stirred my longing to travel and learn. Kashmir became less a setting from another writer's book than a chapter of my own education.

I came to see that the contemporary story was more in need of telling than the old one, and that I had put myself in a position to try to tell it. I began to research a book on what was happening in Kashmir. I might have been daunted if I had known how ill prepared I was to bring it to fruition, or if I had known how thoroughly uninterested American publishers were. Jason Epstein, for example, noted in declining my query that Random House was about to publish another book on "that part of the world"—*The Ends of the Earth* by Robert D. Kaplan, whose over-ambitious scope encompassed countries from West Africa to Southeast Asia. But there's no substitute for being somewhere interesting at an interesting time, and my sustained attention to Kashmir in the mid-1990s bore fruit a decade later.

My earliest aspirations were high-minded and literary, but in Bangkok I had become steeped—or pickled—in an anti-intellectual macho culture of journalistic beer-swillers and he-men. I supposed that I might write a Kashmiri version of Michael Herr's *Dispatches*, but before I could do that I thought I had to prove myself as a straight-ahead newsman. I was stringing for *The Globe and Mail* and the *South China Morning Post*, plus this and that. I was still filing stories by fax, but back in America the Web was kicking in, and the authority of traditional periodicals was already crumbling along with their economic foundations. I didn't know it yet, but the very lack of the institutional support I yearned for was standing me in good stead.

As I crossed the shadow-line in Asia and later in England, I imbibed the great tradition of English essayists, the lineage of practitioners of "the higher journalism" that runs from Johnson to Hazlitt to Chesterton to Orwell, and that disregards the odious American cults of objectivity and professionalism, euphemisms for a sinister scrubbing from public writing of personal perspective and responsibility. It was my unwillingness to be scrubbed that did me in as a newsman. And it was the unpublished Kashmir project that helped me shed my callow discipleship of a dubiously worthy role model on one hand, and the heavy hand of the compulsions and conventions of straight journalism on the other. Kashmir helped turn me into a travel writer: a subjective narrator of personal history. And my Kashmir work didn't go entirely unpublished. In 2004 I distilled it into the early chapters of *Alive and Well in Pakistan*. We want to look at a line on a map and know that it means something. But often it doesn't. And beginning a story of Pakistan with a long prelude about Kashmir agreed with my experience.

What lingers in memory from my times in Kashmir is what exists now only in memory. One day in July 1995 I traveled to Charar-e-Sharief, a village where the fifteenth-century Sufi shrine of Sheikh Noor-ud-din Wali had been razed by fire overnight on May 10–11, after a two-month standoff between militants and the Indian Army. The local people claimed the army had set the fire, and they showed me mortar shells clearly marked as from an Indian ordnance factory. But who can know? And once something is gone, remembering what it was all about can take more effort than people can muster. The old man who was my guide and protector remembered, though. "Every prime minister of India used to come to this place," he said. "One crore [ten million] people were visiting this shrine every year, from all over Jammu & Kashmir State. *Many* thing Sheikh Noor-ud-din gave to Kashmir. He was the *great* man of Kashmir. The Kashmiris are indebted to these saints, for the reason that

Valley Community Library
739 River Street
Peckville, PA 18452-2313

they have Islamize-ed this whole region. 'My grandfather was Hindu,' Sheikh Noor-ud-din used to say, 'and I am his grandson.' Therefore Hindus used to come pray here. They pray their way, we pray our way."

But all I saw that day was a stone foundation five meters or so square, covered with a cloth tent; a few charred beams; bricks and lumber piled neatly on the stone floor; and the red-brick remains of dozens of houses on the hillside beyond. I had seen ruins and aftermaths already before this, in Haiti and in Detroit. Kurien had felt too young at twenty-four to see such things. The day I saw what remained of Charar-e-Sharief I was twenty-nine, but I learned some things that day: that it's easier to destroy than to create; that loss is inherent in the passage of time.

* * *

Fourteen years later, I wasn't going to get back to Kashmir. The best I could do was to speak to Kurien's friend Mahrukh Inayet, deputy news editor of Times Now, the channel whose breathless coverage of the Lahore cricket attack we had watched at Kurien's house. Mahrukh was well known nationally, especially since the previous November, when she had extensively covered the Mumbai siege. "After the blast we went out for a drink," Kurien told me. "And she's a huge celebrity, and people were asking for her autograph. That was a very famous photograph of her lying on the ground."

Mahrukh was a young, stylish, intelligent woman, self-assured and thoughtfully candid. She was also Kashmiri, and her views were different from those of most Kashmiris I had met. It was a different time and place, and different circumstances.

"The Muslims in Kashmir are a far more affluent lot," she told me at a coffee shop near Kurien's neighborhood. "They're educated. There's a sense of alienation from the rest of the country, but that doesn't come from being Muslim; it comes from being

Kashmiri. There's a historical context to why they feel angry with the Indian state. And that is the overriding sentiment. It might have ebbed over the years, especially now. I don't really see that sentiment coming through. With a couple of generations older to me, there was always the sense that we had an historical problem, we had been betrayed by our own leaders and the Indian government, the promises have not been kept."

"Pakistanis claim Kashmiris as Muslims," I said to her. "I think Kashmiris are not impressed."

"They're not impressed. What happened in the early part of the nineties, when this movement—as most Kashmiris would call it—when the troubles started in the Valley, there was a section which was being supported by Pakistan. Mostly the training of these kids happened in Pakistan. But there was a section called the Hizbul Mujaheddin, the hardliners, that was being supported by Pakistan. And the sentiment that they were going with was being part of the big, huge Muslim brotherhood."

"Whereas the JKLF ..." I prompted her. The Jammu & Kashmir Liberation Front was led by Yaseen Malik, whom I had met.

"Whereas the JKLF was all about independence," she said. "And it wasn't about Muslims or Hindus. It was about Kashmir, and Kashmir was an identity, and that needs to be protected, and we were promised something which hasn't been delivered. So in that sense, Kashmiri Muslims have never felt that because they are Muslims they're being targeted. But if you come out of Kashmir and you travel anywhere in the country, most of the Muslims, for one, are not as educated. And I'm not trying to sound standoffish or snobbish when I say this, but in Kashmir by and large, almost 90 percent of the population has at least two square meals a day, they have a home to come back to, they have clothes—things that Muslims elsewhere in the country cannot take for granted. There is poverty, there is ignorance, from which comes radicalism. You can easily be completely brainwashed by people who think that they are your messiahs and they will get you out of your squalor.

"That is something that I cannot relate with. I can see it as a third person and understand the anger. As a journalist, as an observer, I can understand it. But as a Muslim I can't. Maybe as a woman I'd be able to understand another woman being Eve-teased or not having as many rights, because I can empathize with her. But there's no empathy as far as an Indian Muslim per se. Because that kind of anger that they feel, I find it jarring."

"So how would you say that Indian Muslims who are not Kashmiri feel about Pakistan?"

"I think that some of them, especially the radical lot, or those who are looking at a big, huge Muslim brotherhood, might be able to relate to them. If you have a cricket match between India and Bangladesh, a lot of Muslims in this country will support Bangladesh, only because Bangladesh is 90 percent Muslim in terms of the team composition. And it's funny, because what's the connection? You might never even go to Bangladesh, or know any of these guys, or like the cricket that they play, but just because they are Muslim, you will support them. It's the same thing for what's happening in Pakistan. Not because they understand the history of the problem, and not because they're human rights activists who are going to be out on the streets. It's because they think it's a pan-Islamic identity."

"You seem as if you're not particularly in sympathy with that kind of attitude."

"I'm not. I am angry about Palestine because young kids are being killed, but I am not going to be angry about Palestine because Muslims are being killed. Because then that's a disconnect. I feel very strongly when it comes to Kashmir, because I have a connection with that place. But even then, I am angry about all kinds of people being killed. I'm angry that there are human rights violations, because women were raped by authorities who were supposed to protect them. Whether it was a Hindu woman or a Muslim woman is irrelevant."

"Are you religious?"

"No." She laughed, a little nervously.

"How do you feel as a Kashmiri, and especially as a Kashmiri who's fairly recognizable on TV, here in Bombay? Are you treated in certain ways or responded to in certain ways because you're Kashmiri?"

"Even in our newsroom there are all kinds of snide remarks that are passed, especially when the terror attacks happen. When the train blasts happened in Bombay, I got an SMS from a colleague that said that, 'Why is it that all Muslims might not be terrorists, but all terrorists are Muslims?' I got slightly upset about it, but I didn't react. Because there are two ways of handling situations. It's not like I haven't faced people talking about me because I'm a Muslim. Either you react and try to convince the other person, or else you just let it be. It's no longer going to be a conversation, a debate. It's going to become an argument. I'm not trying to convince other people of what I think. If they're ready to listen, that's fine. But people aren't ready to listen yet."

"Have you ever been to Pakistan?"

"No."

"Would you like to?"

"Yeah."

"Why?"

"Because I'm very fascinated by this place which is like a complete failed state, as far as I'm concerned," she said. "There's absolutely no rule of law, people can get away with anything, you have a system where a person who is a nobody is today the president of that country. If you want to get rid of the opposition, you make the judiciary come into place, and you have Supreme Court judges and chief justices who are working at your beck and call. And then you have a group like the

Taliban that has a peace deal. A peace deal! I mean, who are you having peace with? They don't even understand what peace means. Tomorrow they'll be ruling Karachi and Lahore, and the next day be in Islamabad. I mean, it's actually scary. And being so close to Kashmir and to India, I think that effect is going to come sooner than later.

"I'm fascinated in that sense, and especially because ever since I've been at Times Now, I've listened to a lot of Pakistani journalists and human rights activists and thinkers and observers. There's a fascinating range of opinions. I think it's creditable that in a situation like what Pakistan is in right now, people have the courage to go ahead—like a journalist, Hamid Mir, he's pretty well known. The other day, one of his journalists was killed in the Swat valley; he was shot thirty-two times, by obviously the Taliban because he was about to expose something. And he came out and he said that, 'We're going to fight them with the pen and not with the sword.' I know it's very dramatic, it's great television. But at the same time, in a country like Pakistan, where anybody can be killed, from the generals down, it takes a lot of courage to say that. And having lived in Kashmir, I know how difficult it is, especially when you know that there are certain groups that might not like the way you talk or what you say. It's very difficult to come out in the open and say it out loud. So I admire that. That's the paradox that I'd want to see, which is why I'm interested in going to Pakistan."

"Despite how messed-up the place is, there are some people who are really rising to the occasion," I agreed.

"I'm very angry with that country, because it's easier to place the blame on somebody else," she said. "Not that I'm not angry with our own Kashmiri leaders, and with the Indian government. But a lot of anger also towards a neighbor which has never been honest. The promises have never been very sincere."

"What is Pakistan's involvement, if any, in the 26 November attacks?"

"I don't completely buy what the Indian government says. Purely as an observer of what has happened, I don't think that the Zardari government per se is even involved in the entire attack, because I don't think it's in their grasp. They're still trying to grapple with what's happening, in terms of gaining power and so on and so forth. But I cannot accept that some members in the Pakistani establishment, especially in the army, have not been part of this plan. Because it's pretty clear that the conspiracy was hatched in Pakistan. And if that is the case, for such a well-orchestrated plan that was put into action, it's impossible that ten kids who are training in a normal terror camp are able to do what they did."

"What about the Navy Chief saying a few days ago that they didn't come by sea?"

"You have the interior minister who, a week earlier, made a statement that 'We have found the dinghies, and we found all the equipment that they used, and then the ship changed its name, and then a trawler changed their name and then took it at sea.' And then the Navy Chief comes out and completely contradicts that. And a day later there's a U-turn and he says that 'I didn't mean to go against the interior minister.' There's a very interesting argument that one of the Pakistani journalists has: He said that he was trying to send across a message to his men. He's saying, 'This is what I'm saying; none of you should talk.' But I think he messed up majorly, because he had to retract his statement the next day."

"Do you think you could get a visa?"

"I don't know. If I tried as a journalist, I don't think I'm going to get it."

"Do you think you're well known enough as a TV journalist that the Pakistanis would know that you're a journalist?"

"I don't know. I don't think so. Not in Pakistan."

"Do you consider yourself a Kashmiri patriot?"

"Depends on how you define the term patriot. I don't believe that Kashmir should be with Pakistan, at all. And I don't believe that Kashmir should be independent, because we wouldn't be able to survive. I think they're both bad ideas. If I say this in Kashmir, a lot of people will say that 'She has sold her heart and soul to the Indian idea.' But the point is that the Indian idea is fantastic. I have never had an issue with being myself, doing what I want to do. I have had no restriction. And I'm not saying I represent all Kashmiris. I'm not saying that Kashmiris haven't faced problems, especially after the troubles started, in terms of getting homes, getting houses, getting places to rent. But show me one place where you don't have Kashmiris still doing their business. You go to Goa, you go to Kerala, you go to any of the tourists spots in the country, the maximum number of people that you see are Kashmiri. And let's look at it this way. I'm not trying to advocate a different philosophy, or trying to say that these guys are fools or that they haven't faced atrocities. But how can you expect a middle-aged Hindu woman, who's living alone in a city—suddenly you come to her house and say, 'I am this young Kashmiri from God knows where, and I want to stay at your place.' What will the normal reaction be? Nobody will give you a room. I wouldn't give a room if I was living alone, not knowing where you come from. I'd be very cagey about giving that to you. Not because—yes, unfortunately, it is because you are a Kashmiri. But you can't say that 'I am being discriminated against.' That's a normal household reaction, and average people don't think about things of saving identity and protecting identity. They're scared. These terror attacks can happen anywhere. The kind of psyche that people in India have now is that we don't know where the next attack is going to come from. They're scared of all Muslims."

"I think the fact that Partition happened bothers Indians," I said. "Indians feel like Pakistan shouldn't have come about in the first place, and if it hadn't, we wouldn't have all these problems."

"I think even that sentiment has gone down. Now they just don't want Pakistan to be an irritant."

"But it is an irritant, and it's going to be one."

"It is. Which is what bothers most Indians. And that too, a section of Indians in the North. And maybe you might have a few radical elements in the South as well. But by and large, they're like, 'Okay, we are on the path of development. We want good money, we want a great lifestyle, we want to travel.' That's the psyche of an average Indian."

"We don't need this headache."

"We don't need this! They're just bringing us down."

I asked her about the Mumbai siege.

"I was just finishing my day," she said. "My show is from nine to ten in the evening, so I had just gotten out of the studio and we heard this news. And instantly we thought that it was another incident, or some stray firing or whatever. I was sent to the Oberoi, so when I reached there, I had no idea what was happening. I had just got the preliminary reports when I left office. You know how Bombay is: You see traffic almost at any given point, and night or day. There was nobody on the road, which was the first indicator that things were not all right. I never imagined it to reach the kind of proportions that it did.

"And then I got there. As soon as I got out of my car, I saw the first burst of gunfire from one of the windows. And it wasn't the gunfire per se that scared me. It was just the fact that it was happening in Bombay. The train attacks might have happened in Bombay; this was very different. The first thought that came to my mind was, 'They can attack any place.'"

"Isn't that the propaganda message of such an attack?"

"It is, absolutely. The message is that we can attack anywhere, any time we want. And I think that's what created the fear psychosis in India. For more than sixty hours, and with the kind of

41

twenty-four-hour news channels that you have, it was reality TV. It was terror, in your face. Voyeuristically you can say it's great TV, right? But otherwise—where else have you seen something like this happen? The message was being reiterated every second, every moment: 'This is what we are capable of, and you can't do anything.'"

"And you as a TV journalist were in a sense being used by the terrorists to convey their message."

"Yeah. We all were."

"Where were you?"

"I was at the Trident at about two-thirty in the morning of November 27, which was the intervening night. I kept getting information because I had the earpiece on, and I could hear what was happening in the studio. And I heard another reporter who was at the Taj, saying that the Taj was on fire. By then there were already two reporters where I was, at the Trident. And I said I'm going to go to the Taj. So I got to the Taj, and that image I will never, ever forget in my life. The dome of the Taj was in flames. It looked as if straight out of a Hollywood or a Bollywood movie. There were these two or three fire tenders that were trying to douse the flames. And it's engulfed with smoke, and against that smoky backdrop, that huge imposing structure. And then the dome, which is like the piece de resistance"—she gave the French phrase an English pronunciation—"is up in flames.

"And there's absolutely no security in place. The entire city should have been put under curfew immediately. I walk around the Gateway of India, to the front facade of the Taj. And I'm standing there with about a hundred other people: kids, bystanders, curious onlookers, everybody looking up. And I look up at this building, and I see faces who are trying to get out. There were women and kids and men, thumping on the windows trying to get out. And I just kept looking up, and I was doing a phone interview, what we call a phoner. Talking to my editor. He was in the studio, and we were doing nonstop with the coverage. And I just stopped, because

I said, 'What are we doing?' And there's one fire tender in one corner, and I'm looking up and I'm waving at them, trying to tell them help is on its way. But I saw people with wet cloths, must be wet towels, keeping them on their faces, because obviously the room was smoky. But I don't know what happened to those people. And that I can't get out of my head.

"And then it was a blur, because I was there for the next sixty hours. I was there till the siege ended at the Taj. And then it was about being calm under the situation, then your sensibilities as a journalist kick in. By the end of it I was hoarse, and you're dead tired, you're exhausted. You're still alert because what's happening around you is unbelievable, and there are so many bomb blasts, and before they'd open each room of the hotel they were triggering all those blasts, to make sure there was nobody inside or whatever. So you kept hearing this the whole time, you kept hearing gunfire, and you're sitting in Colaba and you're right in front of the Taj. It became slightly bizarre."

"Kurien told me that he and you and some others were out a couple of nights after that, and people were asking for your autograph. What was that like?"

She laughed. "That was slightly—I don't know how to react. It obviously felt very good; I'm not going to say that it didn't feel good. But coming as it did on such a tragedy, it felt like you were kind of—not degrading, but kind of bringing down what had happened. But, to be very honest, at the personal level it felt great that people were able to appreciate what I did. Though I don't think anybody who was there did anything that was very difficult or different. Because you were there, you were in a situation, you're not adding to it, you're just giving the news, right? Your being there is not personally adding to what is happening, because what is happening is far bigger. So in that sense I didn't personally feel that I had done something exceptional. Yes, I survived the sixty hours and was there the whole time, which is possibly what I think people appreciated."

* * *

We had met Sanjay Jha, the director of *Deshdrohi 2: 26/11 War in Mumbai*, at the home of a young woman named Vidha Saumya. Vidha in turn I had met through the artist Salima Hashmi, whom I had known at Beaconhouse National University in Lahore, where she was Dean of the School of Visual Arts.

The period I had been at BNU, from September 2003 to February 2004, had been a relatively quiet time. The shock of the World Trade Center attacks and the Afghan war had subsided, Musharraf seemed calmly and confidently—and, to many, benignly—in control, and the next wave of upheavals was scarcely more than a vague sense of foreboding in the disgruntled minds of a few liberals. Musharraf had been welcomed widely, if not universally, when he overthrew Nawaz Sharif in 1999, and his middle-class origins and habits were appreciated by many Pakistanis who resented the preceding decade of vindictive, high-stakes plutocratic gamesmanship between Nawaz and Benazir Bhutto.

I was one of those who appreciated Musharraf, albeit from a figurative armchair; it's easy to tell other people what kind of government they should be prepared to live under. The truth that, as A.J.P. Taylor wrote in Bismarck, "In every state power rests with the armed forces; and whoever controls these forces controls, in the last resort, the state itself," seemed self-evident in Pakistan. And I had learned, at firsthand in Phnom Penh in July 1997 and in Pakistan, that coups happen when political situations have become untenable. So I was not out of sympathy with Musharraf, or with the compulsions that might have forced him to seize power. He had nimbly and shrewdly kept his country from getting (as State Department official Richard Armitage reportedly put it directly to him) bombed back to the Stone Age in the aftermath of September 11 by cooperating with the Bush regime's war in Afghanistan, and he had presided over several years of what to many felt like peace and prosperity. By late 2003 my teaching colleague Taimur-ul-Hassan could tell me, as an aside during a long rant about how severely Benazir had disappointed him, "If you talk about merit, I think Musharraf has served the interests of secular classes more than she did."

Vidha had studied at BNU in 2007–08, when Pakistan's chickens were coming home to roost. Musharraf's protracted and undignified demise had begun around the time he arrived in America, hawking his self-serving and ill-advised memoir on *The Daily Show*, in the fall of 2006. Within six months, he would pick the fight of his life by dismissing the Chief Justice of the Supreme Court, Iftikhar Chaudhry. He would also have his hands full in 2007 with the standoff at the Red Mosque in Islamabad, but Musharraf cannot have known what forces he was unleashing in March when he acted on the historically justified assumption that, like dictators before him, he could control or intimidate a reliably meek judiciary. That was the moment when his professed personal liberalism met the mindset of a military man accustomed to being obeyed.

The groundswell of civic activism and constitutional patriotism that captured the world's imagination as the lawyers' movement would be dramatically vindicated in Lahore almost exactly two years later. The country arrived at that moment by way of a lurching series of alarming crescendos, from Musharraf's desperate imposition of emergency rule on November 3, to Benazir's assassination in Rawalpindi on December 27, to the delayed but startlingly peaceful February 18, 2008 elections, which signaled the ascendancy of Benazir's husband Asif Ali Zardari, who eventually became president after Musharraf was finally shown the door.

Vidha had been living in Lahore, as a visiting student, during all these events. It was her father, Ajay Brahmatmaj, a film journalist with a leftist background, who introduced me to Mahesh Bhatt at the *mahurat*. I liked him for his gentle manner and for the twinkle in his eye that suggested adventures enjoyed and lessons learned. I asked him if he felt Pakistan had been good for Vidha.

"Yeah, sure," he said. "Every Indian should visit Pakistan once in a lifetime. Some of our friends asked me why I was sending her. Some of them asked me, 'Do they have higher studies in Pakistan? Most of the people going to Pakistan learn terrorist activities. How come your daughter is going to learn art?'"

"Are they joking when they say that, or serious?"

"The mood is a little bit serious. But our family is not a common Indian family. My wife is from a different caste, and our marriage is a love marriage (and that is 26 years ago!). We married and we fled from Bihar," he added with a laugh. "We are friend to anyone, and we want to learn anything. That is the motto of our family."

I asked him how Pakistan had affected Vidha.

"Culturally she's more mature now," he said. "As well, you must be knowing that her boyfriend is a Muslim."

"Ali."

"Ali, yeah. He's going to marry her. It's my thought, or my perception, that in some ways she's preparing herself to be ready to accommodate another family's religious tradition."

I asked if the rest of his family was more traditional.

"They are not more traditional, but they are not exposed," he said. "They are living their life in a secular way. They are not fundamentalist, they are not religious, and they are not orthodox, but their outlook is very limited. But in that limited exposure, they are very much open. From my younger age, I was a little bit rebel kind of a boy. I was not good in study, and my parents were very worried: What will happen to him? My father had very traditional thought, that if you are graduating from a university, you do your postgraduation from there, and then go in teaching line, be a professor, be a teacher. My idea was different. I did my graduation, and then I thought that Bihar is not a good place for me, or what exposure I want. So I just took a train and wrote a postcard to my elder brother: 'I am going to Delhi, and if you are ready to accept my decision, just send me two hundred rupees for my immediate expenditure.' Two hundred rupees that time was big money. And that time my father was retiring. And he said, 'I don't have enough money to afford you, for your study. So if you can manage yourself, then go and study there.'"

"Did he send you two hundred rupees?"

He laughed. "Yeah, my brother sent. And that's why I am saying that he's very open to my decision and very supportive, though he's not so exposed. But in his limited world, he's open. All of my brothers are very supportive."

In Delhi he had joined a student group affiliated with the Communist Party of India (Marxist). "I have that germ still in my mind," he volunteered. "And it's a very useful tool to judge a person, to judge a situation, to take a decision, and it's helping me all my life. Though I'm not very active now, and I'm not practicing left ideology, but it is behind my mind."

"It's influencing your daughter I think, too."

"Yes, of course. She is not so politically active, but that thought is there. What limited knowledge I had, I inculcated in my daughters: Be independent, be individual, don't be religious but do respect all religions, and eat everything. I always say—this is a law in my family—that if I'm going to Kerala or I'm going to Pakistan, you must eat their food."

On our last morning in Mumbai, Vidha met us for tea in Kurien's neighborhood.

"My mother would keep telling me that, 'You can choose anyone when you get married,' she said. "'Just don't choose a rickshaw-wallah or some *paan*-wallah or something. Choose somebody who is decent, somebody who is educated. It doesn't matter, you can choose a person from any religion, just don't choose a Muslim. Just don't fall in love with a Muslim guy.' And then when I finally started going around with a Muslim person, slowly she is now saying, 'Oh, it is okay if you get married.' I mean, obviously she knows I would not walk out on a Muslim guy just because he's a Muslim. You know, what a stupid reason."

"So your mother's okay now?"

"I think she has very reluctantly accepted the fact. Though she projects that she is quite pro-Muslims or whatever, I think this is something that comes as upbringing, from the kind of place that she is from. Something that is instilled so deeply takes a lot of time. And all the time, when you're even saying that you're pro, you're probably denying something. And you would want to take a certain decision because that is probably the right thing to do, but not maybe willingly."

"And how about your father?"

"He's been okay from day one."

I asked Vidha about the events she had lived through in Lahore.

"The only real knowledge of an emergency that I had was of the Emergency that was in India in 1979, I guess," she said.

"Seventy-five," I corrected her.

"Seventy-five, yeah. So I had heard stories. So I was a little scared then, and I came back, and the warden [at the student hostel] told, 'Don't go out.' We were going to celebrate Diwali in a week's time, so I wanted to buy a few things for myself. And I wanted to go to the market just that day, and we weren't allowed. But then I still took my friend, and the guard said, 'Don't go too far away, just come back.' And the market seemed quite normal. But just that thought in mind that there's an emergency, there's something that has probably changed. And from the next day there were these protests in college, and all that."

"Protests at BNU?"

"Yes, at BNU. All the students. And there's this one student called Ubab Mamina. She was in the second year at that time, and in her own way she was somebody who took that responsibility, or just took that charge, of getting things organized, getting talks organized, getting people to come and speak to the students, and organizing the silent protests. She was someone from whom we would hear the updates about everything. She's just this really skinny, thin girl, who otherwise talked about clothes and shoes and fashion and makeup, where you would least expect her to do something like that. She had slogans written on her t-shirt that could get her in trouble, but she went everywhere wearing it. And we were advised, because we were students who had come from outside, to not participate in all that, because if we do that, there's nobody from family who can take any kind of a measure, and the only person responsible there was Salima Hashmi. She was the only one we could have looked up to, and she was under house arrest.

"I couldn't eat food for the next two days, and I just got so depressed. I was so scared that 'What if they send us back? What is going to happen?' They said, 'They've been put in jail.' That's all we would hear. And there was food served, and you would feel how can you even have dinner, when somebody is not having—one didn't know what the condition was. Days passed, and I had a presentation also that time, and I just couldn't concentrate, and I was just so lost. Maybe because it was the first time I had experienced something like that. And probably I'm not too strong emotionally that way; I just got really disturbed by the whole thing. And that was the time I spoke to my father. I was really scared, and he said, 'You don't have to get scared. These kind of things keep happening. And don't worry, they'll not send you back. And even if they send you back, they'll send you back. Nobody's going to attack you, nobody's going to kill you, nobody's going to do anything to you, so don't worry. And it's a very important time also, something that will teach you a lot. It's a good time to understand things, to know things. And be prepared for whenever next something like that might happen.' So then I got a little calm, and I was okay."

Salima Hashmi was under house arrest for about a week. "And they had a gala of time," said Vidha. "There was singing, and there was just so much of food coming from everywhere, because everyone was concerned. They distributed the food amongst the policemen and their guards, and there was people singing and talking of stories, and all that kind of a thing."

"She's a cool lady," I remarked.

"Yes, extremely cool. If I was stuck in a situation like that, I think I would probably start crying or something. She said things that weren't just protesting, or saying, 'Okay, don't do this to me.' She was hitting nail on the head all the time, with every statement she said."

"Your father told me that his perspective was affected by his experience of China," I told Vidha. The family had been living in Beijing during what Ajay called "that Tiananmen incident." The Indian embassy "declined to take us away from Peking to India," he had told me, "because I was working for Foreign Language Press, editing a magazine called *China Pictorial*. It was in Hindi. They said, 'You are a liability of the Chinese government.' That day I was in Bhopal, and some of my friends called and said, 'Emergency has been declared in Pakistan, and how is your daughter?' So I had that memory, and here she was an independent scholar who went to Pakistan with not so much help from the Indian government. So just for that flash of moment, I thought if there is some problem with her, what will I do, and how I will manage to take her out from Pakistan? But then Vidha called me from somewhere, just to say that 'I am fine, I will call you later.' And that was enough for me."

In Beijing in 1989, Vidha's parents could hear gunfire from their home. In Lahore, she said, "nothing like that happened to us. It was just that everyone around seemed very not certain as to what was going to happen. It was that kind of a silence. And in a city which is always bubbling with energy, to see something like that was not too great. But I think what I really learned during that time, and what really made me stop getting affected by it so much, was the fact that there were just so many students—and students from well-to-do families, students who are used to a certain level of comfort—who came out on the street. Whether it was for fun, just for the adventure of it, but still, to spend a whole night in the winters of Lahore, outside. To actually do that, or to go early in the morning and put these posters all over the market: That is something that really inspired me and made me feel happy."

I asked her about the assassination.

"We had our winter vacations happening," she said. "And we had a lot of power cuts happening. Because it did not rain in Lahore that year, so there was less water, and the hydroelectricity is what gets provided there. There was very little water. We had these extreme power cuts, where the electricity would go out for an hour, they stay for two hours, and again go for an hour. But since it was a vacation time we were all glued to the TV, and everyone was watching. I think we saw it on the news first, that Bhutto has been assassinated. And nobody in the hostel knew, and we just started telling everyone."

"The foreign students' hostel?"

"No, this was a hostel with Pakistani students as well. Earlier it used to be only foreign students, where the boys and the girls would stay together, then they made it into a girls' hostel and boys' hostel, since there were Pakistani students as well. Benazir Bhutto has been a very important personality, even for India, just as a lady, and in terms of her representation from Pakistan, being Bhutto's daughter, and just a very important person that way." Benazir's father, Zulfikar Ali Bhutto, was Pakistan's charismatic but arrogant and demagogic prime minister until 1977, when he was overthrown by the army chief he had appointed, Zia ul Haq. Zia went on to concoct a trial against Bhutto for murder, for which he was hanged after a 5–4 verdict in the Supreme Court in April 1979. "We had all read about her, seen her interviews. So there's always this close association that one had, even though one was not from Pakistan. So it felt like a very personal loss. I was quite sad, and I called my parents also, and they had already got the news. Then we were all under sort of warden-imposed hostel arrest; we weren't allowed to go outside of the hostel at all. I think she was assassinated on the twenty-fourth or twenty-fifth?"

"Twenty-seventh," I said.

"The thirty-first was the day we were allowed to go out, and that was towards the new year. The thirty-first itself felt like a new year, because we had seen the outside world after four days. We met Salima Hashmi, because we were all planning for an exhibition. And we had to go again in the evening. There was an exhibition by Faiza Butt, and Asma Jahangir"—the internationally prominent human rights lawyer—"was to come and give a talk. Not really a talk, but just her time with Benazir, and we were remembering her. Attending that also made me realize that there were lots of things we didn't know about Benazir. It's on YouTube as well; it's uploaded there. She did not talk about how Benazir was in politics. She spoke about the time when she first met Benazir, and how she would call Benazir a really boring girl, and how somebody would not really enjoy talking to her, and how she transformed with her whole entire study period, and she came back. And how she would be with her daughters—because Asma's daughters were studying where Benazir's children were studying. How she would take care, and take them to shop for sweets and chocolates. And if she would invite somebody for dinner, the dinner would just have things that she liked; they need not necessarily match. So there would be a *haleem* with probably a Russian salad, and something that she just liked. She was just talking about all these things, and I felt that it is often this side that is neglected about any known personality: How they are when they are so normal. Because everyone has that side."

"Between then and February 18 was everything to do with the elections," I prompted her.

"The elections, surprisingly, happened very, very peacefully," said Vidha. "The elections were originally going to happen in December, or the first week. There was a group from Lahore which was planning to come to India, so that trip got delayed. There was this teacher of mine who was coming from India. He stays in London, and he had come to Bangalore to do a course, and he was planning to come to Lahore. So his trip got delayed. My parents were planning to come there. People suddenly got a little anxious. I had my first exhibition at that time. We were just a little, 'Should we keep the exhibition, not keep, will people come?' The election was the talk of the town. All the media was just talking about the elections. So we were just wondering if there will be any press or media that will come for my exhibition." She giggled charmingly. "But I got a good response; there were a lot of people who came."

"All this political stuff was incidental to your decision," I suggested, "but it became part of your experience in Pakistan. What do you feel, looking back on it now, that you gained or learned or absorbed from all that?"

"I was just thinking about these things," she said. "What is it? Why do I like Lahore so much? I think on a purely emotional level, it would be like how the younger child in the family is. He is somebody who is more entertaining, cuter, smaller, does these funny things, and does naughty things, but you would still have a higher degree of attachment. But he'll be irresponsible, and he'll not do what you ask him, he'll be really menacing, but you'll still be attached, purely because of the joy he brings to you. So all these incidents that happened, and people say bad things about Pakistan—it just doesn't affect me, because it's something that I just love so much. Probably it's a wrong thing also, that I don't really start putting down facts, don't discuss the negative and the positive, and become really biased in my opinion at times. That does make me take sides at times. But then I can't help it. I just love the city so much."

"I have similar feelings," I admitted. "That's why I write affectionate things about Pakistan." I turned the subject to the attack on the Sri Lankan cricket team. "You must have been shocked when it happened."

"I just went, like, 'Oh please.' It's just getting bad to worse. Things were going on really well, it had become so easy to go and come, and everyone had started taking kind of a positive stance. And then this happened, and I was like, 'Oh God, please don't do this again.' It's like they're just spoiling it all. Because nobody is going to really try to understand what probably was the reason—you know, who did it. It just becomes 'Oh, Pakistan.' Like on the radio the other day—I was telling you over the chat—there was this conversation happening between these two radio jockeys. And they said, 'Will there ever be peace in Pakistan?' So this girl said, 'Yah, I don't know why are they doing all this all the time.' Then the guy asked this girl, 'So do you want to go to Pakistan?' She said, 'Yes, yes, I am from Sindh, so I would like to see that part of the country.' So he said, 'Okay, do you think you will get a good welcome there now, after 26/11 and after this whole attack on the cricketers?' So then she said, 'I will go if I'm greeted with flowers, not obviously when I'm greeted with bombs.' To say something like this over the radio is a very, very irresponsible act."

"Some Indians are saying, 'Oh, these Pakistanis, they're going to portray themselves as the victims now, but actually, they're the problem,'" I said.

"People will probably say something like that. But just yesterday or the day before, I heard this Pakistani journalist, he was also on the radio. He was saying this is the time Pakistan needs that kind of support from everyone, to fight these people who are creating all this havoc. So then the radio jockey said, 'What about when the attack happened in India? You did not support us, and you were acting so aloof.' And he explained his point: the kind of pressure, the way people have been used to living there, because of such a long time under dictators. If there is even one person who is even trying to be democratic, there's so much pressure from all kinds of people. When you are at home and you have pressure from just, say, two people in the house, the way you function becomes so disarrayed. Imagine somebody who's heading an entire country, being pressurized with somebody who has a greater influence with people. How is he supposed to respond and take decisions?"

"Have you been to Liberty Market?"

"Yes," she said. "In fact, when the attack happened I was just remembering this time. The last five Saturdays I was with this friend of mine, and we used to just travel the entire night in Lahore. We would meet at around nine-ten o'clock, have dinner somewhere, then just take a rickshaw, go somewhere else. Then just roam around, maybe have a Coke, or have some coffee, then take a rickshaw, go somewhere else. That whole last one and a half months is when I have seen the whole night life of Lahore. And, maybe because I was with a male friend, it was really safe. Around three-thirty, four, we would go to Gaddafi Stadium and be there till around eight o'clock, because there are lots of practices, and there are lots of children who come there. It's just very nice to see all of that: these cycling matches, and people come with bikes. It would be Sunday morning; everybody has a holiday. From kids to college students to older men and people coming for their walks, or to play cricket. It used to be a very nice time; I used to really enjoy myself. We would make it a point to get there by three-thirty, four in the morning, and see that whole turn from twilight to bright, sunny morning. By 8 a.m. it started getting really hot; this was around May–June. And then we would go to Capri, which is also in Liberty Market, and have our breakfast there, and then I would go back to my hostel."

"Wow," I said, impressed.

"I did not take pictures," she said. "I sort of decided that I'm not going to take them. Because people start getting conscious, and you also start getting a lot of attention, and I did not want that to happen. It was just such a lovely time. At around twelve-thirty or one o'clock in the night, we would go to Chaman, It's an ice cream place quite close to Anarkali Market. And it used to be filled with people, mainly large families. The place would be abuzz with people, colors, and lights. The entire street would be lit up."

CHAPTER 2

A Little Bit All Over The Place

"You live in Seattle?" said Mrs Baig, politely. "My other son lives near Seattle, in Redmond."

Whenever South Asian parents told me this sort of thing with pride, my heart sank. How could I convey the gulf that separates the worlds on either side of the SR-520 bridge?

What I said was, "Oh! Does he work for Microsoft?"

"No, he doesn't work for Microsoft, thank God. They just laid off all H-1Bs."

"Really? Wow."

"Yes, I think so."

We had arrived in Hyderabad by overnight train, because that's the only way to travel in India. In the rickshaw on the way from the station to the Baigs' house I looked for signs of the "India rising" tech economy, and found these:

> My dad is the best
> He wears a helmet
>
> Don't rule the road
> Follow the rules of the road

And, on the side of an office building:

> Hiring freshers!
> If you are looking
> for a career, we
> have the right
> job for you.

I had been unsure whether we would be able to make the entire trip overland, but in the end we did: from Mumbai in a long arc all the way to Karachi, via Hyderabad, Delhi, and the Attari-Wagah border crossing between Amritsar and Lahore. I shouldn't have doubted it, but my traveling chops were rusty, and I made the mistake of taking seriously the well-meaning advice of affluent Indian and Pakistani friends who were horrified at the prospect of our traveling by train. After the interminable flight to Mumbai, to hug the planet was a relief.

Air travel is violent and disorienting, especially if you fly halfway around the world in one jump. The human body and soul aren't built for it. You wake up very early one morning at home in Seattle, drive across the city, sit on a plane for five hours, sit several more hours in airport purgatory in Atlanta, then sit and read and sleep and eat like a caged animal for what feels like forever, until you arrive in a different world. It's like space travel, except that the planet you finally land on is in fact the same one you left way back when. To see the world from above is a privilege and a joy: "If you can see a thing whole, it seems that it's always beautiful," says a character in *The Dispossessed*, Ursula Le Guin's great science-fiction novel.

> Planets, lives ... But close up, a world's all dirt and rocks. And day
> to day, life's a hard job, you get tired, you lose the pattern. You need
> distance, interval. The way to see how beautiful the earth is, is to see
> it as the moon. The way to see how beautiful life is, is from the van-
> tage point of death.

And as the vast reddish conurbation of Mumbai loomed out of the dark and then rose toward the descending plane, it was wondrous to see. But once back on the ground I wanted to stay there, even though I immediately lost the pattern again.

I was rereading *The Dispossessed* because it's about twin planets separated by ideology, mutual paranoia, and self-enforced exile, and because I had first read it in India. Finding it at a used bookshop in Varanasi in 1994 had led to many good things for me. It was partly a shared love of Le Guin that brought me and Jenny together, and through Jenny I had met Pete, and here I was in India again, with Pete. When Jenny and I had attended a rare public reading in Seattle, standing in line I had struggled with what to say to the little old lady sitting at the book-signing table. There are few authors I simply revere. When we got to the front of the line, what I decided to say was: "*Thank you* for giving us so many wonderful books."

She beamed up at me and replied: "Well, it's my pleasure!" It was like a benediction.

I had found other guides and friends in India too, and in fact it was the enriching of my reading life that was my happiest memory—and not only or especially Indian writers, but A.J.P. Taylor, and Orwell's four-volume *Selected Essays, Journalism and Letters*, and Czeslaw Milosz, and Octavio Paz, and Norman Mailer, and Carlos Castaneda. But the deepest and most enduring literary love I found in India was for Ursula Le Guin. So at night and on trains I was rereading *The Dispossessed*:

> The Odonians who left Urras had been wrong, wrong in their desperate courage, to deny their history, to forgo the possibility of return. The explorer who will not come back or send back his ships to tell his tale is not an explorer, only an adventurer; and his sons are born in exile.

We were in Hyderabad because a friend in Chicago, Jafer Hasnain, had urged me to include it on the itinerary. Jafer was a tall, urbane fellow with owlish glasses; his job was something or other to do with finance. He was a quiet but important presence in Chicago's Pakistani community and a board member of a nonprofit called the Human Development Foundation (HDF), which channeled money and other resources from concerned U.S.-based expats into needed education and health projects around Pakistan. I had been a panelist at the convention marking HDF's tenth anniversary in May 2007, and since then I had returned to Chicago several times and rediscovered the city as a hub of Pakistani-American life. Walking down Devon Avenue on Chicago's north side was like being in Lahore or Tooting in South London. Chicago had changed since I had ridden the train there alone from Milwaukee, for weekend visits to my Aunt Polly. Maybe I had changed, too.

It was at that HDF convention that Jafer had introduced himself and told me the story of the circumstances in which he had read *Alive and Well in Pakistan*. The previous year he had returned to Pakistan for the first time in eighteen years, because his father was ill. He had found my book at Mr Books in Islamabad's Super Market shopping area and had read it over several days at his father's hospital bedside. It had helped him reconnect with his country, he said.

Any author likes anyone who likes his book, but I liked Jafer especially for having sought me out to share a very personal story. I had seen him after that whenever I went to Chicago, and in December 2008 I had accepted his wife Arshya's invitation to speak at their son's private high school. It was over a rushed lunch that day that I confided in Jafer and Arshya that I might write a second book. They egged me on and encouraged me to start the trip in India, and Jafer introduced me to his Chicago-based Indian Muslim friend Aamer Baig. As a result, Aamer's mother was now sweeping us off our feet in Hyderabad.

One purpose of visiting India was to get a sense of the situations and perspectives of Indian Muslims. It was this purpose that Jafer felt Hyderabad would serve. It had been a center of Muslim life in colonial India, ruled as one of the largest of the so-called princely states by a Muslim king, the Nizam. After independent India and Pakistan came into being in 1947 the status of Hyderabad, as a large Muslim-majority territory not contiguous to what was being defined as Pakistan, had been resolved by Indian military action. Jafer was dismissive of Lucknow in North India, where I had gone in the mid-1990s and proposed going again. "Lucknow's been declining for a hundred and fifty years," he said. Hyderabad, by contrast, was part of the new Indian tech economy. And it was in the South, where I had spent very little time. I didn't need much convincing.

"Hyderabad is one of the success stories in the new India," Aamer told me by phone a few weeks before I came. "It's an oasis in a broader ecosystem that is not that healthy. You see a lot of Muslim presence there." It had, he said, "a long history of coexistence." There were many Shia Muslims in Hyderabad, including his family, and many Hindus there attended celebrations during the Shia holy month of Muharram. In a reciprocal spirit, many Indian Muslims were not averse to believing that the Buddha might have been a prophet.

I had discovered that, hobnobbing with Pakistanis in Chicago or San Jose or Pasadena, you might be surprised to learn that the person you're talking to is actually an Indian Muslim; the two communities blended and overlapped through marriage and religious and social institutions. Aamer gave me an insight into the differences. "I think people who grew up in a more pluralistic society have more advantages integrating here, in the West," he said. "We grew up participating in a lot of Hindu festivals and traditions." Most Indian Muslims thought that the Partition had been "not a good idea." It had left them worse off than before, stranded, dogged by lost power and a feeling of guilt at not having opted for Pakistan. "I was brought up to think Jinnah"—Pakistan's founder—"was evil because he broke up the subcontinent." He recommended a book, *Jinnah and Islamic Identity* by Akbar Ahmed, from which he had taken two ideas.

One was that because "the Hindu mindset is caste-based," Muslims in post-Partition India would be "relegated to a caste-like status." The other was a sense that "Pakistanis believe that an Indian Muslim is a defeated Muslim."

* * *

Aamer had left me with a warning: His mother was "a little bit all over the place" and, if we accepted her hospitality, we should expect "a fair amount of chitchat." Mrs. Baig went to some effort to set up interviews for us in Hyderabad with Muslim lawyers and politicians, and a short visit to a Muslim girls' school. All of these were useful and consistent with my purposes, and I dutifully and gratefully went along to them all. But most interesting of all was Mrs. Baig herself. In car rides with her I found myself, more often than not, hunched over my notebookin the back seat, hoping for a traffic jam.

Which is to say that five days with Mrs. Baig reminded me that the chitchat was the whole point. I felt chronically nagged by a self-imposed need to prove my rigor as a reporter, but I had found my vocation as an unofficial listener at the grassroots. Better to be a ste-nographer on the streets than in the corridors of power. Pakistan is the subject, not to say the victim, of too much scholarship and too much journalism, and most books treat it less as a place where people raise children and suffer and listen to music and attend weddings than as an issue or conundrum for makers of U.S. foreign policy. I find such books tedious to read, so I avoid reading them if I can. The avatar of this attitude for me was a literary agent in New York whom I told, over lunch, that I had published a book about Pakistan. "What's your argument?" he had asked. I was so nonplussed by the question that I could scarcely blurt out the answer: I'm not making an argument; I'm telling a story. If I have an argument, it's implicit.

"A Pakistani woman does not have a chance of being a woman in her own right," Mrs. Baig asserted. "I don't think they have a holistic view, the way we do. They can't afford to. They just have to focus on their money-making activities. I find them very mercenary. They are very large-hearted when we go there."

"Pakistanis look down on Indian Muslims, because we did not join them," said her husband.

Mr. Baig was quieter than his wife but seemed to hold his own in marital banter. He had been a banker and was clearly an intelligent and competent man; he just didn't have as much to say—or he left some things unsaid, because she did most of the talking. His brother, Abbas Ali Baig, had played on the Indian national cricket team. "He was a chocolate-box hero," said Mrs. Baig. "A girl came and kissed him on the pitch. He is still very charismatic today. There are so many Muslim boys in the first twelve, the cream a la cream of the cricket. Cricket is like a religion; the whole country comes to a stop. My mother will not move out of range of the TV when a match is on."

Her husband was the same way. One evening, at the home of a remarkable retired woman lawyer they took me to meet, he had taken it on himself to turn on her television to watch Australia v. South Africa. "He can't wait to watch the match," Mrs. Baig said to me, then turned to scold him: "Without so much as a by-your-leave!"

"By your leave," he answered with a smirk.

The next day at lunch we chatted about the lawyer's distinguished career. "And she did it without a husband," said Mrs. Baig in admiration.

"Her husband might not have allowed her," said Mr. Baig.

"Yes, husbands are obstacles," she retorted.

"Well, with her kind of wife ..." He glanced complicitly across the table at me and Pete.

Mrs Baig hadn't heard him—or maybe she had. "What did you say?"

He grinned at us again. "Men only."

The running conversation started over breakfast the morning we arrived, and it didn't really let up until we left for Delhi five days later. One subject was the national elections that would be starting the next month. Mrs. Baig had a stern, unillusioned view on her position in the Indian scheme of things. "I will vote for Congress," she pronounced. "I think we all should vote for Congress, because at least it stops the BJP in their tracks. Muslim vote bank, they call us. We were always separate."

"But not anymore?"

"Not anymore. If BJP comes to power, who knows? They don't want the CPI"—the Communist Party of India— "to come in. All the capitalists are very happy with the RSS and the BJP." These were the main right-wing, Hindu nationalist groups: the Rashtriya Swayamsevak Sangh, and the Bharatiya Janata Party or Indian People's Party.

"And how does that affect Muslims nationally?" I asked.

"Less Muslims get jobs. And there are policemen who cannot function because of the atmosphere. There is a Muslim commissioner of Bombay. I'm sure he couldn't put a Quranic verse on his office wall, even if he wanted to."

Still, she was patriotic on principle. "I am an Indian first, and I am a Muslim, and I am living here," she said. "There's no two ways about it. And you can also live here." But, like many Indian Muslims, she felt taken for granted by the long-dominant Congress Party. "When Sonia Gandhi went to Gujarat, she started her procession at a Hindu temple," she recalled. "And she would not even go to condole with the family of her own man." This was a reference to Ehsan Jafri, a Muslim former Member of Parliament who had been killed and dismembered by a Hindu mob in a Muslim suburb of Ahmedabad, capital of the state of Gujarat, in February 2002. "He was burnt alive. They killed him at point blank range, and they burned the building down." She cited the Muslim community's response when N. Chandrababu Naidu, the former Chief Minister of Andhra Pradesh state, had switched parties. "En bloc, from the down and out to the high and mighty, everybody voted against him. Very far-sighted, a wonderful administrator, he brought Hyderabad onto the world stage. But he stepped on our toes when he went with the BJP."

We had scarcely finished a substantial breakfast featuring goat tongue that first morning, when Mrs. Baig whisked us off for lunch with a contact at the Nizam Club. "When we were small this was a small path in the woods, and there were many trees," she said in the car.

"Well, things have changed everywhere," said Pete.

"How do you spell your second name?" she asked him.

"S-a-b-o," said Pete. "Sabo."

"Are you French?"

"No, my grandparents came from Czechoslovakia."

"That is such a pity that it is being split up. All the Balkans."

She asked about his family.

"I have six brothers and three sisters," he said. "My parents passed away."

"And you all keep in touch?"

"Yes," he said in a way that I knew actually meant "sort of."

"I just gave my younger one a lecture about that," she said with satisfaction. "And you still have relatives in Czechoslovakia?"

"Yes, some great-aunts and distant cousins."

The Baigs had booked us a room at the nearby Golden Glory Guest House, because their daughter-in-law was staying with them. Farah was young and pretty and soft-spoken, becomingly deferential but with a twinkle in her eye. Her husband was Irfan, the Baigs' younger son in Redmond, Washington. They had only just moved there, and Farah asked our advice on local attractions. The only sight they had seen so far was the Space Needle. "It was a very nice view," said Farah. "But we have hardly gone out of Redmond. We went to Bellevue." Pete and I talked up Pike Place Market and Gasworks Park, and we urged her also to see Vancouver and the Rose Garden in Portland. I just scribbled, as unobtrusively as I could, while Mrs. Baig talked. Sometimes I egged her on. She talked about America, where she had made a fifteen-day Amtrak journey from Buffalo to Los Angeles via Dallas: "We met a cross section of Americans that we would not have met otherwise. Mostly old people and students. I thought only in banana republics and Third World countries elections were rigged! Everybody celebrated when Obama came to power. It can happen in our lifetime! I pray for him. I just hope some redneck doesn't get him."

She talked about her sons: "When Aamer was going to America I took him to his grandmother, my husband's mother. And she said, 'Where are you going to college?' And he very proudly said, 'I am going to Austin, Texas.' And she said, 'I've never heard of that place. I only know Oxford, Cambridge, and Harvard!' Such curly hair he had. Now he has hardly any hair, poor fellow."

And she talked about the tech boom and its effect on young Indians: "Because of these horrible call centers, the children have stopped going to college. And all this newfound wealth, they don't save money. In the olden days, before the call centers, lower middle class, they would struggle to send even their daughters to college. There is a respect that goes with education, and these children are going to lose it." Because of the global economic crisis, the new malls in Hyderabad were suddenly emptier than they had been in years. "It used to be so nice to see these youngsters frittering away their money," sighed Mrs. Baig.

I must have made some remark about the state of the American media, because she said: "Even the *New York Times* is in dire trouble, I hear."

"Yes it is," I confirmed. At the time, it was not certain whether the *Times* would be able to pay company debt that was coming due in a couple of months.

"But the *New York Times* is owned by Jews, no?"

"Well, the Sulzberger family that owns the *Times* ..."

"They are a Jew family, right?"

"Yes."

"Then they must be having pots and pots of money!"

This led to the subject of Jews in general, and inevitably to Israel. "The Jews are doing to the Palestinians what Hitler did to them," said Mrs. Baig. "I have no personal thing with Jews. I admire them, I know some of them. They made the desert bloom and this and that. But how did they do this to people? My aunt went to the Gaza Strip. She said every day people are being taken away, people are dying."

In the car on the way to an appointment she told me about a friend, a professor in Pakistan, who had asked her to help give a book he had written to the great Indian writer Khushwant Singh. "He said, 'I just want Khushwant Singh to read this.' And I felt very bad that I did not do that for him."

"Well, Khushwant Singh must have many demands on his time and attention, because he's such a popular guy," I suggested.

"Yes. But I didn't try hard enough."

"I just really admire him as a writer," I said, "because he's done everything." Khushwant Singh is the Samuel Johnson of India, a man of letters extraordinaire: novelist, historian, journalist, jokemeister, bon vivant. His wonderful autobiography, *Truth, love & a little malice*, includes moving stories of his youth in pre-Partition Lahore.

"I admire him as a human being," said Mrs. Baig. "Because you know, he says he's an agnostic. But when the Blue Star operation was going on, the Golden Temple, he returned his Padam Bhushan, the honor of the state that was given to him. He returned it. He said, 'I don't want to be associated with a state that does this.'"

"Well, that's honorable," I said.

"Yes. And he has always taken up for the Muslims and the Muslim causes."

"He has lots of friends in Pakistan too," I pointed out. "He's been there a lot. He was in Pakistan for the hanging of Bhutto."

"Was he?"

"He reported that, yeah." I had made my Beaconhouse National University students read Khushwant Singh's account of that dark moment in Pakistan's history.

This reminded Mrs. Baig of a story. "You know, when Irfan was being born, he was eight-nine days overdue, so they induced labor," she said. "So I was going, and some prayers were being said before I went out of the house. My grandmother-in-law—I showed you her picture—she was a voracious reader. She used to read the paper front to back, and she would discuss the news and everything. And she said, 'When you start your labor, pray for Bhutto.' I said, 'Why should I pray for Bhutto? I need to pray for my father!' My father wasn't right. I said, 'I'm going to pray for my father. I don't care what happens to Bhutto!' She said, 'You don't understand! It's not for one person, it is the whole country!' I said, 'I'm going to pray for my father, and that's it.' Because they say that when a woman is in labor, she thinks of nothing but 'When is this pain going to end?' But if she asks for something other than the cessation of her pain, that wish is granted."

* * *

"Tomorrow there is a musical evening at my friend's house," said Mrs. Baig one day. "Would you like to come?"

"Oh, yes please," I said.

"It is in Urdu, but you can imbibe the atmosphere."

We walked to the Baigs' house at the appointed time and knocked on the door. "Come in," said Mr. Baig. "I just finished my prayers. I'll be ready in five minutes." In the car he asked: "When will you be in Hyderabad next?"

"I don't know," I said.

"This might be finished when you come," he said, nodding at a construction site on a street corner.

"What is it?"

"Even bigger mall."

A group of Muslim families held an evening of traditional *ghazals* every two months, each time at a different home and employing different musicians. It seemed a convivial custom, and it turned out to be a delightful evening. The musicians were a singer who also played the harmonium, a chubby young player of the *tabla* drum, and a dour-looking man who sat behind the singer and seemed to be their roadie. Pete and I sat with the men in one wing of the L-shaped living room; the ladies sat separately in the other wing. One middle-aged man with a full head of hair dyed a striking red with henna kept exclaiming appreciatively at the exquisite lyrics.

Midway through we broke for snacks and tea, and afterward the men showed us a set of framed vintage photographs on a wall downstairs. "The negatives are on glass," Mr. Baig said several times. "The negatives are on glass." The host's grandfather had been prime minister of Hyderabad under the Nizam.

"Wow, that's very distinguished," I said politely.

"That was him," he demurred. "I'm not distinguished!"

"That's Wellington," said Mr. Baig.

"*The* Wellington?"

"Yes, the Viceroy. Lord and Lady Wellington. My father was chief engineer under the Nizam. He was behind the scenes," he added with cheerful self-deprecation. "Not in these pictures." That was when it came out that Farah, the Baigs' daughter-in-law, was a direct descendent of the Nizam.

"Mr. Wasim Ahmed really seemed to be enjoying himself," I remarked in the car on the way back to the Golden Glory Guest House.

"Wasim, Wasim," said Mr. Baig. "Oh, *Nasim* Ahmed."

"Nasim?"

"Yes, Nasim. It can be a girl's name also. We call him LBW."

"Leg before wicket?"

"*Laal baaluun wallah.*"

"It means red-haired guy," said Farah, with a charming laugh.

Back in our room, Pete told me: "Did I tell you I might have royalty in my blood? Apparently when my parents went to Czechoslovakia, some great-aunt told 'em some story about how we're descended from some prince. Unfortunately, my mother couldn't remember the details."

* * *

"How did you enjoy last night?" asked Mrs. Baig the next morning.

"It was wonderful," said Pete.

I told her I had enjoyed chatting with her aunt. "Yes, the one in the blue sari," she confirmed.

"Is that the aunt whose son works at Dell?" I hinted.

"Yes, but he's very sorry, he cannot meet you. He's too busy."

"That's all right."

"He wakes up at about five o'clock every evening, goes to work, and works until next morning. He's not just one of those call center guys; he's a professional, an engineer. But those are the hours he has to work. He was offered to go to America, but he refused. He has his mother and grandmother here, and his wife works too, and they have the family support."

"Maybe we'll just go over to Hi-Tec City and look around," I said with a glance at Pete, who nodded with acquiescence if not enthusiasm.

"Well, that you can do on your own," said Mrs Baig. "I have no interest in Hi-Tec City. I only want to get online to check my Hotmail and back off. My husband doesn't want to use a computer at all. He used a computer at the bank; it's not that he can't. He doesn't want to."

* * *

"You country?" asked the auto rickshaw driver.

"America," I told him.

"America!" he said. "Obama."

"You like Obama?"

"Yes."

"You like Bush too?"

"No!"

"I also don't like Bush."

"Obama is ... friend," he said. "Bush is a fighter."

We had left Hyderabad too soon. Starting this trip in India had been a good decision, but we had only so much time, and I was itching to catch up with events in Pakistan. We didn't make it to Hi-Tec City. Instead of Hyderabad we had almost gone to Gujarat, site of infamous anti-Muslim riots in 2002 that had left more than a thousand people dead and a quarter of a million displaced. During our week in Mumbai I had lost touch with Mrs. Baig and, without confirmation that she was expecting us in Hyderabad, I had sought alternatives and sent out an email appeal for contacts in Gujarat. It made sense geographically—the capital, Ahmedabad, was on the way to Delhi and the Pakistan border—and the state's name had become a byword to Pakistanis and other Muslims for the bigotry and violence associated with Hindu chauvinism.

Tushar Gandhi had told me about his own visit to Gujarat. When I asked if he had ever been to Pakistan, he replied, "No, unfortunately not, not as yet. But I had a very nice interaction with Pakistanis. In

2005 we celebrated 75 years of the Salt March, the one that my
great-grandfather led in 1930. And to commemorate it, we reenacted
the whole Salt March, the exact same way. I called it the International
Walk for Peace and Justice. The entire route was inside Gujarat, and
Gujarat was just recovering from those very severe anti-Muslim riots
that had happened in 2002. Have you heard of Khan Abdul Ghaffar
Khan, who is known as the Frontier Gandhi, from the North-West
Frontier Province? He had an organization of Pathans called Red
Shirts. These are all Baloch people. That organization still survives.
And I invited them to join me, and about 90 representatives came
and walked with us throughout that route. And for me what was
astounding was the way the people of Gujarat opened their doors to
them. I thought there would be a very hostile reception to them,
because there was a lot of animus between Hindus and Muslims in
Gujarat. And here were these Pathans in their red Pathan suits,
marching with us. And all these simple village folk, Hindu village
folk, opening out their doors and inviting them into their homes,
treating them to food and allowing them to use their homes for rest-
ing. I was surprised, and that was something that really showed me
how my great-grandfather was able to pull off these kind of things.
He would just throw a challenge, saying, 'Here I am; do your worst.'
And people were forced to do their best."

But Mrs. Baig had resurfaced just in time and, not knowing anyone in particular in Gujarat, and not confident I could do any measure of justice in a few days to the enormities that had taken place
there, I had reverted to the original plan.

We had taken an overnight train to Delhi and now here we were,
stuck in traffic.

"Three times light," said the driver. The light had changed three
times, and we still had not gotten through the intersection.

"Bad traffic," I remarked.

"Yes."

Pete took an instant dislike to Delhi, and he was ever vigilant with its rickshaw wallahs. "They use the meter for locals," he said. "And we pay four times the price."

"We're not locals," I pointed out.

"When the Metro gets finished, a lot of these guys are gonna be hurtin' real bad," he said with relish. Like the Sky Train in Bangkok, the Delhi Metro was something that a decade earlier I would have considered a science-fiction pipe dream. The Sky Train had remained mired in the muck of Thai politics for thirty-some years, including the entirety of my five years enduring Bangkok traffic, but when I returned for a visit in 2001, lo and behold you could ride the length of Sukhumvit Road in a few minutes. Similarly, the Delhi Metro made getting around an enormous Asian city sometimes startlingly easy, depending on where you were going.

For now, though, we were going by auto rickshaw to the Citywalk shopping mall in south Delhi, where we ended up spending a fair bit of time. "That's a bad sign, when you're getting to know a mall," said Pete. It wasn't by design or preference, but it was a convenient meeting place, and the offices of *The Sunday Indian* were nearby. *The Sunday Indian*, which billed itself as "The Only News Magazine on Earth in 14 Languages," had published an article of mine. An acquaintance had recommended me to one of its editors who was looking for an American to write about what the election of Obama might mean for Pakistan. The pay was a lot higher than I had ever known an Indian publication to offer, and I appreciated the challenge of writing about Pakistan for Indian readers, so I said sure. I made a mental note that there seemed to be more money in India than before.

"Barack Obama has a lot on his plate," I had written.

Far be it from me to downplay the centrality of Pakistan to the world's fate in our time. But the good news is that there's so much wreckage to sift through, on so many fronts, that it is hard to imagine President Obama picking a fight with Pakistan any time soon.

To be sure, his words of August 1, 2007 were pointed enough to be alarming. "There are terrorists holed up in those mountains who murdered 3,000 Americans," he said. "They are plotting to strike again. ... If we have actionable intelligence about high-value terrorist targets and President Musharraf won't act, we will." To many Pakistanis this sounded like a threat, and it is understandable that they took umbrage at it. ...

Those of us who thought it didn't make much difference who the President of the United States is have been proven very wrong since 2000. The personal character of political leaders matters, and nowhere has this been clearer than in recent and current U.S. and Pakistani leaders. Bush was eager to start wars. Not only does Obama have a mandate to try to get America out of the wars Bush got us into; he seems personally inclined to do so.

My many Pakistani friends are entitled to mind the suggestion that a foreign power would infringe on their hard-won sovereignty, especially given the history of U.S. involvement in Afghanistan and Pakistan. Equally, though, an American presidential candidate is entitled to give fair warning that we need Pakistan's cooperation in the tribal areas. The elephant in the living room is the Pakistani state's inability to exert full control over its own territory.

"There used to be hustle and bustle in this mall, every day," said Asad when we met on the terrace outside Citywalk. To get there from the street, you had to walk through a metal detector.

"Is it a new mall?" I asked him.

"Yes."

"Well, it's quite a mall."

"This is Europe. It is not India. Outside is India."

Asad was the editor who had asked me to write the article. I wanted to meet him because he was a Muslim and a contact, and because his magazine still owed me money. To his credit, he was embarrassed and apologetic about it. He was bearded and youthful, round-faced, serious. He came originally from Bihar, one of India's poorest states. "It is undeveloped. It's a banana republic," he said.

"You don't mind saying that about your own state?"

"No. But you should say the truth."

He had lived in London. "Did you enjoy London?" I asked.

"Yes, yes. I miss London a lot."

"Could you have settled down there?"

"Yes."

"Why didn't you?"

"Nostalgia!" he said. "When I was there, I used to miss India. But life is different in Delhi also. It's expensive. Other difference in London is that it's a welfare state."

"I think you're a sentimental guy," I suggested.

"I used to be sentimental. But you have to be realistic. If you are sentimental, you suffer."

That certainly rang true. I filled him in on the purpose of our trip and my fondness for Pakistan. "So that is your love story with Pakistan," he said.

"Yeah, but it's a tragic love story," I admitted.

"It's a country that if it blows up, it will bring down a lot of other countries with it. But the thing is, when you talk about Pakistan in India, there is no middle."

"Everybody's anti-Pakistan?"

"Yes. That is very unfortunate I think so. And I blame the media for that."

His own magazine was an example of what Asad was talking about. In the lead article of *The Sunday Indian*'s current issue, pegged on the Lahore cricket attack and headlined "Allah, Army, America ... Anarchy," managing editor Sutanu Guru called India "the biggest victim" of Pakistan's "descent into chaos":

They say that hope is a flickering candle whose flame survives the fiercest of storms. The flames of hope may still be burning in Pakistan; but it is running out of wicker and wax. They talk about

Dr Frankenstein creating a monster that eventually devoured him. Blighted and benighted Pakistan is stalked by multiple monsters; but you will find it hard to find out who the real Dr Frankenstein is. Fareed Zakaria writes in a recent issue of *Newsweek*, "The veil is not the same as the suicide belt." The mother of all rogue states is now · in a situation where the veil and the suicide belt now hover over Pakistan like menacing and murderous symbols of satanic savagery.

"So what do you see as the difference between India and Pakistan?" Asad asked me.

"India is more self-confident," I said. "And confident in its own diversity. It seems able to accommodate most of its communities, even though there are sometimes severe problems. Pakistan is so caught up in its national ideology and its geopolitical situation that it can't be as confident."

"The interesting thing is that if you take away Muslims from India, India will be in the same situation as Pakistan," he said. "So Muslims are the unifying factor. That is why the RSS uses Muslims as a scapegoat, to unite all the Hindus on one platform. The Muslims don't have a good situation now. They are suspected of terroristic activities, of anti-national activities. So therefore Dalits [Untouchables] don't convert so much to Islam." Things could be worse, though. "Things were different when the BJP was in power. But when Manmohan Singh came in, when Congress came to power, things have changed."

"For the better?"

"For the better. And I think there's a realization by the Hindus that they cannot alienate the Muslims. And I think there's a realization on the part of the Muslims also that if we have to live in India, we have to be patriotic. Any country that gives room to people with different views–this is what India has, and Britain too, and I think America must have it too. But this is lacking in most Muslim countries. Democracy teaches you this: to live with people and to respect people with different views."

Asad compared India's right-wing RSS to the British National Party. "They think that if we give leeway to people with different views, then we are going to lose," he said.

"This is what Bush was about," I said.

"Yeah," he agreed. "Actually there is fear also. As V.S. Naipaul wrote in his book *Wounded Civilization*, Hindus feel this as a wound on their body, that Muslims came in and invaded, they destroyed our civilization, they destroyed our culture, and then in 1947 they took away Pakistan, they took away Bangladesh, and now there are still twenty crores [200 million] of Muslims in this country, and we have to suppress them."

I went into the mall to get drinks for us at a coffee shop, and when I returned I found Asad interviewing Pete about stem-cell research. "I got a question for you," Pete was saying. "What is the Muslim view on embryonic stem cell research?"

"I have no idea," said Asad. "I have the idea that it's embryonic, and it can be used to help people who are very ill ..."

Pete explained how it works. "But a lot of these embryos are frozen in tanks," he said, "and if they're not used, they'll die. And the right wing says that it's murder. So it's the old question of when does life start, and what is a human being?"

Asad was reminded of Maneka Gandhi, animal rights activist and widow of the late prime minister Indira Gandhi's late son Sanjay. "A guy wrote back to her and said, 'What about plants?'" About stem cells, he said to Pete: "It has to be destroyed. So why not use it for good purpose? I think it's going to become a non-issue. But it has to be regulated; I agree with you. And it also has to be something that's not just for the rich."

"I agree," said Pete.

"But Muslims believe that abortion is wrong," said Asad. "I could never do abortion. Best thing is not to have that situation in the first place. Use contraceptives."

* * *

Also at Citywalk we met Afshan Anjum, a television cricket reporter recommended to us by a colleague of hers in Mumbai, Faisal Shariff. Afshan was a bubbly, enthusiastic woman and, like Faisal, a Muslim. Both had covered the Indian national cricket team's instantly legendary 2004 tour of Pakistan.

"If you take all the big stars in India, like Shahrukh Khan and Amir Khan, and all of them, they're not really practicing Muslims, or Muslims as such, you know," she told me. "But the fact that they're Muslims makes lots of people happy and very connected to them. That will even happen if you go to Peshawar. Shahrukh Khan is originally from Peshawar."

"Faisal was telling me a story ..."

"Yes. We traveled to Peshawar together. Actually, Faisal was doing only hardcore, pure cricket, and I was doing a bit of feature stories as well. So I went to this place in Peshawar which originally belongs to the family of Shahrukh Khan. And you have his relatives and you have his cousins, and I was so surprised, they all have something in their face which resembles Shahrukh Khan so much. And everybody was telling us stories about him, and how everybody in those hills and those distant places, villages, just connects to him. Just his name—it isn't that he's doing anything that will make them happy. He's just an actor; he's just a star. But they feel that 'He belongs to us.' So that was very interesting. And in Pakistan everybody used to ask us that, 'Okay, so all these Khans and all these Muslim stars are marrying Hindu girls. Why do they do that?' I said, 'I don't have an answer to that. They just fall in love and they marry anybody they like!'"

"It's because they're in India, and I think the Pakistanis don't quite ..."

"Yes, Pakistanis also feel that we are slightly corrupted Muslims, we are not so pure when it comes to Islam. Well, you know, that's just a way of looking at it. I feel that in Pakistan, because they're not so exposed to such a versatile society, which is so complex and complicated, and which is a mix of so many cultures, a lot of people cannot imagine what it is to grow up in a place like India. It's very difficult to explain it to my friends in Pakistan."

"How do you try to explain it to them?"

"I just say what I just said to you."

"And it doesn't register, it doesn't compute?"

"Not really. You know, very few people actually understand why we are like this. I came across a lot of people like makeup artists in Pakistan, because we were doing a few shows out of Lahore, on cricket. Makeup artists who come and do your touchup and your hair and all, they keep talking to you. So they asked me, 'Why don't people in India like us? Why are they so much against Pakistan?' So I told them that I am not like that. But they said, 'No, but when we go to India, everybody looks at us like, "Oh, you're Pakistanis." And why is it like that?' I said, 'You know, there is no clear-cut explanation I have for it. There are like one thousand kinds of people in India. They have a different idea about everything. Some of them know Pakistan, some of them don't. Some of them know Pakistan through TV, some of them have heard stories about you.'

"And when I came back from Pakistan for the first time, I had a fight with so many people, that 'It is not like what you think, it is just not.' And I really felt bad at certain points, while we were traveling in Pakistan the first time, which was after fifteen or sixteen years that India went to Pakistan for cricket, for a bilateral series. So it was big, in 2004. And people hadn't seen Indians for a very long time. So when we were on the roads people used to stop their cars, come running to us—because they can differentiate the way we look, the way we dress up, certain differences. They used to come and ask, 'Where from India? Oh, have you ever met Shahrukh Khan? Have you ever met all these actors and actresses?' And they used to tell us that, 'Oh, I have my friends there, and I have a chat friend there on Yahoo,' and all kinds of things. And I also found certain people who just came, and the first question was that, 'What do you think about Pakistan? Did you like it?' And you say yes, or no, or whatever. And the next question was that, 'Madam, we are not terrorists, did you see that? We are very normal people.' And my heart used to just break. Imagine a society which has to say and prove it directly in words, that 'We are not terrorists.' Can you imagine what psyche they have, the kind of impression they have in the world?"

"So how did they respond to you as a Muslim? When they say those things to you as an Indian, are they aware that you're a Muslim?"

"They used to ask me what my name is, and the moment I said Afshan—it's a very typical, well-known Urdu word—they used to say, 'Oh! Are you a Muslim?' And when you said yes, they had this big smile on their face. 'Oh, that's very nice.' Suddenly they have this cord of connection, and they can ask you all kinds of questions that were there in their head, and probably they can never ask an Indian. Questions like, 'How are Muslims treated in India? Are you actually deprived of a lot of things? Is your life normal? Do they torture you?' All kinds of things that they must have heard or read or imagined about India."

"What do you say when they ask you questions like that?"

"It's very difficult to answer, because there is no direct yes or no to it. Because we grew up in an environment where everything was normal for us. I make them happy by saying that, 'No, we are absolutely fine. It's perfect for us,' so they don't feel worried for all the relatives they have, or just for the community they come from. But it's slightly complicated. We live a very normal life, where there is no problem at all. When I was a child it was *slightly* abnormal sometimes, because maybe in a bunch of fifty children, I was one of three or two who were Muslims. And it wasn't that I was being deprived of anything, or I was thrown out of any kind of get-together or anything. Just that when children ask what your name is, they say, 'Oh, you're a Muslim! Oh, okay! So, what do you do on Eid? So your mother wears a burqa?

So you chop mutton at home?' Strange things, which make you think that, oh, okay, I am not like everybody else. I'm slightly different. You grow up with that in your head."

"I'm the same as everybody else, only different," I paraphrased. One thing Pakistan offered Muslims, especially of older generations, was relief from that feeling of being different.

"You don't have to explain anything to anybody," said Afshan. "Everybody is a Muslim. That's one comfort factor, I think, which was there for my parents. I don't think like that, because I grew up in this environment, and I'm comfortable. My father used to say, whenever he used to get emotional, that 'I wish we were Pakistanis, and it would have been so much better for us, and our children would have grown in a proper environment where we were not different.' And I always used to believe him, most of the times. But now I think, in the past twenty years, India has changed a lot. Our generation doesn't know too much about Pakistan. It doesn't carry the burden of that history, you know? Although there is sometimes a fear factor when there is a huge riot happening somewhere in Bombay or Ahmedabad. Then suddenly you feel that, 'Oh, maybe it isn't so normal.'"

"There is the BJP and the RSS and all those people," I reminded her.

"Yes, the rightists are always there to remind you that it's not such a democratic country also. I get very scared when a huge riot happens in Bombay or Ahmedabad, or wherever the RSS is. I am scared somewhere inside. I saw the '82 riots with the Sikhs. They were killing all the Sikhs."

"Here in Delhi?"

"Yes, in Delhi. We used to live in old Delhi that time, and all the shops were being burned, and the women were taken away and raped and molested, and all the money was being looted. I've seen all that as a child. So sometimes it comes to your mind that maybe it's not so flowery and rosy and nice, even if you are educated, even if you are contributing to the society."

I thought of what Naipaul had written in *An Area of Darkness* about how, growing up in Trinidad, "at an early age I understood that Muslims were somewhat more different than others. They were not to be trusted; they would always do you down; and point was given to this by the presence close to my grandmother's house of a Muslim, in whose cap and grey beard, avowals of his especial difference, lay every sort of threat." I paraphrased that passage from memory and asked Afshan if she had read the book. The guy kept popping up in conversation in India, like a bad penny.

"I haven't read it," she said. "I have it, I have to read it. I have been to Port of Spain, and I have met his relatives; I was covering the World Cup in 2007. Those Indians are such a story in themselves, who live in Trinidad. I was doing a story on the temples, and I went to this particular temple, which belongs to this trust owned by the Kapil Dev family. And this Kapil Dev family is directly related to V.S. Naipaul in some way. They were telling me that, 'He's our cousin,' or something. Their whole idea is to save the Indianness in Trinidad. So I did a feature around this: That there's a temple, and there are children coming with flowers, and worshipping, and all that."

"Did you meet any Muslims in Trinidad?"

"In Trinidad I didn't. But you know, Indian South Africa isn't very different from us. The Indians who went to West Indies went much, much before the ones who went to South Africa. So South Africa is still closer to what we are in India. But yeah, I met many Muslims in South Africa. And they are generally Gujeratis. And it was so surprising, and in fact very nice also, that they are really respected in South Africa, and nobody looks at them with that terrorist kind of a view that, 'Oh, this is a Muslim, Islamic extremist.' They are respected, they are loved, and they are given the space that they need."

"How do you like being known as a cricket reporter?"

"It is very irritating! Because people stop me on the streets, and they expect me to tell them what the score is." I laughed. "Yeah it has actually happened like that! 'Ma'am, what is the score?' How would I know? I am off today, I'm not working!"

"But this tells you something about how important cricket is to people, I suppose."

"It is like the heart and soul of this country. Even Pakistan, for that matter. In fact, just now when that whole thing happened with the Sri Lankan team, I was so upset. Because all Pakistan has to follow, in terms of heroes, is just their cricketers. And I was talking to the Pakistani cricket team's captain, Yunus Khan, who comes from Mardan and Peshawar. He came out with a statement, and then I called him: 'How are you?' and this and that. And he was telling me, 'In our country, you all know that there is nothing that we have to follow. There is no Bollywood, there is no theater, there is nothing great being done. It's just cricket that has taken us to the international forum and we have been recognized. And if you really go to the north, Peshawar and the area around that, children don't have anything to do. Children don't have a world to look up to or follow.' And I know that Yunus and all those cricketers who come from Peshawar, they were such examples for the children there. Yunus was saying to me that, 'I am so upset that if these children don't see us playing anymore, if they don't see anybody coming to Pakistan, they will pick up the guns.' It's the easiest thing for them. And there'll be nobody to tell them that this is not right.' And he was sounding so sad.

"But the saddest part is that there's a lot of hypocrisy between India and Pakistan, specially sometimes from the side of India. Because we try and be very nice, that we are friends, we are the same, there is a just a border between us, we are brothers. And the moment something happens" —she snapped her fingers— "one little thing, you become enemies. How is that possible? Are we so frivolous inside? That's my question. When I'm sitting in a group and talking with my friends, and we're having a discussion about Pakistan, it just takes them one second to start criticizing Pakistan, and to start proving that it's a terrorist country and it's a failed state, and it should be bombed, and all kinds of things. And I don't know what to say then. These are the same people who could have gone to Pakistan and had great meals with their friends there. I don't know what kind of hypocrisy is this."

"The isolation is part of it," I suggested. "If you don't have direct experience of a place, it's harder to humanize the other person. And the separation is a big part of that."

"I was traveling in a bus when I was in college," Afshan remembered. "Two old ladies saw me, and they thought that I'm very cute-looking, and they just said, 'Oh, what a nice-looking girl. Come come, sit next to us.' And then they went on chatting. Some news had happened in Pakistan, and then something had happened in India. And they said, 'Why the hell these Muslims are here in India? Why didn't all of them go to Pakistan, when we had made a Pakistan and given it to them? Go, live! Why are they here in India?' And I was sitting right next to them and thinking that they think that I'm such a cute little girl, and they offered me this seat, and this is what they think. And what will they do if they come to know that I'm a Muslim? I just kept quiet. This is a joke between all my Muslim friends. Whenever I meet them I say to them, 'We made a Pakistan for you. Why are you still here?' We keep telling each other, 'Why are *you* still here? Why are *you* still here? Why are *you* still here?'"

I asked what differences she had noticed during her visits to Pakistan.

"For them, being modern and being more developed and forward-looking is about being anti-establishment and against the basis of that country," she said. "I've seen lots of people who rubbish Islam in Pakistan."

"Well, Islam is getting shoved down their throats," I said.

"Yes. That is why they want to get anti-Islam, and prove that they are actually modern. An Indian Muslim will never do that, because nobody is forcing Islam on them."

"And Islam in Pakistan comes in large part from the state," I said. "It's closely identified with the state, and the state is very dysfunctional."

"That creates a lot of confusion and complexity, specially for the youngsters."

I sketched the theme and plot of *The Dispossessed* to her. "So it's about the people who are really the same people," I summarized, "and the isolation they've endured, and how they have to come back to trying to understand each other, and trying to reconnect, but they also have totally opposing ideologies."

"I think that Pakistan is actually us," she said. "It's not so different."

"It's what we might be, if we weren't who we are."

"One important thing is the language. My parents used to speak beautiful Urdu. And I have never really studied Urdu; I just know the basics. And I speak Hindi and I speak English, that's it. So Hindi and Urdu are almost the same, you know. But when I go to Pakistan, and I see them with this wonderful vocabulary of Urdu, and the best pronunciations in the world, I think, 'Oh God, all this just went away from India.'"

"Do you think you'll have another chance to go cover cricket there any time soon?"

"I don't see it happening. In fact, I was telling my parents the other day that maybe I've been very lucky, that I went there so many times, and I went there when India was going to play cricket after fifteen or sixteen years, that great tour. And now, maybe if it happens after ten years, it'll be again a whole media *tamasha*, where you do stories on everything, and all those postcards start coming from Pakistan, and we are both happy countries and friends and everything, all this pseudo behavior."

85

"Your timing was good."

She giggled. "Yeah."

"What do you see coming for international cricket?"

"The basic result is there will be no international cricket in Pakistan. Which is the worst thing that can happen to that country. Nobody is ready to go to Pakistan—Australia, New Zealand, England, everybody has refused. The only thing that England has done is that, 'Okay, Pakistan can come play in our country.' But nobody is going to Pakistan. That's the most horrible thing that can happen to cricket in Pakistan, because if nobody goes, people will stop playing cricket. This is the worst possible thing that happened, because Sri Lanka said that, 'Okay, we will go to Pakistan, because everybody thinks that there is LTTE [the long-running Tamil Tigers rebellion] in our country, and nobody comes to Sri Lanka, so we want to set an example, so we will go, and then others will come.' And what happens is these Talibanis come and shoot them, so now nobody is going there."

Then she asked me a question: "Why do you think they have formed this alliance with these people in the Swat Valley? Because they couldn't control?"

The question threw me. A young Christian Pakistani had done something similar to me in Lahore in 2003, during a conversation about his family and the girl he wanted to marry. Like him she was Christian, but her family were modern-minded "Anglo-Indians" whereas, as he put it, "We are the simple Punjabis." The issue was that the Punjabi joint family system entailed crowded and complicated households, and his fiancee didn't feel up to that. "For last three-four-five years, I am in this situation," he had fretted. "So you tell me one thing: What do you suggest?"

Afshan's question nonplussed me in a similar way, although its awkwardness was not personal but political. A journalist claims license to be nosy without committing or exposing himself. But by asking my view of a delicate current issue, Afshan was gently and justifiably rendering our interview mutual. She was a journalist too, after all. And even if she hadn't been, why shouldn't she ask? Put differently, why shouldn't I be asked such a question? I'd rather not be, but why shouldn't I be?

What was delicate was that she was asking me to pass judgment not on the Taliban forces that had asserted control over the previously idyllic Swat Valley, but on President Asif Ali Zardari. How fully any civilian leader controls the state or the military in Pakistan is always an open question, and in Zardari's case it was complicated by the history and baggage that he brought to the role. When his wife, Benazir Bhutto, had been prime minister during the 1990s, he had been widely despised and lampooned as "Mr. Ten Percent," for his alleged corruption. Cases had been pressed against both him and her, and he had spent time in prison. Many in the press and elsewhere wondered aloud where the couple had found the money to purchase the "Surrey *mahal*," a multi-million-pound mansion near the village of Haslemere in a salubrious area of southern England. Insinuations were made about, for example, the rumor that the bodyguards of Benazir's estranged brother Murtaza had forcibly shaved off half of Zardari's mustache on an airplane flight, only days before Murtaza was killed in a gunbattle with Karachi police in September 1996. Zardari's and Benazir's relationship was widely believed to have been chilly, few Pakistanis liked or admired him, and now, somehow, it had turned out that she was dead and he was president of the country and co-chairman of the ostensibly liberal Pakistan People's Party that her father had founded. The nation was still digesting that turn of events, and Zardari had resorted to banning jokes about himself sent as text messages on cell phones. Was it—to adapt a memorable line from Raja Anwar's book about Murtaza, *The Terrorist Prince*—"yet another farcical episode in the comic opera of Pakistan politics"? It certainly seemed to be. But I didn't consider it my fight.

I would have preferred not to tip my hand, because Zardari's place in the scheme of things was officially none of my business. Like all the other skeletons in the country's closet—like Bangladesh and Kashmir and Bhutto and Zia and nuclear proliferation and terrorism and Afghanistan and Musharraf—it was a family affair for Pakistanis to settle among themselves. Wasn't it? I might have views on the guy, just as any Pakistani might have views on my country's president; but if I was invited into the national conversation, it was as a guest. Pakistanis are as hospitable in their political debates as they are in their homes—friends were always calling me an honorary Pakistani, intending it as a compliment—but in neither case is it advisable to presume. And in this instance, to boot, the person asking my view was not a Pakistani but an Indian.

I could have declined to reply, or I could have silently omitted the exchange from this book. I could have written around it. I am writing around it, in fact. I could have fictionalized it. When Mohammed Hanif's instant classic *A Case of Exploding Mangoes* burst on the scene in 2008, I conceived (but never actually wrote) a novel in a similar vein, which I would have titled *The Widower*. It would have been a worthy successor to my previous unwritten bestseller *Killer App*, a tense and tawdry murder mystery set on the placid campus of a fictional enormous software company in Redmond, Washington. It's probably just as well that I never got around to writing either of those books.

What I said to Afshan was: "Yeah, I think Zardari is really not in control. And because he's desperate, and because they're stupid."

* * *

Pete's and my feelings about Delhi were colored by the fact that bad timing and glitches in our forward planning compelled us to stay in Paharganj, the tourist ghetto near New Delhi Station. We had an invitation to stay in a private home—with a man a Pakistani acquaintance in Dallas proudly called his "Hindu friend"—but the emails

Mumbai

Kurien Abraham

Mahrukh Inayet

Bollywood filmmaker Mahesh Bhatt

Tushar Gandhi

Ajay Brahmatmaj (left) and Sanjay Jha (right)

Vidha Saumya

Hyderabad Deccan, India. Above, a Muslim girls' school.

A *ghazal* evening in Hyderabad

Mr. and Mrs. Baig with their daughter-in-law, Farah

Char Minar, Hyderabad

Scenes from an Indian train

Cricket journalist Afshan
Anjum in Delhi

Asad, an editor at *The Sunday Indian*

Pete Sabo, intrepid photographer

Scaling the Red Fort, Agra

Raj Bindra and his wife, Ruma

The Golden Temple, Amritsar

The Wagah border to Lahore

At the Lahore Gymkhana

Aslam Mughal

Aaqib Javed, Chief
Coach at the National
Cricket Academy, Lahore

misaligned, and we arrived in Delhi and had to stay somewhere. So, between meetings, we went ahead and acted like tourists. Walking toward the Red Fort and Humayun's Tomb early one morning, Pete saw some dogs and said: "Boy, man's best friend. They take so much abuse." Some strides later he added: "When they actually get garbage service here, *then* this'll be a real city." We walked past the Delhi Stock Exchange, where people were sleeping wrapped in blankets along the covered sidewalk. "These are the stockbrokers," said Pete.

"Well, the market just crashed," I said.

"I shouldn't joke," he said. "It's Saturday, so the market's closed."

The same afternoon we endured an incident that was infuriating but ultimately edifying. We let a young hustler on Connaught Place con us into paying far too much for a hired car to take us to Agra to see the Taj Mahal. When we realized that we had been had, Pete insisted on returning to the travel agency—by foot, a mile or so back from New Delhi Station, in the heat of the day—to force them to give us our money back. As the seasoned Asia hand, I felt ashamed to have let Pete down; I wasn't about to talk him out of it.

"Please sit down," a man said to us when we barged in and launched our first salvo.

"I want to stand up," said Pete. "I'm angry." He was glaring.

"Don't give me American eyes," said the man. "This is India!"

"We want to talk to Jana."

"Please sit down."

"I'll stand."

The young man who had scammed us was in his office with the door closed. Next thing I knew, Pete was bursting in and shouting at the couple sitting across the desk from him, "Don't believe a word he says!" It was Pete at his righteous best.

The incident echoed some of my earliest experiences in India, back in my callow youth. This time it was more aggravating and more humbling, because I should have known better. But it was a helpful reminder of the gulf across which one would always be perceived in Asia. I would never be Indian, or Pakistani, or Thai. Nor, frankly, did I want to be. I thought of something a dyspeptic Australian friend from my Bangkok days had said: that sometimes you might as well just go ahead and act like a white man, because that's what they're always going to see you as. Or, as Kipling put it:

> And the end of the fight
> Is a tombstone white
> With the name of the late deceased
> And the epitaph drear: "A fool lies here
> who tried to hustle the East."

Having been caught red-handed, they were already coolly preparing to refund our money, but no apology was forthcoming. An older man—he was stout and rather short, and had a mustache and a dot on his forehead—started counting out cash, and I turned to Pete and started asking him if he would accept rupees. But when I turned forward again, someone was producing the two traveler's checks we had used earlier to pay and handing them to Pete. We had won. But the fight wasn't over.

"Please sit down."

"I don't want to sit down. I want to stand. I'm angry."

Suddenly the stout man was shouting and wagging his finger in Pete's face. This astonished me, and the sheer gall and offensiveness of it snapped my will to stay cool. I grabbed the man's wrist, then wagged my own finger in his face. "Don't wag your finger in my friend's face!" I cried. I wasn't yelling—not quite. I wasn't out of control—was I? But if I hadn't stood up for Pete in that moment, I wouldn't have respected myself. My usual inclination would have been to urge calm—*jai yen yen*, as they say in Thailand. But why the hell shouldn't Pete be angry, and why shouldn't he stand if he wanted to? *You* lied to us, I thought. *You* ripped *us* off, and now we've busted you, and you presume to wag your finger in our face?

We got out of there in one piece and made it onto a train to Agra, which left several hours late and didn't arrive until one-thirty in the morning. On three and a half hours' sleep, we dragged our asses out of bed and down the street to see the Taj Mahal at sunrise.

"This is great!" exclaimed Pete, and the multiple exhausting hassles of the previous day were suddenly worth it. And all I had to do that morning was sit in the shade on the cool marble, as the sun rose in the sky and the shadows shifted in the alcoves of the famous mausoleum, and watch Pete do his thing with a camera. This was his element; there were times when I wished I could take pictures of Pete taking pictures. But behind the camera was where Pete wanted to be, where he was happy and purposeful.

To me, a camera is an encumbrance. Writing and photography require different kinds of attention, and having to think about taking photos, much less actually taking them, is a distraction from what I should be doing. For Pete, it was the point. I had no pictures from my previous times in India and Pakistan, and as a writer I believe people should want to read the words in a book, never mind photos and other ornaments. But enough readers had asked me why *Alive and Well in Pakistan* didn't have pictures that I decided this time I'd better give the people what they want. And traveling with someone who actually enjoyed taking photographs was a luxury and a load off my mind. "You didn't bring a camera?" a Pakistani woman said to me later in the trip, in Rawalpindi. "I brought Pete instead," I told her.

I asked Pete to take some pictures I knew I was going to want, but mostly I left him to do his thing while I did mine. And watching him was a window into a different way of looking at the world. He had a strange thing for statues and monuments, which interested me very little, but otherwise his eye was selective in ways that I felt reflected well on him. He sought out natural beauty, and he had a knack for finding wildlife in the interstices, like the hawks' nest on the minaret of a mosque in Paharganj, the parrots at the Red Fort, the puppies in the village near the Line of Control, the feral cats on the pile of garbage in the fishing village outside Karachi. There were swallows, egrets and plenty of pigeons, as well as parrots galore at the Red Fort in Delhi and at the Taj Mahal. The famous monkeys at Murree near Islamabad were a treat for Pete. As our trip progressed, I enjoyed fancifully imagining a pair of coffee-table books that would offer an idiosyncratic vision of the subcontinent: *Pete Sabo's India* and *Pete Sabo's Pakistan.*

But Pete wasn't one to put himself or his work forward very aggressively. And photography was an avocation that suited not only his love of gadgets and doohickies but also his taciturnity. "I'm not a words guy," he said to me. "That's why I'm a photographer. Worth a thousand words."

"You don't have to write," I acknowledged, a bit enviously.

"I used to do that," he laughed, "but I graduated."

※ ※ ※

"Okay, I think I'm getting to saturation point, where everything's starting to look the same," said Pete around nine o'clock that morning, after a good three hours of photographing the Taj and its gardens and outbuildings. "Plus, I'm hungry."

"You were like a kid in a candy store for a couple hours," I said.

"Oh man, no kiddin'!"

Our day in Agra, and the effort of getting there and back, drained our capacity for sightseeing in India. Basing ourselves in Paharganj and Connaught Place hadn't helped our attitude either. We were eager to get to Pakistan, where at least we wouldn't be treated like tourists.

But our last couple of days back in Delhi were retrieved when Raj Bindra, the "Hindu friend" of my Pakistani friend in Dallas, reached me and invited us to stay with him. Raj lived in Karol Bagh, not far from New Delhi Station, with his wife and grown son, Raghav. He was slightly built, with a little mustache, and he had lived so many years in the United States that he spoke with a distinct American accent. Raj had been born before Partition in Sialkot, a city that was now in Pakistan. "When I applied for my U.S. passport in 1992, I put 'Pakistan'"—he pronounced it the American way— "on the form as my place of birth, because I assumed it had to be the name of the place as it's called now," he told me. "When I renewed it ten years later I asked them to change it, and they wouldn't do it. They read 'Pakistan' and they give me another look. And for that reason, I think, my bags at the customs get opened every time." He was philosophical about this annoyance. "Maybe it just happened that way to protect me in the future, maybe. Maybe I'll get caught up in a situation where those credentials will help me."

Stories like his were very common here in the Punjab, on both sides of the border. "We had property back in Pakistan," he told me. "And *this* house was evacuee property, that used to belong to rich Muslims. My grandfather was a lawyer, and he was appointed by the government as a chief claims officer, to adjudicate. Since he had the information, and we had claims that were government-approved, my father was able to buy it. We only had one part of it, the upstairs. Downstairs was all refugees. Then my father filed lawsuits against the rest of the tenants, and finally, after thirteen years, he was able to evict them. By that time it was 1970, and I came back from London, and my father told me to think about renovating it, to make it liveable."

Raj had been very small when his family crossed the new border under duress, like millions of others. "All I recall is that I was about three years old," he said. "I recall too that while we were transitioning into India, we were camped out. Partition happened in August; I think we left in July. It was hot, and I was in my mother's lap, and I was crying. I remember Mother trying to put me to sleep, but I couldn't, because of the conditions in the camp."

"It's amazing that you remember even that much," I said.

"Yeah. I was three years old. And I remember women washing clothes in the river—the Tavi river—in Jammu or Pathankot. One or the other. I think it was Jammu. And a woman washing clothes on the rocks: she wasn't bit by a snake, but a snake came up on the rock, and there was a lot of screaming because of the snake."

"Did you come straight to Delhi?"

"No, no. We were at different refugee stations. We were at Kapurthala. That's the name of a little princedom. Then we were in Amritsar; we stayed with relatives several months. My paternal aunt, you know, my father's sister, we stayed at their house."

"And your family left everything in Pakistan?"

"Yeah. We left everything."

"Have you ever been back to Sialkot?"

"No. But I would love to go. I heard that the house there was so big that it was subsequently turned into a government office."

"So when did you come to Delhi?"

"We came to Delhi in '52, when I was about eight years old. My father found a job."

"What job?"

"I think as an office manager."

"And you grew up the rest of your childhood in Delhi?"

"Yeah, until I was nineteen years old."

"Where did you go when you left Delhi?"

"I went to London, in 1963, when I was nineteen years old. I went to study there."

"Had you ever been out of India?"

"No. It was an eye-opener. It was a whole different world. But I was very enthusiastic, because I felt I was released from prison. Because I had my mother and three sisters, and there was a lot of quarreling. Being the only male, I felt a little left out. My father didn't talk much, wasn't very approachable. That's how Indian fathers used to be."

"You're not like that," I remarked.

"No, I'm not. Maybe that's part of the problem—I over-compensated with my own kids."

In 1976 he was living in New York and stressed out by a job in accounting. "In the subway I saw the posters for this Maharishi Mahesh Yogi, and I took that up. And would you believe it? Within four or five days, my palpitations stopped. So I thought 'I owe it to my life to keep doing it.' And my consciousness has expanded a lot because of it." Hinduism was a generous buffet of traditions and practices that he felt he could define and use any way that worked for him. "There is no central institution," he said approvingly. "There's no Vatican, there's no Church of England, there's no Mecca, Medina, Jerusalem."

"What does that mean to you?"

"It means that I can take a very open view of everything. I don't have to be restricted. I can be Muslim, I can be Jewish. When I was in the jewelry business in New York, my wife used to wear a Star of David ring, and I used to tell the Jews we did business with that my grandmother was Jewish."

"Was she?"

"No! And they used to give us special prices because Jews, they help each other out."

In India it was possible to be oblivious to what was happening in Pakistan, but at Raj's house we caught the news on Times Now, and it seemed momentous. The lawyers' movement had planned a Long March from Lahore to Islamabad to confront Zardari over his broken promise to restore Iftikhar Chaudhry, the Chief Justice of the Supreme Court whom Musharraf had illegally dismissed two years earlier. If it had reached Islamabad, the march might have been so large that it would have overwhelmed the capital's barricades, and who knows what might have happened. But former prime minister Nawaz Sharif had busted out of house arrest to join the marchers, Chief of Army Staff General Ashfaq Kiyani had probably

intervened quietly to bring home the point that, if he chose confrontation, Zardari could not rely on the support of the military, at
the last minute Zardari had caved in, and the marchers had declared
victory.

This was, intoned the Times Now anchor, "Pakistan narrowly
pulling back from total anarchy." Another way to see it was as "the
coming of age of the Pakistani political process," as a Pakistani inter-
viewee described it. "Is there going to be an all-out power grab?"
asked the Times Now anchor. It was, countered the Pakistani, "an
assertion of middle-class civic activism at its best in Pakistan."

"You never know what's going to happen there tomorrow," Raj
said. "That's the way it's been for many years."

"Do they give us cause for hope?" I asked him, referring to the
marchers.

"Maybe briefly and temporarily, but I think some very complex
things are going to unfold in the coming weeks and months. It looks
like some major events are about to happen. They're contained for a
while, but they're going to explode."

"Like what?"

"The Army would be pointless if it didn't have India to fight with
over the Kashmir issue. If they didn't have the Kashmir issue, the
Army would be redundant."

"But what about the Frontier? Doesn't that give the Army a new
purpose?"

"They're really manipulating the U.S. into making them believe
that unless the U.S. gets involved in resolving the Kashmir issue,
most of the Army would have to be deployed on the Pakistani side
of the Kashmir border. Enough manpower is not available to them
to fight the Taliban. They will keep the pot boiling, too."

"What's the significance of Obama in this context, if any, and the
change of administration?"

"Oh, it presents an opportunity of transforming the country's image. Because all the goodwill that America had had been drained during Bush's administration."

"But I mean specifically to do with Pakistan."

"Well, he has a real opportunity to reach out to the Taliban. They have an opportunity to sift them, the good from the bad from the ugly. Like they did in Baghdad. They're hoping they might succeed. But I doubt it. He has to exhaust all peaceful channels, but if they appear to be pliable, it's only to their advantage to buy time."

* * *

On our last day in Delhi, Raj drove us all the way across the city during evening rush hour to Nizamuddin Station, to catch our train to Amritsar.

"Next time you can't pull that shit, staying a day and a half or whatever," he said. "Next time, you have to stay your whole stay here."

CHAPTER 3

THE GUY WHO KEPT COMING BACK

"What is your profession?" asked the customs man at the Wagah border crossing, between Amritsar and Lahore.

"I'm a biologist," Pete told him.

"And your profession?"

"I'm a journalist," I said.

"I think you are a gentleman, sir." The man smiled through his mustache, the way Punjabis do. He was welcoming us, not grilling us, and my fears and worries fell away.

"I try to be," I said.

"And you, sir? Are you also a gentleman?"

"Uh, yes."

"You don't have any alcohol in your bags? It is not allowed in Pakistan. If you have any, don't tell anyone!" And with that, he cheerfully waved us in.

* * *

I had spent most of 2008 planning to come to Pakistan. The journey had begun in a sense the morning after Musharraf declared the state of emergency, in November 2007, when I awoke early at home in Seattle and wrote a synopsis for a feature-length documentary film I would have titled *Musharraf: Man of Crisis.*

Any project covering contemporary Pakistan will be overtaken by events. What I've relearned since that morning is that, although things often don't turn out as planned, they do have a strange way of turning out as they should. Sustaining that faith can be difficult, but the alternative is bitterness, paranoia, and despair. I also believe that, while Pakistan is specifically itself, it really is little different from anywhere else. If Pakistan is corrupt and maddening and dangerous, that says something not about Pakistan but about people and the world.

A couple of weeks after Musharraf declared the emergency, I was a speaker at a day-long seminar on Investment Opportunities in Pakistan, hosted by the Pakistan Club of the University of Chicago Graduate School of Business. The timing just turned out that way. My subject was tourism. What do you say to a room full of Pakistanis on that subject, two weeks after their country's military ruler has suspended the constitution? Now that it was pretty much too late, pondering what-ifs was a form of self-flagellation, though maybe not without usefulness: What if Pakistan had not come into being in the blood-soaked way it did? What if Mohammad Ali Jinnah, the founder, hadn't died little more than a year later? What if Pakistan and India had not fought three wars? What if Z.A. Bhutto had not banned alcohol in the 1970s? What if the Soviet Union hadn't invaded Afghanistan in 1979?

What I tried to say that day in Chicago was that maybe Pakistan's failure ever to have developed a proper tourism industry was a historic missed opportunity. Anything that increased human contact and sympathy between Pakistanis and Americans was good and important, and tourism was one such thing. I cited Emma Duncan's insight in *Breaking the Curfew*, her book about the transition in the late 1980s from the Zia dictatorship to civilian rule under Benazir Bhutto, that post-British India enjoyed "a monopoly on imperial nostalgia." I noted that India was still called India, whereas Pakistan wasn't—India had the "brand." And I wondered: What if Pakistan had decided, early on, to make a priority of marketing the heritage of the Mughal

Empire and the ancient ruins at Taxila, not to mention the Himalaya and the Hindu Kush and the annual Shandur Polo Festival and Alexander the Great, assertively or even shamelessly to moneyed Westerners? And what if the country had built world-class roads and resorts to serve such an ambition? More what-ifs.

Afterward, a youngish man in a suit bought *Alive and Well in Pakistan* and told me his name was Fawad Butt.

"Are you Kashmiri?" I asked him.

He was impressed by the question. "Yes, I am," he acknowledged.

"Is it true that all Butts are Kashmiri?"

"Yeah, it is."

I told him there were Butts in the early chapters of the book. Like most Pakistanis, he had never been to the Kashmir Valley but had wistful feelings about it. Then he told me about his infant son: "My wife and I decided that if he was going to go to school in America, we had to give him a different last name." The name they had decided on was "Kashmiri." Fawad was an enthusiastic and creative entrepreneur born in Lahore, raised in Saudi Arabia where his father had worked as an engineer, and based in Chicago since he had landed there at nineteen knowing no one. I came to learn that his was a fairly common Pakistani story. Our first encounter launched a whirlwind of planning and scheming, public speaking and dinner parties, midnight eurekas and hare-brained capers concocted in Fawad's basement, that hasn't let up since.

I returned to Chicago three times within five months, Fawad jumped on board the documentary film project, and it morphed away from a focus on Musharraf. The original title was an allusion to something Hassan Iqbal, a young man I met in Islamabad, had said to me in 2003. I was staying with Hassan's family in Rawalpindi when the scientist Abdul Qadeer Khan was exposed for having sold nuclear secrets to Libya, Iran, and North Korea. With Hassan and his parents I had watched the televised press conference in which Musharraf, wearing a camouflage uniform with "Pervez" on the name tag, had manfully duked it out with foreign journalists. "This is an independent nation," he retorted to a Reuters reporter who asked whether he would allow UN inspectors into Pakistan. "Nobody comes inside and checks our things. We check them ourselves."

"Do you think this is a major crisis for Musharraf?" I asked Hassan.

"Oh yes," he replied. "He is the man of crisis."

"Every year he has crisis," Hassan's mother added cheerfully. "Two years before, Taliban crisis. Then last year, Iraq crisis. Now this Qadeer Khan crisis."

It was tempting to personalize things, especially with a personality as vivid and assertive as Musharraf. But the point was that Pakistan is a country of crisis, no matter who's in charge. "Events are moving so quickly and rapidly that you can't keep up," Hassan had observed way back then. It wasn't really about Musharraf. And soon enough, it wasn't even ostensibly about him anymore.

By the spring of 2008, Fawad and I were focusing instead on personal stories of ordinary Pakistani people with representative experience of recent history. The film was going to be a sequel to *Alive and Well in Pakistan,* but eventually we concluded that writing a second book instead would cost a lot less in time, money, and heartache. Not that writing a book isn't a lot of work, but at least there are fewer moving parts.

I began introducing myself to Pakistani communities around the United States and Canada. In April I returned to Chicago to speak at a fundraiser for Greg Mortenson's Central Asia Institute, and in May I spoke at a fundraiser in San Jose for the Human Development Foundation. There I took the opportunity to argue, in a talk Fawad and I co-wrote, that Pakistani Americans had both a responsibility and a historic opportunity to participate more actively in American political and civic life. "This is a crucial historical moment," I said, "because the demonization of Pakistanis and Muslims will affect not only the current generation, but generations to come. And the damage will be not only to Pakistanis and other Muslims, but to all of us and to our shared human future." I pointed out that complaining to each other on Pakistani news channels like Geo and ARY "does not constitute a media strategy." And I asked: "HDF and several other Pakistani organizations that we support do excellent and important work not only in Pakistan but elsewhere, including here in the U.S. Why don't other Americans know about it? The Pakistani community in America is an American community, after all."

Fawad and I spoke together in Washington, DC at the big annual convention of the Association of Physicians of Pakistani Origin of North America (APPNA), and I started driving up the coast to Vancouver, to meet the long-established Pakistani community there. In our minds all this was preparation for a joint trip to Pakistan in the fall to scout and begin filming stories for the documentary. We had never made a film before, but we were going to teach ourselves how, and Pete was going to join us as a photographer. Things didn't quite work out as planned.

What happened instead was that Pete and I applied for visas in August, then waited. Then we waited some more, until it became obvious that we would have to reschedule the trip. It was an especially fluid political time in Pakistan, not everyone in official Islamabad was inclined to welcome American journalists, and our lack of institutional affiliation didn't help. And the truck bomb that killed at least fifty-four people and severely damaged Islamabad's iconic Marriott Hotel on September 20 can't have helped either. It was demoralizing, but also helpfully humbling, to be reminded that my unofficial status as a friend of Pakistan didn't entitle me to anything.

So we made new plans and called in favors, and eventually Pete and I were granted visas. In the meantime, Fawad went without us to Lahore for a month. He returned in mid-November, just in time to join me for two speaking engagements in Denver. The main one, at the Episcopal cathedral, was a prototype of the kind of mainstream American audience we wanted to begin reaching.

Fawad's mood in Denver was distinctly downbeat. In Lahore there had been a spate of bombings of juice shops, where extremists suspected teenagers of meeting in private booths for trysts. "The important thing to know about the juice shop bombings is that, one, they didn't happen in the rich parts of town," he told me. "They happened in old Lahore. People in Defence weren't affected by them. Pakistanis have become so resilient that they've developed a sense of who the target is. If you went to a cafe that was in either Gulberg or Defence, where plenty of dating occurs on a regular basis, there was no sense of fear. The fact that these bombings occurred in the poorer part of town, on the other side of Mall Road—on the other side of the tracks, so to speak—gave the rich and the affluent a sense of security."

Of more direct significance to Fawad was "load shedding," the rationing of electricity by power suppliers because of the government's inability to pay its bills. I had been irked by the infrequency of our email contact during his trip; now I learned the reason.

"The fact that electricity was rationed made everything less fun and more complicated," he said. "Simple tasks became complicated, like using the Internet. If I had gone there for just two weeks, all I would have remembered about this trip would be that it was dark there. In the middle of Lahore, right outside of Defence, at eight-thirty or nine at night, it would be absolute silence, and absolute darkness. You could sit on your balcony and see the stars. And in a major city, that never happens. That feeling that you're living in a rationed environment—not just the poor, but everybody. And the physical sense of darkness. It was kind of scary. And you have to understand, this was also in the aftermath of the Marriott bombing. You could equate it to 9/11 occurring in the U.S., and right after that the electricity situation would occur."

"Remember those blackouts on the East Coast, not long after 9/11?"

"Except this was constant," he said. "It was every hour. You couldn't shake it. That was something that I had not seen in Pakistan. The funny thing is that you get used to it. And literally, at 11:45 or 9:45 or 7:45, you start to panic. You start thinking about all the things you have to get done while there's electricity. The other major thing about Pakistan this time around was the sense of an impending financial crisis. Many Pakistanis have foreign currency accounts in banks. And once before, during the Nawaz Sharif time, those accounts were seized."

"Yeah, I remember that."

"So everybody I would meet would advise me to take my money out of the accounts."

"Did you?"

"Yeah. And that's an adventure in itself. One of my accounts is at Standard Chartered Bank. My brother-in-law, who is a branch manager at a bank in Lahore, finally convinced me to go get the money out. So I go to Standard Chartered, to the biggest one on Gulberg Main Boulevard, and they asked me whether I was a regular customer or a priority banking customer. I didn't know, and it turned out I was a priority customer. So they take me into this room, and this beautiful girl asked me how she could help me, and I told her I was there to withdraw some dollars from my foreign currency account. When I told her that, she immediately had that look on her face that told me there was something wrong. And when I told her I had to withdraw a significant amount of money, she told me that was not possible."

"So then what?"

"When I was like, 'Why not?' she said, 'We have no dollars, sir.' Which was surprising to me, because I had a dollar account. It wasn't like I was there to buy dollars. I was there to take my dollars out. And I asked her when they would have some dollars. Her answer was, 'I don't know, sir.' And, confused as I was, I said, 'What do you mean?' And she said, 'We'll take your information, amongst others who are looking for dollars, and when we have some, we'll give you a call.' And really, that was when I was in a state of panic. That's when it occurred to me that there might be a real crisis at hand."

"So maybe now that the country has $7.6 billion from the IMF, you'll be able to get some dollars," I suggested.

"I sure hope so," he said. "But this was only the beginning of my adventure. Over the next ten days, I had the same conversation with all eleven of the Standard Chartered branches in Lahore."

"How were you feeling by the end of those ten days?"

"I was feeling very disappointed in Pakistan. And then a funny thing happened. Then I got used to it. So finally I went to a branch one fine morning, asked for the manager, and told him I wasn't leaving until I got my money back. And after five and a half hours of sitting at the bank and threatening the bank manager with this silent protest, and him making at least twenty-five calls to his management and the state bank and God knows who else, he finally gave me the good news. And the good news was that I could have my money back, except it wouldn't be in dollars. And he offered me my money back in pounds."

"Not rupees?"

"Well, I had refused to take rupees, much earlier. And I was so frustrated by that point that I figured I would take whatever I could get."

"I hope you weren't too mean to that young girl."

"No," he assured me. "She was my first encounter."

"Ten days and eleven branches earlier."

"Yeah. And the eleventh branch, where I finally got my money back in pounds, was in Islamabad. I had to drag my ass to Islamabad and spend five and a half hours ..."

"Did you go to Islamabad just for that?"

"I literally had to borrow Amber's uncle's car, drag my ass to Islamabad, and spend an entire day at the bank to get my money back."

"Did you drive there the day before, or did you get up early in the morning?"

"Oh my God. This adventure is so long. I got up early in the morning to get to Islamabad in time, during banking hours. The branch I was supposed to go to was the Diplomatic Enclave branch, which was the branch where I had opened my account many years earlier. Islamabad is such a different place now, because of the Marriott bombing. The entire Diplomatic Enclave is in a protected zone, which is equivalent to the Green Zone in Iraq. After three checkpoints, when I finally reached the street that the branch was on, I was told that cars were not allowed on that street, and that the bus service wasn't running that day. I said, 'But my account is at this branch.' And he said, 'I'm sorry, sir, but we're not allowed to let anybody in.' And I was frustrated as hell, because I had just driven five and a half hours to get there."

"So you got to the branch eventually, though?"

"No. It's such a long adventure that it's never-ending. Out of frustration I called the bank manager, and he was very apologetic. He said, 'I'm sorry, sir.' And I said, 'But I just drove from Lahore.' And he said, 'Well, what I can do for you, sir, is I'll transfer your account to the F-7 branch, which is not in the protected zone.'"

"Maybe he had already learned to do this for other people."

"I think so. And the next day I went to the F-7 branch and did my silent protest, and got the British pounds instead."

"Well, that's quite a story," I said.

"I've got twenty like it," said Fawad.

* * *

"Amjad told me there are some *goras* sitting there," said Adnan with a big grin, when we found each other on the Pakistani side of the border.

106

Our train from Delhi had arrived early that morning in Amritsar, capital of India's Punjab state. We had quickly toured the Golden Temple and its museum of startlingly violent paintings depicting scenes from Sikh history, and the park commemorating the infamous Jallianwala Bagh massacre of 1919. But we had no other business in Amritsar and I was eager to get to Pakistan, so in the early afternoon we headed to the famous "Wagah border," the only land crossing between India and Pakistan. I had first crossed at Wagah in 1995. In 2004 I had visited it from the other side with my students to sit in the bleachers and watch the border closing ceremony, in which the two countries' soldiers vied in pomp and ersatz ferocity. It had become a legitimate daily event, almost a sporting event. It was a bit goofy, but fun and certainly preferable to an actual war.

"You sir, press reporter?" asked the young driver Raj Bindra had arranged through relatives to drive us to the border from Amritsar.

"Sort of, yes," I admitted. I always resisted the tag, but it was hard to avoid.

"You America?"

"Yes."

"Obama," he said.

"Everybody likes Obama," I remarked.

"Yes."

"I'm sure glad we didn't come here last year," said Pete, not for the first time.

Adnan Latif had not been the brightest of my students, but he had been the most enthusiastic and eager. Beaconhouse National University charged high fees and catered to Pakistan's economic and social elite. Adnan's business-oriented family was well off, but social distinctions set him apart from my other students. Besides Adnan and a young Indian in the visiting students program, I had two other male students. The rest were young women. The girls nagged and bullied the boys, especially poor Adnan, although it was true that he irritated them by making rude remarks and generally being a bit of a galoot. He also had a reckless streak, which was alarmingly apparent when you rode in a car with him. Adnan was tall and lanky, dark-skinned, with stringy hair and a sharp nose. He had arrived a couple of weeks into the semester, which I had not been happy about, but he had taken to my class with alacrity. Something must have struck a chord in him, because he started talking about actually trying journalism as a career. This desire was not evident in his classmates, nor did I encourage it; if there was anything I had learned from the freelance racket, it was that writing good journalism is not readily compatible with making a living. This didn't deter Adnan, but he had a shrewd business head and a lot of moxie, so I figured he'd do well for himself one way or another.

Five years later he had a notepad impressively full of phone numbers of famous and powerful people, which he proudly shared with me after we had reached Lahore and sat down. "How do you know all these people?" I asked him.

He beamed. "I am a journalist!"

Adnan had proven the best of my students at staying in touch. "good to see you sir you are looking still young and we people are going old," he had written to me when I joined Facebook. "I'm very keenly waiting when you will visit Pakistan for the documentary project. Hope you are having a good life there." And three days after the Marriott bombing, he had written: "hello sir hope you are good … I just share my worries with you that you are coming or not in these circumstances … If you are coming then be careful I don't want to see you in danger." I had written back to assure him we were still coming. "I can arrange prominent personalities for interviews," he replied. "my all time is for you in Lahore. I can do my best during your stay."

I wasn't as eager to meet prominent personalities as Adnan was for me to meet them, but his loyalty was touching, and it was comforting to know a friend was waiting for us. At the border I had left Pete sitting at a soda-pop stand while I went in search of a phone to call Adnan, but his driver had spotted us first.

"He is my father's very trusty man," Adnan told me. Amjad was taciturn and had little English, and he rode shotgun because Adnan enjoyed driving, the way some people enjoy things like jumping out of airplanes. "I called Amjad just for your protection," he said.

"Thank you," I said. "Do you think we need protection?"

He left a longish pause. "I don't think, but ..."

"Just in case?"

"Yes. Otherwise I come alone."

His vehicle was a Mitsubishi Pajero. "Actually it's my father's car," he said. "I rarely use it."

"Did you ask him if you could use it?"

"Oh, he say, 'Do what you want.' Even though he is going to Faisalabad today, he take smaller car." Adnan basked in his father's indulgence. During the fasting month of Ramadan in 2003, I had spent an afternoon with him in Lahore's Moghul-era old city. When he nearly collided with another car and I winced, he told me he had once had an accident with a bus. "When he went to police station, my father angry," he said. "He say, 'Why you break the bus mirror?' But otherwise he not angry. He always love me. He say, 'Anyone hit your car, just let them go away. Forget them.'"

"You're the same kind of driver that you were five years ago," I said now, and he smiled proudly.

His driving wasn't the only thing Adnan was proud of. "I was invited for tea by ex-governor," he said. "After I wrote article about him, his milit'ry secret'ry called me and said that he appreciated my work very much. I am very happy!"

"Is Shahbaz Sharif going to come back?" I asked him.

"*Inshallah*!" God willing. "He is my leader." Adnan was a pukka Lahori.

"What do you think about everything that's happened the last few days, with the Long March and Nawaz?"

"It's good for democracy," he said.

"It's good for Nawaz too, I think," I said.

"*Sudden* it happened. Because he did not expect so many people to come out."

"Have you been to India?"

"Yes."

"When?"

"New Year Night in 2004, I was there."

"How did you go there?"

"That was a goodwill trip for Beaconhouse National University, and I really enjoyed it. Actually, my forefathers came from ..."

"From Indian side?"

"Yes."

"Where?"

"In Punjab. In some rural areas. They were landowners."

"Where did you go in India?"

"Fifteen days we went, and we visited seven cities."

"Which teachers went with you?

"Taimur ul Hassan." Taimur was my teaching colleague and fellow founding faculty in BNU's School of Media and Communication. "Ayela Deen." Ayela had been the bossiest of my girl students, leader of the clique I called the Gang of Three, but she was likeable and a strong leader. She had returned to BNU as an instructor.

"I'm very happy to be back in Lahore," I said, and I meant it.

"Lahore is Lahore!" cried Adnan, quoting a smug local saying.

"That's true."

"This is my city. I feel comfortable like a king. No tension."

I felt an inkling, and gave voice to it. "So, are you going to be Chief Minister one day?"

He didn't deny it. "Inshallah," he said, beaming. "Inshallah."

* * *

Adnan treated us to a late lunch at the Salt 'n Pepper restaurant near Liberty Market. It was here, early in my stay in 2003, with time on my hands before the semester started, that I had wandered alone one afternoon, wallowing pleasurably in the sounds and smells of an Asian city. I had felt then that I was returning full circle, completing an experience begun nearly a decade earlier. A few months before that, I had not known if I would return to Pakistan; I had last been there in 1999 and my life was elsewhere, or so I thought. In '98 I had hit a wall, broke and demoralized by the perpetual travel and thankless exertion of trying to make a living as a freelance journalist in a part of the world the triumphalist West found too remote and exotic to be relevant. After five years in Asia, I had gone to live in England. I fell in love with a woman there and told her, because it was what she wanted to hear and what I wanted to believe, that I was done with journalism and with Asia. I was well and truly burned out. What I hadn't counted on was that, in an English suburb, I would be bored.

Those were different times, the nineties, the days of the Asian Tiger economies. In September 1996 my friend Anthony Davis, a leading authority on Afghanistan, had been compelled to pick a fight with his own editors at the Hong Kong-based newsweekly *Asiaweek* to get his eyewitness account of the Taliban's capture of Kabul to the Taliban published. *Asiaweek* is now defunct. But in '96 Hong Kong and Southeast Asia were riding high, I heard rumors that America was doing well too, Windows 95 was the greatest thing since sliced bread, and everyone was all excited about the Internet. Within a few days in early July 1997, the Thai baht crashed from its longtime peg at 25 to the U.S. dollar, a coup d'etat made a mockery of the international community's most audacious and expensive attempt at liberal political engineering—the May 1993 UN-sponsored election in Cambodia—and Britain gave Hong Kong to China. I was present at the first two of these events. Even at the time it seemed clear to me that an era had ended; we just didn't know it yet.

My precocity didn't do me much good. "You're ahead of the curve," an editor who positioned himself as my mentor advised me. "Don't dumb down your work in order to place it; it's only a matter of time." I was still too inexperienced and hopeful to know that that's actually not true. And even if it were, how much time can a person afford? Hemingway had a good answer, in *A Moveable Feast*: "Oh sure, I thought, I'm so far ahead of them now that I can't afford to eat regularly. It would not be bad if they caught up a little." By early 1998, I had decided to give up and come in from the cold.

A year later, I cobbled together assignments from the Observer News Service and the *Boston Globe* and made two long trips to Pakistan. Given new expectations premised on maintaining a middle-class lifestyle payable in pounds sterling, this was treading water at best. But it was what I had to offer and, if I was honest with myself—which I wasn't—I found Pakistan much more interesting than England. Another four years later, in a transformed global context and still struggling to find my feet in a country I didn't belong in, and to prove myself in a relationship that was becoming a perpetual audition, I found the invitation to teach in Lahore too liberating to pass up. It was what Graham Greene would have called a way of escape. That was when I began to appreciate the incompatibility between my work and my tenuous life in England. I sent almost all of my BNU salary back to West Byfleet, and it still wasn't enough.

When I was in England I missed Pakistan, but not vice versa. And it was right here, in Liberty Market, days after the second anniversary of the World Trade Center attack, that I had smelled Asia again—the exhaust fumes from honking auto-rickshaws, the neon shop signs, the mangy street dogs— and it smelled like home. And here I was yet again: the guy who kept coming back. The timing of our arrival was dictated in part by an appointment I had made with a man named

Aslam Mughal. My friend Tauheed Ashraf in Chicago worked with a guy named Tony Couris, whose company did business with Tauheed's company. Tauheed had given Tony a copy of *Alive and Well in Pakistan*; Tony liked it and hosted a dinner party for me. Tony in turn introduced me to Umar Mughal, a young Pakistani he worked with in San Francisco. Umar came to Seattle on business, we met at a coffee shop near my house, and he invited me to meet his father in Lahore.

I had learned to take care with Pakistani introductions. For one thing it was easy to end up with too many of them, and if you weren't sufficiently vague and noncommittal, you could find yourself overloaded with obligations. Many Pakistani acquaintances in the United States urged us to look up and even stay with their relatives and, like Adnan, they usually emphasized and sometimes exaggerated the importance of their connections. It was necessary to stay mindful at all times of sensibilities and relationships, and to tiptoe around social and political minefields. You never knew who knew whom, or how. Then again, most Pakistanis I knew were remarkably generous and gregarious, sometimes even touchingly unguarded, regardless of their commitments or connections. Their country was perpetually a cauldron of schemes and theories; and their families, army batches, and alma maters encompassed everyone from ardent democrats to religious nuts to pro-military authoritarian nationalists. They knew from experience that until the day one or another faction finally prevailed, which would probably be never, somehow they had to live with each other. So they could be remarkably indulgent of each other on a personal level, even as each staunchly defended his or her wicket. In the abstract realm of drawing-room speculation and disputation, Pakistanis tended toward absolutist pronouncements and solutions and long-winded, hectoring disquisitions. In practice, they gave each other a wider berth and de facto benefit of the doubt.

So the day after we arrived, we had a lunch date with Aslam and several of his friends at the Lahore Gymkhana, a colonial-era athletic and social club where I had played tennis almost daily in 2003–04. BNU was across Zafar Ali Road from the Gymkhana, and at 3 p.m. most days I had grabbed my tennis kit and stolen over to the grass courts, where gents played doubles until sundown. I lost twenty pounds and improved my backhand, and—so I told myself—got a valuable close-up look at the Lahori elite. It wasn't always pretty; there were large egos and longstanding animosities among the men I played with, and they weren't all kind to the downtrodden ball boys. But it was a memorable enrichment of my life in Lahore, and I wrote about it fondly and at length. Back at the Gymkhana five years later for lunch, I led Pete over to the grass courts and found myself recognized and greeted by Suleiman Khan and Imran and the other ball boys. We took pictures and they led us over to the new junior courts where the coach, Tariq, was instructing some boys. Tariq and I had had good times together, and he had been a patient teacher. "Your game one month ago and now, very different," he had told me. "*Much* better." Now, he gave me his big sporty smile and hearty Punjabi handshake, and it was as if I had never left.

Aslam Mughal had been an eyewitness to the short Long March of March 15–16, less than a week earlier, and he was still gushing about it. The morning after our lunch at the Gymkhana, Pete and I went to his house.

"When the people at large join a movement, it is very difficult to stop it," he told us. "And that is exactly what happened. It was amazing. People from all walks of life. Children, women, older people. I have never seen anything like it."

His feelings were so strong and apparent that I wondered where they came from. "How would you define yourself in class terms?" I asked him.

"I'm, uh, upper middle class."

"Do you feel that people from your class are economically and politically secure?"

"Economically, yes. I don't know politically."

"Do you feel represented politically?"

"Not really."

Aslam had enjoyed an international career as an urban planner. "I came back in 2000, after eighteen years of just wandering around here and there, with the United Nations," he said. "And I've been trying to make certain changes in the system of Pakistan in my field, which is housing and urban development. But I failed. I mean, eighty percent of the population in urban areas, they cannot afford their own transport. Which necessitates that the public transport system should be strong. The pedestrians should be safe, the cyclists should be safe. They should be able to move very safely and securely and pleasantly. But a pedestrian cannot cross a road, even at the intersection, because the left turn is there. The people who have to travel on the buses, they cannot get the buses. And everything is being dictated by the car. Where is the democracy?"

"Could there be a metro here, like in Delhi?" I asked.

"I don't think we need a metro. I would go for a strong bus system, which we can afford and we can manage. Even that we are not managing properly. There is a very good model, where they have a bus system which is just like a railroad—two buses joined together. The infrastructure is changed and there are bus stations, proper bus stations like a metro."

"Like light rail."

"Yeah. But it's very flexible, because you can shift the buses from here to there and there and fix the road system. But first you have to make a decision that you plan and do things for the majority of the public. This has not happened. And housing also: eighty percent of people cannot afford housing. But if you go out, there's so much land subdivided, lying vacant, developed and semi-developed and fully developed, for speculative purposes, in nearby suburban areas of major cities: Islamabad, Lahore, Karachi. I'm talking about my field."

"You really have to have a political revolution, though, to ..."

"To change things. And policy being formulated for the majority of the public. Once this decision is taken, everything will start working for the general masses."

"People speak highly of Shahbaz Sharif as an administrator," I said.

"Exactly. That's the reason: because he's hitting at the middle class, and the lower middle class, and the poor people. All his focus is on this segment of the population, which is really, really deprived."

"People in the West see the Sharif brothers as quote-unquote right-wing or conservative," I told him. "Is that accurate? Everybody in the West thinks Benazir Bhutto was wonderful."

"Yeah. I think the perception is very good about her. But Nawaz Sharif is probably not perceived properly. In fact, Bush made a very derogatory statement against Nawaz Sharif: that he doesn't know the realities of the ground, or something like this."

"And Bush does know the realities of the ground?"

"Ha ha ha ha ha! He's the American president, so he can say anything. But I think in the present political scenario, the people who are well-meaning for the general masses are the Sharif brothers and Imran Khan. I cannot really pick even a third person, unfortunately."

"What if Benazir had lived?"

"I was in government when her father was the prime minister. We were at the delivery level; I was with the Punjab Department of Housing Development. I was a director there. And he was very good at raising slogans; he was a wonderful orator. He could really sway the crowds in any direction he wanted. But he had contradictions in his mind, in his delivery. He was always talking about the poor, but he did not deliver to the poor."

"He was a *jagirdar*," I suggested—a landowner.

"He was a jagirdar. In the heart of his hearts he was a *big* jagirdar. And so was Benazir."

One of the paradoxes of Pakistan is that while it never achieved rural land reform after independence, thus the tiny landowning class remains powerful today, it's also a self-made, frontier country. Because both Britain and India begrudged Pakistan its very existence, it never inherited its full share of the colonial bureaucracies, institutions, and budgets. And because of the massive uprooting of people at Partition, Pakistan needed talent in many fields. This created opportunities for young men who happened to have been born at the right time, and Aslam was one of these.

"I was born in a small town about eighty kilometers from here," he told me. His family was lower middle class. "Even lower than that. I remember my childhood in this small town, the way we used to live, and the way we used to go to school. We were just sitting on the floor, because our school could not afford furniture. I think that where there is a will, there is a way. I know personally so many people of similar background. So it was through struggle, through education, that I got admission to one of the best institutions in Lahore in '57, got good education, scholarship from Ford Foundation, this Michigan State University."

"So you really are an example of the middle class that came up."

"Self-made. I could never *ever* imagine what I have today. This is the reason I think the best empowerment of poor people is education. I believe in that, because it happened to me. I am not doing any professional work now, although if I do my consultancy I can make lot of money. My international rate is quite high. I make about five hundred dollars per day; that's my rate. But I'm not doing that. I associated myself with educational institutions. I enjoyed my professional career, and now I want to see things happening in my country. There has been a deliberate attempt, on the part of the landowners, not to have educational institutions established in their villages. Because they think that if the people are educated they'll leave the village, and they will not be able to exploit them."

* * *

Aslam had gone out early on the morning of March 15, to play golf. "Coming back I saw these barricades," he said. "I said, 'Oh my gosh.' In fact, I had to deviate back to my house. I could not take the straight route, the Mall and the canal bank, because they diverted me to some other place."

"They closed off the Mall?"

"Yeah, they closed off the Mall, near Gymkhana. So I took the canal bank in front of your university, Zafar Ali Road, and then I took this Jail Road, and then I had to go onto the service road, and then somehow I got onto the canal bank. That was eight o'clock in the morning, and the procession had to start at eleven o'clock. So three hours before, they had barricaded this area, which was not supposed to be the scene of clash. It was going to be the Mall in front of High Court building. I came home and sat in front of the TV. When we realized that Nawaz Sharif has gone out of the house and he's coming to this GPO Chowk, then we rushed there. I saw with my eyes. Glad I saw that."

"You saw him come out?"

"No, not him. He had passed. We were little late. But we saw the big procession, people following, and the enthusiasm, and the flags, and these children, and these policemen, and all walks of life, which was amazing. It was really across-the-board representation of the society. That was a fantastic scene, which I can never forget."

"This is the heart of the Punjab," I said. More than sixty percent of Pakistan's population lives in Punjab, which skews national economic and political priorities in its favor and leaves residents of the country's three other provinces feeling neglected and resentful. "Do you think this meant something for people in Balochistan and Sindh and the Frontier?"

"I'm sure," said Aslam. "Because justice is the problem of everybody. Although the political control of People's Party and MQM in

Sindh, they tried to double-play it. They were not probably joining the path as Punjab would, because of the close proximity of Islamabad. There were going to be thousands and thousands of people coming from Frontier. They sneaked through other areas, and they were on the outskirts of Islamabad. They would have overtaken the city. Maybe [General] Kiyani delivered a message [to Zardari] also, that 'You are on your own.' Definitely I think he delivered a message. That did the trick."

The next morning, March 16, he was awakened early by a knock on his bedroom door. "I was sleeping, and my brother came from our hometown. He woke me at quarter to three. I thought maybe he wants to show me that the Long March has reached this point and this point. He said, 'No, the government is announcing the surrender.' So we sat down in front of the TV at quarter to three. And the prime minister was going to speak to the nation. They said in fifteen-twenty minutes' time, but he came on air at quarter to six. Five-fifty. So we were just sitting there and sitting there and sitting there. But it was so important that I forgot about my sleep. And I think many Pakistanis would have done the same."

"How can this be conveyed to the West?" I wondered. "You know how Pakistan is perceived in the West."

"Yes."

"Americans don't understand the domestic politics of Pakistan very well," I told him. "They think about terrorism, and they think about the Frontier and Afghanistan. What just happened on March 16 seems like such a historic event."

"But it has not been reported in the West. Is it deliberate?"

I laughed nervously.

"No, I'm just asking you. I don't know."

"I think it's semi-deliberate," I suggested. "I think it's that the Western media have a certain story that they intend to tell about Pakistan."

"I think, Ethan, you are right," said Aslam. "I remember there was a lead story in *Newsweek*, that the most dangerous country in the world is not Iraq, or Afghanistan, it is Pakistan. And Pakistan was at that time very peaceful. How the hell they could say that the most dangerous country is Pakistan, unless they knew a plan which is to be implemented? It makes me think."

"Pakistanis tend to think in conspiracy theories," I cautioned.

"That is also wrong. I don't subscribe to that. We want to shift the blame to somebody else. This is not correct. I don't buy the conspiracy theories. But there are sometimes interventions. Basically, it is us. We have to take charge of our country, and we have to see where we want to get and how we get there. And I think I see some beginning, after sixty years."

"Do you think that's going to be remembered as a historic day?"

"Exactly. They are already giving it different names. I think it's going to be remembered in the history of Pakistan. I for one have not seen this kind of movement."

"It had the effect of bringing down the government," I suggested—wrongly, as it turned out.

"Yeah, but bringing down the government was not the aim. But I think that Zardari resisted to the last."

"The Sharif brothers were no longer in power in Punjab," I said. "So Zardari's man ..."

"... is Governor."

"It's Governor's Rule in Punjab right now, right?"

"Yes. And they had changed the entire bureaucracy: the police chief, the chief secretary. And they brought people who they thought would be *really* against the Sharif brothers. This police chief they brought from Balochistan. And this Lahore police chief was also brought from Balochistan, so that they can really take a tough stand. And then there were about two hundred police officers who were sacked by Shahbaz Sharif on the basis of corruption. They reinstated all of those people. When you are fired by somebody and then you are reinstated, you come with a venom."

"This is the kind of thing that historically happens routinely in Pakistan, right?"

"Yeah. Bureaucracy changes every time."

"But this time it didn't work."

"This time it did not work. Normally, it works."

"Where are your political loyalties?"

"Well, I'm inclined to Imran Khan and Nawaz Sharif."

"You were certainly talking up Imran Khan yesterday."

"Yes. Brigadier Siraj and I, we have been talking about joining his party, but we have not yet."

"Maybe he needs people to join his party."

"I think so. The system is so corrupt that good people need lot of courage to get into the political game in Pakistan."

"He didn't have to do that," I said. "He was already a national hero."

"And he was doing good work. He established one hospital in Lahore, he established another one in Karachi, he established this university in Mianwali. He could do more and more, and this is what people wanted. In fact I spoke to him, when I was in Riyadh, Saudi Arabia. I said, 'Why are you getting into politics? It's a very dirty game.' He said, 'I can establish one hospital, two hospitals, ten hospitals. But what about thousands of hospitals, which are not delivering to the masses? What about thousands and thousands of educational institutions? How many I can establish? It is only with the change of government that you can really impact the grassroots.' I was not convinced. But I started seeing some reason for his jumping into it. And he faced lot of difficulties, with all these corrupt politicians. He's very blunt and straight. He would say that, 'Zardari, you are corrupt. Prime Minister, you are corrupt.'"

"And he refused Musharraf's offer to be prime minister," I said.

"Uh, well, to tell you the truth, I think ... Musharraf came with a very, very good agenda. A six-point agenda. You should get hold of it. It's excellent. Somehow, Imran Khan got convinced, and I think Musharraf gave him the impression, that 'I'll make you the prime minister.' That 'I'll have the power, the control, and you'll deliver.' And during that time, I met Imran Khan at his hospital, in some other connection. As I told you, I'm associated with that and go to their fundraising dinners, and—sugar, Peter?"

"Yes, one," Pete said politely.

"None for me, please," I said.

"And Imran said, in so many words, 'I'm going to be prime minister.' This is just sitting across the table. I'm sitting here, he's sitting there. And I said, 'Khan sahib, how you are going to become the prime minister? I fail to understand what mechanism.' He said, 'I don't know. But I am going to become prime minister, and we are going to change Pakistan.' I knew that Musharraf would never, ever appoint Imran Khan as prime minister."

"Maybe he didn't mean under Musharraf," I suggested.

"No, no, he meant under Musharraf," he insisted. "And then with the famous referendum which Musharraf had, he went out of his way to support Musharraf publicly. And he's still apologizing to the nation for this. 'I'm sorry. I'm sorry, I made a mistake.' Please taste something. This is a typical sweet."

"At least he's apologizing," I said.

"People like me should not be really complaining about anything," said Aslam. "Because we can afford anything we want. But at times there is so much depression at what's happening in the country. We are just upset. I mean, we have a beautiful country. You know. We have all the resources in the world. We have wonderful people, and they have lot of potential. Given a proper system, this country can really rise. But the system has been hijacked."

"By whom?"

"By the vested interests. It started with jagirdars, with these land-owners, soon after independence, because they were the ones who were in politics. Then came the bureaucracy—civil and military. The business community, which was left out, came a little late into politics. It was in eighties when Nawaz Sharif was inducted by Zia ul Haq into Punjab government as finance minister. He wanted somebody from the business area, the private-sector know-how. I think he brought him in with good intentions."

"Zia's intentions were good?"

"I think so. But still, the businessmen's representation in the parliament is not very significant. The landlords, military, bureaucracy, they're all very much into each other, through marriages and other relations, business deals, things like that. So this is the group which has hijacked the country. What is happening now, I think this is great, if the independence of the judiciary can be achieved. There's still question mark. I think there's going to be a lot of resistance still."

"Do you think they can continue it?" I asked him. "A lot of the lawyers lost a lot of money over the last two years. They haven't been able to run their practices."

"But according to my assessment, this is going to continue. Because they have tasted the success of their movement. They have been on the roads for two years. This is a long period of time. Lawyers, you see, they say they cannot tolerate even loss of one penny. They're always eating at the expense of the client, even drinking at the expense of the client. But the mere fact that they have suffered this loss, and now they have tasted success, I think this is going to make them rejuvenated. A pressure group has been created in the country, which hopefully—hopefully—is going to impact the political system."

"It's an urban, middle-class pressure group," I noted.

"Yes. Highly educated class. And for any movement, it has to be led by educated people. And, in addition to the lawyers' community, there is a civil society, which was completely missing in Pakistani society. It was simply not there. It has started to make its presence felt. It's still not very strong, but I think that, along with the lawyers, we are seeing the participation of civil society for this cause."

"You mean NGOs and media?"

"No. I'm saying civil society per se. People from the general public, who are concerned."

"Like yourself?"

"Yes. Why this is happening to my country? We have lived our lives, you see, very comfortably. We have enjoyed it. But what about my children? I want Umar to come back and do something for his country here. But I really don't feel comfortable talking to him that we'll come back. When you're not even feeling secure, you see. And the system doesn't let you perform."

"The country needs people like Umar."

"Absolutely. If you can put a proper system in place, political and administrative system, a lot of Umars will be coming back. They want to come back. When I graduated in '64, from Michigan State University—I did my master's—I was offered a job and Green Card before graduation. I was not interested. I did not take it. I did not even consider it. I wanted to come back and do something for my country. And I suffered a lot. Believe you me, I suffered a lot. Life would have been much more comfortable. But I have no regrets. Looking back, I would have done the same thing all over again."

"But you don't recommend it to Umar."

"No, no. At that time, country was in a different situation. Still, it was very difficult for people like me, who came with ideas and education to introduce into the system. The old guards would not listen to us. But I was young and enthusiastic, and I would just bang, you see, and throw ideas and fight, and sometimes I would succeed. Mostly I would fail. But we made headway. And I was in government for fifteen years, sixty-six to eighty-one. And I did lot of things. Within the same system, system which was tough, which was difficult to operate, we were able to do lot of things."

I asked Aslam if he had played golf again on March 16, after hearing the prime minister on TV.

"No," he laughed. "Then I was too tired. I wanted to go, but I had no strength left. So I felt relaxed, and I lay down in bed, dreaming for a better Pakistan. And it was so relaxing, his announcement. We felt so good. And the entire nation: small, big, woman, man, older man, businessman, farmer—everyone I met, you could see the glow in their eyes. This is what we want."

* * *

"So who are you looking up here in Islamabad?" asked Isa.

"I'm making a point of seeing the Minallahs," I said.

"Oh, good! Athar is quite big-time now. You'd better make an appointment. I hear he has a sunburn from all the cameras."

We had stayed only two nights in Lahore, because we had an invitation to attend a wedding in Islamabad. As soon as we arrived, I regretted having accepted it. Pete and I had been on the road for three weeks, living out of our packs and recycling three of four shirts each. I had one pair of long khakis, and my only shoes were open-toed sandals. We were barely presentable, and every other man there was in a suit. Pete didn't even own a suit. I had hoped to buy a nice *shalwar kameez*, but we had not had time to shop before rushing here from Lahore. We sat around at the elite home where the evening began, and the son of the man who had invited us was kind enough to make conversation with us for a few minutes. Then we followed the wedding party to the Marriott, where we sat in a large room while many photos were snapped in the front and everyone else chatted with each other but not with us. Reinforcing our unease was the Marriott itself: the high walls and sandbags and razor wire and metal detectors that we had had to negotiate just to get in the building. "It's times like this that I could use a drink," said Pete. After a tedious hour or so, we slipped away.

It was through Isa Daudpota that I had gotten to know the Minallah family, back in 2003. Isa was responsible for a lot, in fact—he was the one who had asked if I knew anyone who would like to spend a semester teaching at the new Beaconhouse National University. Isa was a physicist, a secular intellectual in a country where that was a lonely and trying thing to be. He was a bit of a loner, but a gentle and generous soul. I had not become close to him—I sensed that wasn't easy or something he welcomed—but I had always been fond of and interested in him.

Isa and I had been email pals for years before we met, and it was by email that he had introduced me to Helga Ahmed, a German woman who had met her Pakistani husband in London in 1955. I had been asked to edit a collection of writings in the immediate wake of the September 11 attacks, and through Isa something Helga had written had reached my inbox. She remembered that, when she had witnessed history living in Afghanistan between 1978 and 1980, "there was no global outcry at the cruelties committed by the so-called freedom fighters, trained and fully supported by the Western world, and now their offshoots are known as the Taliban." Afghan friends had told her about atrocities committed by the U.S.-sponsored extremists, and she had been "keen to get these stories published and willingly shared them with Western journalists."

"I'm sure you all would be able to guess what their reply was," she wrote. "But for those of you who perhaps are too young to know about the complicities of Western politics in the Third World, the reply was: 'Oh no, this goes against our present-day political interests.'"

Visiting Islamabad in 2003, I had stayed with Helga and her husband Jamil, a retired civil servant. In their early years together, Jamil had been posted to remote parts of Pakistan, often without electricity or running water. Helga was not one to respect the taboos of her adopted society when they clashed with her own Teutonic sense of right and wrong. When I asked if she had converted to Islam, she replied: "I did. But it didn't make any difference, because my parents had already left the Church. We were neither Catholics nor Protestants. But I use it when I have arguments. I quote the Quran and say I am a very good Mussulman."

Helga's son, Temur, had married Fauzia Minallah, a spirited woman who was an artist and an outspoken environmentalist and preservationist. Fauzia was frankly admiring of her formidable mother-in-law. The day we visited a village outside Rawalpindi to look at vats that fermented animal dung into gas for cooking, she told me: "Other women of Auntie Helga's—how shall I say? —age and class, they are busy in coffee malls, having chitchat. She spends her time here." Fauzia showed me a plant and said, "That's basil. That's Auntie Helga. You will see it at my mother's house too. Auntie Helga is always telling us to grow it. So you can see the influence of one person."

Fauzia had invited me to celebrate Eid, the festival that marks the end of Ramadan, with her family in their home village of Sirikot, in the hills a couple of hours' drive from Islamabad in the North-West Frontier Province. In long conversations over several days with Fauzia's brother Athar and sister-in-law Ghazala, I had soaked up some fascinating personal history. Athar had been Minister of Law and Local Government in the NWFP provincial government until the 2002 elections, and Ghazala taught law in Islamabad. In February 2000, when—three months after his coup—Musharraf required Supreme Court justices to take a new oath, Athar had delivered a handwritten petition asking them to refuse.

"There's one question you haven't asked me, and that I think you should ask me," he had said to me. "If I took this petition to the Supreme Court, why did I take a position in the same government?"

It was a good question, so I asked it.

Musharraf had promised elections within three years of the coup. "Everyone had accepted that timeframe of three years," said Athar. "There was no protest. I was probably genuinely convinced that what General Pervez Musharraf was doing, he was doing to improve the situation." "At the time, it seemed to be the right decision," added Ghazala. "But as time has passed, all this accountability stuff has turned out to be a farce." "This is a very fertile country in every way," lamented Athar. "And there are so many intelligent people here. They need good leadership."

"All the flaws of the system and of the man notwithstanding, can Musharraf provide that leadership?"

"The system does not favor him. I think he has missed that opportunity."

It was all the water under the bridge since then that had compelled me to return to Pakistan, and arguably the most significant thing that had happened was the lawyers' movement that erupted in the wake of Musharraf's dismissal of Supreme Court Chief Justice Iftekhar Chaudhry in March 2007, and that had just culminated with the dramatic events in Lahore. Athar had emerged as the embattled Chief Justice's spokesman, and Ghazala had also been in the thick of things.

"You've become famous since we last met," I said to Athar when I reached him by phone. "You're in the *New York Times* every week."

"No, no," he demurred. "You made me famous by putting me in your book!"

But getting a meeting with Athar proved as challenging as Isa had predicted. Ghazala was more available, so one evening we went to their house and spent three hours with her. Her English mother, Jean Shah, whom I had not met before, sat with us.

Ghazala's father, Syed G. Safdar Shah, had been Chief Justice of the Peshawar High Court, then an associate justice on the Supreme

Court. The dictator Zia ul Haq had appointed him because of his known animosity toward Zulfiqar Ali Bhutto, the prime minister Zia deposed in 1977. "You could say there was a personality clash," Ghazala had told me in 2003. "He didn't dislike Bhutto as such, but when he disliked anything that Bhutto did, he openly criticized him. Bhutto had a major problem with that." When Zia concocted a murder case against Bhutto, he appointed justices he thought would support the trumped-up charges. "He thought my father would be an ideal candidate, because of his grudge against Bhutto," said Ghazala.

But Justice Shah had refused, on principle, to join the slim majority that voted to hang Bhutto. As a result, he had been compelled to take his family into exile in England, where he died in December 1986. Earlier that year, the day before she returned from her own exile, Benazir Bhutto had phoned him. "And he was advising her, because maybe he thought she would do better than her father," said Ghazala. "They used to visit us quite often in London, her and her mother. You could say that she and her mother had a special thing for my father, because they knew he had reasons to go with Zia, but he didn't. They had a lot of respect for him, for that reason. I remember him telling her that, 'Don't surround yourself with sycophants.' I remember that word. And he told her to listen to criticism, and not to make the same mistakes which her father did. The vote bank for the PPP is still there, because of her father, despite the fact that she blew it twice."

I summarized this background to Pete while we waited for Ghazala to join us. Her mother didn't catch my words. "I beg your pardon?" she said politely. Mrs. Shah was thin and prim, very English, very self-possessed.

"I gather that he and Bhutto were not friendly," I said to her.

"No, they were not," she confirmed.

"I remember Ghazala telling me that Benazir phoned and took advice from your husband when she was planning to return from exile."

"Yes. She was very young then. We landed at the end of November, beginning of December of 1980."

"A year and a half or so after Bhutto was hanged."

"Yes. We left the country because I was uneasy about my daughters."

"You must be proud of your kids and your whole family, what's become of them," I suggested.

"Oh, yes. Actually, I think that episode was a good thing for them, in a way. Because they had a very sheltered life here. They were sort of thrown in at the deep end."

"And they were little kids then?"

"No, no. They were not small. They were teenagers—mid-teens. And very sheltered, not like a teenager, or even an early age teenager, of England. They were brought up mostly in Peshawar, and we moved here later, just when my husband joined the Supreme Court. They were very sheltered."

Ghazala returned. "I was saying how different it was for you there, and how you were really thrown in the deep end," her mother said. Ghazala gave a sad little laugh.

"Were you proud of the stand that your husband took?" I asked Mrs. Shah.

"Oh yes, of course."

"That can't have been easy for him."

"Well, he did what he had to do," she said with a sigh. "I think probably the consequences were a little bit tougher than he hoped they would be. Because he didn't want to leave this country."

"The country has come through another couple periods of trauma since then," I said. Thinking of their family's historic connection with the Bhuttos, I told them how I had learned of Benazir's assassination. "My parents have this really nice cabin in the mountains," I said. "It's away from the world."

"Oh, how wonderful," said Mrs. Shah.

"That's where I was," I went on. "And this friend of my mother's, who thought she was being helpful, phoned me at the cabin. I didn't want to hear this kind of news up there. I wanted to be away. And she said, "Did you hear Benazir Bhutto's been assassinated?' It kind of ruined my vacation, needless to say."

"Did you ever meet her?" asked Ghazala.

"No, I never did. I always wanted to; I would have loved to. I met Murtaza; I interviewed him at 70 Clifton." Murtaza Bhutto was Benazir's estranged younger brother, and 70 Clifton is the family home in Karachi.

"Really? When was that?" asked Ghazala.

"It was in March '95, on my very first visit to Pakistan."

"Was Benazir in power?"

"Yes."

"That must have been shortly before he was assassinated."

"I was very new to the country," I remembered. "I didn't know much about all the ins and outs. And then next thing I knew, he was dead. And she fell from power very soon after he was killed." Murtaza Bhutto died in a gun battle with Karachi police in September 1996, and Benazir's first government fell two months later. "But how did her assassination affect you?"

"My mother was here also," said Ghazala. "She comes every winter. So we were just watching TV. We knew that she was going to Liaquat Bagh that day to give the speech, and it just suddenly came: news alert that there's been a blast there, and that Benazir is injured, and she's being taken to the hospital, and the next thing we knew was that she was dead. I was very upset. Because whatever her faults, whatever her shortcomings, no one's perfect. But out of the lot that we had at the time, I think she was the most promising."

"She seemed to be channeling the hopes of the nation at that moment," I said.

"Yes, she was. Because when she came back after seven years, I think she came in a totally different frame of mind. When you're outside, you look at things from a different perspective. But when she came back, I think the ground realities hit her, particularly regarding the Chief Justice and this movement. Because she'd been very critical of the movement and the Chief Justice when she was outside the country. But I have friends who were very close to Benazir. They were with the PPP, but they have distanced themselves since Zardari has come into power. So they were with Benazir. And one of my friends says that she actually sat and one day asked everyone who was sitting with her, that 'This Chief Justice thing really seems to have taken a grip of the nation, and it's really something which everyone wants.' So because my friends were part of the movement as well, they told her what everyone thought about it, and how strongly everyone felt about it, and that was how she then changed her stance as well.

"So whether she ever truly believed in it or not, that's irrelevant. The point is that, as far as the public eye was concerned, she did come out open about it. And what she said outside the Chief Justice's house, when she went up there with a procession—and it's all on camera—that has been the argument for us, throughout this campaign, to convince the People's Party to fulfill what she wanted. That was her promise to the nation."

"Because she was on camera saying it."

"She was on camera, in the Judges' Colony, saying that, 'When we come into power, we will hoist the Pakistan flag on the Chief Justice's house. He is still the Chief Justice of Pakistan today.' This is all on record. And it's like a slap on their faces, every time they show it. That's why they slammed Geo shut. Geo was off the air just a short while ago. Because Geo was amazing, you know? They dug out all this footage! When Nawaz Sharif, in a speech in Punjab, said to the police that, 'Don't obey unlawful orders,' the government came out with, 'We're going to charge you with sedition.' So the next thing we see is Geo, with Benazir over there, telling the police, 'Give way, police! Do not obey illegal orders! You do not have to obey illegal orders!' But the worst thing about this government is that they lie through their teeth. I mean, they can sit there on television, and they can just ..."

"Zardari," her mother interjected.

"Mummy, *everyone*. All of their supporters who come in these talk shows, they lie through their teeth. I've been on talk shows with PPP representatives. They show a clip of Benazir over there, talking about the Chief Justice, and then there's this woman Fauzia Wahab. She turns around and says, 'Oh, that's just one aspect of what Benazir used to say. She used to say something totally different.' I said, 'Okay, so you're trying to prove that she was two-faced, and that she was a liar!' I mean, that's the kind of people that we're up against."

"Do you feel the PPP has been sort of taken over?" I asked.

"I have always maintained, in public also, and I'm on record having said this, that the PPP has been hijacked. And as far as I'm concerned, Zardari and the morons around him, they are out to destroy the PPP and just finish it off once and for all."

"Is that their intention?"

"That is what I feel, and what *many* people feel. It's not just me."

"I'm interested in the personal and professional and political dimensions of everything you've been doing the last two years," I said.

"For me it was very, very personal, Ethan, because we had seen this judge in action. We didn't know him personally. But his judgments, in the two years that he was the Chief Justice, they had stirred up such an interest in everyone. It was something new for Pakistan. For the first time, we had a Chief Justice who was delivering judgments which were almost human rights issues, which was unheard of in Pakistan. And in Pakistan mostly human rights are violated by your elite class. It's the pseudo elite class, or your landed gentry of the rural areas, against the poor and oppressed. And it was amazing, the kind of decisions that he was giving.

"The federal Education Minister, Mr. Bijrani, was responsible for a *jirga* decision in Sindh. There's this horrendous custom, in all parts of Pakistan, in which to patch up a feud between two families, they give away small girls of the enemy's family, as a token of peace. To hell with what those little girls go through for the rest of their lives. They're just a peace token. And that's all over. It's not just Sindh—it's in the Northwest, it's in Sindh, Punjab, Balochistan, it's by different names. And Athar's sister, Samar, had been a party to these cases, in the sense that she was the one who actually filed the petition. The Chief Justice took notice of it, and he took such an interest in these cases that he even issued an order that from there onwards, if any jirga decision was carried out and implemented, it would be the local police incharge, and the local administration, who would be held responsible. You see, previously the administration and the police were all conniving with these jirgas; they were taking money! So once they were made responsible, that immediately changed the whole scenario. And it was amazing the number of cases which were pouring into the Supreme Court on these type of issues."

"So there's a lot at stake in this Chief Justice issue."

"A lot. This is just one tiny drop in the ocean I'm telling you about, but one tiny drop in the ocean which involved thousands upon thousands of innocent little girls who could see a bright future all of a sudden. And I tell you—I'm just jumping, fast-forwarding it a bit—that the day of 9th of March, 2007, when the Chief Justice was removed for the first time by Musharraf, there were phone calls from Sindh and all over Pakistan that these big landlords were distributing sweets, *mithai* all over, celebrating, that 'At last he's out of our hair, and we can get back to what we were doing in peace.' That is just one type of case. There are so many other human rights violations for which he took a stand. And he would always stand for the oppressed. People would send him handwritten notes, and he would take notice and take action on them. And then, of course, there were some very,

very controversial decisions which he gave—controversial as far as the government was concerned. Like he started taking an interest in these missing persons issues. The missing persons were the persons who had been picked up on terrorist charges, no trial, no access to a lawyer, no appearance in court—they just disappear, and the families are suffering. It's horrific what those families are still going through."

"You said you don't know the Chief Justice personally. What's your sense of him?"

"I didn't know him on a personal level, but we got to know him as a judge. And then I'm going to give you another personal aspect of it: I didn't know that his daughter was in my class. I teach A-level law. She was my student in my class; I didn't even know who she was, and he was Chief Justice at the time. And for Pakistani culture that's very unusual, because whoever comes from those high-ups, they make it known to everyone who they are. (Please, you must help yourselves as well. We can talk, and you can help yourselves as well.) It just so happened that one day we were discussing something in class. And we were talking about the Supreme Court. So one of the students said, 'Why don't you ask Ifra? Her dad's in the Supreme Court.' So I said, 'Okay, Ifra. What does your dad do in the Supreme Court?' So she said, 'Oh, he's the Chief Justice.' Now, this was just soon after he was appointed as Chief Justice, before he started establishing himself as the person whom we now admire so much. So I came home and I asked Athar, 'Who's the Chief Justice of the Supreme Court?' He said, 'It's a new guy who's been appointed.' He said, 'He was the Chief Justice of Balochistan High Court, and blah blah blah.' He said, 'Why are you asking?' So I said, 'Well, his daughter is in my class.'

"Oh now, I've missed out something very, very important actually. Before this conversation in the class, we had a parent-teacher meeting. So this guy comes and sits in front of me with his daughter, I don't know who he is, and I'm talking to him and discussing, and he's saying that 'We've just moved to Islamabad, and she will have a bit of problems, and I hope that she'll be able to sort them out.' Just discussing generally, and just 'Thank you very much,' and blah blah, very polite. I didn't know him from Adam, and he goes away. And then, a few weeks later, this conversation in the class, and I said, 'Okay!' So I told Athar, 'He came to the school for a parent-teacher meeting.' He says, 'What!? He came to the school, and you didn't even know who he was? Didn't the principal tell you?' I said, 'No.' So that's the kind of person he is, you see? That's when I first got to know that he's a very humble man, very down to earth. And then after that, when we started hearing about his judgments, that's when we got interested. I even took my students to the Supreme Court, which I do on a regular basis. For the past two years I haven't, for obvious reasons. And then the steel mills case."

"I keep hearing about the steel mills case."

"That ruffled a lot of feathers! He basically saved the country billions and billions. They were going to sell off the steel mills thing for peanuts, basically, and everyone, including the then-prime minister, Shaukat Aziz, were beneficiaries of that deal."

"So Shaukat Aziz's reputation has been sullied."

"Oh, everyone who was in Musharraf's government's reputation is questionable."

"How do you feel about Musharraf in retrospect?"

"I think he should be tried under Article 6 for treason."

"On the record?"

"Definitely on record, he should be tried. Set this on record, and I repeat, he should be tried for treason. Because one excellent precedent has been set in Pakistan, and that is the restoration of the Chief Justice. Because all odds were against this movement, Ethan. All odds. You think about it: After 9th March, every atrocity has been unleashed on the lawyers' movement which you can possibly think of. And every possible step was taken to try and dishearten everyone and discourage it. People have lost their lives. The first person to lose his life in this movement, in order to pressurize the Chief Justice, was a young man who was appointed as a registrar in the Supreme Court, and his name was Hamad Raza. And he was a young man who was serving in Balochistan, and he picked him up on merit. Everyone who knew him knew he was a brilliant young officer. And he was very, very close to the Chief Justice. And he was the first person who was murdered."

"What happened?"

"I got a message early in the morning that Hamad Raza has been murdered. Samar and I had worked with him on a project the year before. We went to his house, and lots of people had gathered obviously, and his wife was hysterical. And his wife is a British citizen. And I was there when she gave her statement to the police, and the statement that she gave to the police was *not* the statement which came out in the media. We were eyewitnesses to what she said to the police. She said that she and her husband and her three young kids—the eldest was six—were asleep in their bedroom upstairs, and Hamad's elderly parents were in a bedroom downstairs. Whoever it was broke in through the kitchen window, and tied up the parents, and asked where the family was, and then they went upstairs, and the door was locked. They knocked on the door, and when Hamad opened the door, she said that they kept a pistol on his head right here, and shot him at point blank range. And obviously the children were in the room as well, so you can imagine what the wife went through. She said the man just ran downstairs, out into the garden. She said, 'I ran after him.' And she ran out screaming for help. And she saw a police van, parked outside. This man jumped into the police van, and it drove away. This is about four or five in the morning. She gave the statement to the police in front of me. It was never, ever reported. So that's how we know that his murder was definitely to pressurize the Chief Justice. The Chief Justice was devastated. He was very, very upset."

"So that's only one example of what the movement has been through," I said, to prompt her to tell more.

137

"That's one example. Then the Chief Justice went to Karachi. He was invited by the bar association there. And they did not allow him to leave the airport. Athar and lots of lawyers were with him. The whole of Karachi was under siege. Before that, the Chief Justice had visited Lahore, he had visited Peshawar, no problem. They would go in procession. Thousands and thousands of people would accompany them, and welcome everywhere. Driving through Punjab, and ordinary people would be welcoming him. And in Karachi—the whole of Karachi was under siege."

"By whom?" her mother piped up.

"By whom? The MQM." The MQM is the controversial party that controls Karachi and claims to represent *mohajirs*, Urdu-speaking descendants of immigrants from India. "Basically it was them that the whole of Karachi was under siege from. Like the container scene which we had in Islamabad, the day before the Long March, when all the roads were blocked and containers had been seized from people, and they were causing billions of rupees of loss to the country, because many of them had goods in them. Perishable goods—can you believe it? They were just seized, and people were coming on TV and complaining that this is causing us billions of rupees' worth of loss. So the whole of Karachi had been blocked with containers as well. And suddenly this firing started, all over Karachi. And over fifty people were killed."

"This was the summer of 2007."

"This was 12th of May 2007, to be exact. And all the evidence is there on camera. These TV stations, they recorded it!"

"That was only two months after the 9th of March," I said. "And there have been ebbs and flows to the movement ..."

"You see, in the beginning they took these drastic measures, so the people would become scared. Hamad Raza didn't work, so then they tried the 12th of May; that was horrific. People's Party workers were killed in Karachi, because they were part of the movement as well. The People's Party was very much a part of the movement. Lots of political workers were killed. Lawyers were killed. Ordinary citizens were killed. There's this channel, Aaj TV. And this very popular journalist who has a talk show called Talat Hussein, you may have met him? Talat was broadcasting live. He was lying on the floor, and there were bullets flying through the office! It was horrific. We were sitting over here shocked, absolutely shocked, at what was going on in Karachi. And then the same evening, Musharraf has a rally at the parade ground outside the parliament. People had been brought in in buses from all around, from Punjab and whatnot. And the media—because the media has played such an amazing role in this movement, I tell you—the media was interviewing these people who had been shipped in. They were saying that they had been paid a thousand rupees each. They had been promised that they would be taken to see Faisal Mosque and probably also go up to the hills of Murree. And that they'd get free meals and this, that, and the other. It was hilarious: This man was standing with a banner, with a picture of Musharraf upside down. So the interviewer says, 'Why have you got this thing in your hand?' He says, 'I don't know. I was told to hold it.' So he says, 'Do you know that you're holding it upside down?' He says, 'Oh, am I?' Scenes like that. And the same evening, Musharraf stands up there behind his multiple glass bulletproof screens, and he shows his fist, and he says, 'Did you see the show of strength in Karachi?' All the channels have this on record."

"I'm tempted to say that's the moment Musharraf turned into a dictator. Is that too glib?"

"He turned into a dictator the day that he sacked the Chief Justice," she said with venom. "The day that he forced him to resign and had five generals there to bully him into doing it. And the man said no."

"How did you feel about Musharraf before the 9th of March?"

"Before the 9th of March I was indifferent, to be very honest."

"He was not Zia."

139

"No, he was sly and cunning. Zia did everything out in the open. He was doing everything behind the scenes. But after the 9th of March he came out in the open also. Because I don't think you could be more open than the 12th of May. That was horrific."

"And so after the 12th of May, what came?"

"In Islamabad, whenever we had rallies and protests, the maximum amount of teargas, shelling, baton charging, water cannoning. We've experienced everything. Arresting people, throwing them into prison. Whenever they wanted to really unleash their horror on us, they would specially ship in the police from Punjab. It was the (Q) League who were in power at the time, and the entire Punjab police was their own hit men, basically. Not the present one. That Punjab police was known to be horrible. So whenever the Punjab police was called in we knew: 'Right, this means trouble.' They're scared of students. They didn't want the students coming out. So in the very beginning there was a big student rally over here, and they arrested about forty or fifty of them and took them to the police station. And they wanted their parents to come in and sign bonds, that they would not be involved in any such activity in the future. Now, we were there in that rally as well. So there were many of us adults who followed them to the police station."

"By students do you mean university students?"

"I'm even talking about high school students. Fifteen-year-olds, fourteen-year-olds. My son, who was fourteen at the time, got a big whack on the back from a baton. Then my nephew, he was hit as well. My nephew was being dragged away by a policeman when my son tried to rescue him and pull him. That's when both of them were hit. So we followed them to the police station. And many of those kids had not even told their parents that they were in this rally. Some of them were the children of members of parliament and government servants. They were *really* scared for their parents. So many of us posed as aunts, uncles, so and so, and went in to get them out.

It was quite funny also. One of my friends, she said, 'Listen, this is the third time I've gone in as an aunt. They're not going to believe me the next time I go in.'"

"You've got a lot of nephews."

"And nieces! So finally then, there's this lawyer over here whom we contacted, and he came over, and he got the rest of them out."

"These are kids who are about the same age you were, not to put too fine a point on it, when your family had to go into exile," I said.

"This, for me, was vindicating my father," she said. "Because I felt that my father stood up for justice. He had to leave his country; he died in exile. And he took to his grave the fact that an innocent man was hanged, and he couldn't do anything about it. Because it was such a sham case, it was such a fabricated case."

"How do you think this will affect your son and other people of his generation?"

"Oh, very, very positively. Because Zia had suppressed the youth of this country. He had banned all student unions. So a whole generation of students grew up since then who were totally apolitical, totally uninvolved in any kind of political scene. Athar was a student in Zia's time. He was a part of the PSF, which was the People's Student Federation, the People's Party student faction. And he was wanted by Zia during his regime, because he was a student activist. In fact there was a warrant for his arrest, and he went into hiding for quite some time. A friend of his, Jamil Abbasi, who was also in the PSF, got arrested and spent seven years in prison. He also spent about six months in the Lahore Fort, where he was tortured. Athar would have ended up in the same place, but got away with it. And then Jamil Abbasi was with us, part of our movement."

"Somebody like Jamil Abbasi, this is kind of full circle for him."

"Definitely. But for Jamil Abbasi it's very very sad, because Jamil Abbasi was the original People's Party. He idolized Zulfiqar Ali Bhutto. And he idolized Benazir. And he cut off with Benazir when she married Zardari. He knew that Zardari was no good from the day that Benazir married him. And even though Benazir pleaded with him, that, 'Listen, forget about him. He's my husband,' he said, 'No, I can't tolerate the man, and he's going to bring you down, and I can't have anything to do with you if you're going to be married to that man.' So for him it's very sad, because he was devastated when she was assassinated. And it made him even more angry that, because of him, he had cut off with Benazir as well."

❧ ❧ ❧

"I'll never forget the 9th of March, when this happened," Ghazala remembered. "Athar and I were driving down Margala Road, and we got a phone call. And Athar said, 'Oh, no. So they've done it.' I said, 'What have they done?' He said, 'Musharraf has kicked the Chief Justice out.'"

"Was Athar close to the Chief Justice before the 9th of March?"

"Not at all. Never even met him, other than seeing him in court."

"How did his association with him come about?"

"Totally accidental. After he refused to resign, he and his children were locked up in the house, all their phones were cut off, their TV connection was cut off. They had absolutely no link with the outside world. For about a week, we had no idea what was going on in there, and they had no idea what was going on in the outside world. And he was supposed to be taken to the Supreme Court on the 13th. That was the day when he came out, when he was manhandled. When he came out, and they were taking him to the Supreme Court, he refused to sit in the car. He said, 'I want the Supreme Court bar president to come and take me.' Munir Malik was the president at the time. This we know now, because since then he's told everyone that this is what happened. But they refused; they wanted to push him into that car. And that is when they grabbed him by the hair also. When that was flashed on the front pages of the newspapers the next day, I mean, that just did it for everyone. I could have strangled that man with my bare hands there and then, Musharraf.

"Athar would be able to tell you more precisely. I might be jumbling up a few events. But as far as I remember, this is what happened: When he was not able to contact anyone, somehow, someone managed to get a message through to Athar, who was with some other lawyers in the Supreme Court, waiting for the Chief Justice to be brought there."

"They got the message to Athar personally, or to that group of lawyers?"

"I think he got a phone call, that 'Has anyone got email facility? The Chief Justice would like to send a message.' Some lawyer who happened to be there at the time wanted to send a message through by email, and Athar's partner had one of those phones that you have the email as well, so he got a message that 'I am being manhandled, and my wife is being manhandled.' She had been dragged away from him physically by the policemen and taken away into Balochistan House. His children were back home, and they had locked themselves inside, and the intelligence agency people were hammering on the door outside. Can you imagine? Young kids inside, and this is what they were doing? It was horrific. I tell you, when I heard about it I just broke down into tears. I said, 'What is happening to this country?' And I was not the only one. Athar was *so* upset. I've never seen him so upset, when he heard about the manhandling bit. He was so upset."

"So this movement really is something extraordinary, that could well not have happened," I suggested. "It could well have been quashed entirely."

"Yes."

"Certain chance encounters, and also the technology ..."

"Even if these chance encounters had not taken place, Ethan, the Chief Justice had become so popular through his judgments, and the stands that he took, that everyone admired him. You see, it was not just a certain class which admired him. His judgments had affected *all* classes. And that's what was so amazing about him. You had the whole Christian minority rallying for him. Why? Because he had given an amazing judgment. There's this Christian—it's called a *katchiabadi*. What would you call it? Like a slum, basically."

"French Colony?"

"French Colony in F-7. And there's a park there. That park was going to be given by the CDA"—the Capital Development Authority—"to a cousin of the chairman CDA, to build a mini-golf course. Which would be entry by ticket only, purely for the elite class. And that was the only recreation place for that French Colony. For years and years in the evening, their children would play there, the older people would sit there smoking their hookahs. It was basically their rights against this person Shah Sharabeel. He's the owner of the Lahore mini-golf course also, and he's a big entrepreneur, he calls himself, or whatever."

"Is this the same Shah Sharabeel who's involved in arts and theater in Lahore?" In 2003 I had attended a performance of his production of *Moulin Rouge* at the Alhamra Theater.

"Yes, yes. So that judgment also he gave against Shah Sharabeel: that this is public property, and it's their right. This was not made for private enterprises. That judgment was such an amazing one, because no one ever expected that judgment. Everyone said, 'Oh, we know what will happen, just as it always has happened, that the elite get their way, and the downtrodden remain downtrodden.' There's so many judgments like that. Then you've got this Hindu chap in Sindh, who's got the Chief Justice's picture up with his god. I mean, he's got his god, and then there's Iftikhar Chaudhry. Manu Bheel, his name is. Ten members of his immediate family, his wife, children, other immediate family members, have been missing for the last ten years, in the custody of a *wadera*. That is a landowner.

They know who he is. No one dares to touch him. And his case had just come to the Supreme Court, and the hearings had started, when he was removed. Then you've got all of the missing persons' families. That was another amazing thing which he had done, because Musharraf's camp was trying to spread the propaganda that he was supporting terrorists, whereas that was the last thing that he was doing. All he was doing was saying that everyone is entitled to a hearing in court. 'Show us what evidence you have.' Which law allows you to torture the family members, for God's sake?"

"That principle has not always been honored in America in recent years," I pointed out.

"I know," she said. "America is responsible as well for these missing persons. But whenever people say, 'America, America, America,' I say, if our own rulers had a bit of integrity or honor in them, no American would dare do what they did. Musharraf in his own book brags, that 'I have sold people for bounties to the Americans.' In his book, *In the Line of Fire*. In his book he's boasted about it, so he can't even deny that now."

"Not to take the responsibility away from Musharraf, but hasn't it been the case that the Bush administration set a lower standard that allowed Musharraf and other rulers to do this kind of thing?"

"I am glad to see the back of Bush, Ethan. I condemn his policies. I condemn everything about him and his regime. But I still hold my own rulers responsible. It's no use crying that the Americans are responsible."

"People in Pakistan have a longstanding habit of cynicism," I said. "Of believing that the worst case is always going to play out. As you said, like the golf course case, the French Colony case. 'Oh, it'll go this way.' And then suddenly it doesn't go that way, it goes the other way. And that gives people a sense that there is justice, or there can be justice after all. That seems to be what the lawyers' movement and Iftikhar Chaudhry represent to a lot of people."

"I am optimistic," she insisted. "If I wasn't optimistic about this movement succeeding, I wouldn't have been able to carry on for two years. I've always been optimistic. Optimistic in the sense that even if Iftikhar Chaudhry is never restored, I still believe that a lot of lessons were learned during this time. A lot of people were exposed. The people of this country were educated in a lot of things. There are so many things which have happened during this movement, which will now serve as a lesson hopefully for the future. That is, if the lessons are remembered. People have short memories in this country. But then, something like this has never happened before in this country either."

"Are those lessons going to bear fruit in coming years and decades?"

"I'm hopeful, Ethan. Time will tell. But I don't think this is something which is just going to die out, or fizzle out. My firm belief is that it was the people's power which brought this around. It was two years of pressure which was building up. And then the last straw was what happened in Lahore on the 15th. They were terrified of the Long March, the government. They went absolutely bonkers, in the stupid measures which they took to try and stop it. It was so immature and stupid on their part. We had a Long March the year before, and they didn't create any hurdles on that, and it was totally peaceful! Thousands upon thousands of people collected in Islamabad that day."

"It strikes me that the government wasn't afraid of violence," I said. "They were afraid of the political implications."

"Yes. And they were afraid that these people who had been going on for two years mean what they say. And this time it *was* a sit-in till the restoration." The previous June, the previous Long March had resulted in 500,000 people—the *Washington Post*'s conservative estimate—gathering in front of the National Assembly, after Zardari promised three times to restore the Chief Justice but failed to do so.

"Did Zardari ever intend to restore the judiciary?"

"Every time, we believed him. Stupid that we were. But if we hadn't believed him, everyone would have said that 'You didn't give them a chance.' It wasn't for us to give them an opportunity. It was for Nawaz Sharif, actually. Because it was both of them who collectively promised the nation."

"Nawaz Sharif has seized the high ground, and he's aligned himself with the lawyers' movement."

"Definitely."

"Is that to his credit?"

"I definitely give him credit. I admire the man for the fact that he has stood by his word, he has admitted the mistakes he made in the past, he admits that he has learned from the past, and he hopes that he would not repeat those mistakes in the future. And the biggest thing is credibility, Ethan. I mean, this government has got no credibility whatsoever. That man has stood by his word. He said that 'The third time Zardari backs out, we will quit the federal government.' And they did. They had about seven federal ministers; all of them resigned. This was a first in Pakistani history. And the Punjab government was functioning perfectly well. It was the only provincial government which was functioning perfectly well. They had absolutely no reason to interfere with it."

I told her what K.C. Singh, the Indian civil servant we had seen interviewed on Times Now in Mumbai on the day of the Lahore cricket attack, had said: that if the Sharif brothers had been in power in the Punjab at the time, the attack would not have happened.

"Yeah, it wouldn't have happened," she agreed. "Because the whole of the Punjab administration, they were focused on trying to discourage the Long March. And it was pathetic. The Zardari government had promised the Sri Lankans the same security which the president gets. Does the president go in an open coach like that? With just one police car in front, and I don't even know if there was one behind them? A fat lot of good that does. They were just sitting ducks."

147

"Are you personally, historically, a PPP person?"

"I am historically a Zulfiqar Ali Bhutto supporter. Even though Zulfiqar Ali Bhutto was responsible for retiring my father prematurely by amending the constitution, so he was no angel either. But being objective, keeping my own personal things aside, I think that as a leader he had amazing qualities, and he was going to take Pakistan ahead."

"So you're not a PML(N) person."

"No, not basically. But now I am, in the sense that I admire the Sharifs for—for whatever they are so far. The real test comes when you are in power. Let's hope we see that day, and let's see how they fare when they're in power."

* * *

"There's so much else to tell you," said Ghazala with feeling. "There's *so* much. And then there was the incident of the lawyers who were burned alive in Karachi."

"Tell me," I said.

"That was also not so long ago. Mysteriously, they were burned alive in their chambers. Locked in and set alight. About four or five lawyers lost their lives like that."

"And they were lawyers' movement lawyers?"

"Yes. Lawyers' movement lawyers."

"What about people who say 'Iftikhar Chaudhry has become quote-unquote too political'?" Just as I asked this question, Ghazala's phone started ringing.

"Oh, I hate that, when everyone says that," she said. "Too political. For them I have one answer: if this is what a political—just let me answer ..." She took her phone call and stepped away, and I made small talk with her mother.

"You must be so proud," I said again.

148

"Worried at times," she said with a laugh. "The first day I arrived last year—not this Christmas, the Christmas before—she was going to a meeting and a demonstration the same day. I said, 'All right.' She came back with a plaster on her head, here and here. I said, 'What happened?' She said, 'They hit us with the sticks.' And in the papers the next day it showed her with blood pouring down her face. I said, 'Well, this is a nice way to start the holiday!'"

Ghazala returned. "The reason why I got whacked on the head was I had snatched the stick of one of the policemen, and he was getting really furious: 'Give me my stick back!' I said, 'You bet you'll get your stick back!' So another one whacked me on the head. I said, 'That's some cheek! Hitting us with it, and they want it back as well!'"

"You were talking about the charge that Iftikhar Chaudhry is quote-unquote too political," I reminded her.

"Yes," she said. "That is a typical story spun by the Zardari supporters. I ask you: What is so political about him? He only ever addressed the bar associations; he never, ever delivered public speeches. And if he is going from A to B, and the whole of the country is showering him with flowers, can the man help it? If that makes him political, then my answer to those kinds of people would be, 'I wish every Chief Justice is political in this country, then.'"

"Another suggestion that's been made is, 'These lawyers' movement people, they're standing on principle about the Chief Justice, but where were they when it was important to stand against Musharraf as an unelected dictator?'"

"I'm not going to defend them, or defend myself," she said. "Where was I, for that matter? Why didn't I stand up then? I'm telling you, because there was no one to give us that push. It was Iftikhar Chaudhry, by standing up to those five generals and saying no, which kindled the whole nation. He brought out that spark in everyone. Because otherwise we were just dead, basically. Dictators have been coming and going for the last sixty-two years, and we've done nothing. But this man finally took a stand."

"Today is March 24," I said. "What is the significance of March 16?"

"March 16 will go down in history as, I think, a turning point in the history of this country. Pakistan is going to enter a new phase. In the sense that now, in the future, the military is not going to be able to take over with that confidence. And political leaders also know now that there is a nation out there, who have found their latent power."

"What should I say to Americans who say, 'Well, this is all very interesting, but what does it have to do with Osama bin Laden and the War on Terror and the fact that Pakistan is a naughty country?'"

"You can tell them that Osama bin Laden and all these other naughty people are playing havoc with us, more than they are with the Americans. We are at least as concerned about it, if not more so, than they are. And if they would only wake up and kindly pressurize their own government not to meddle in our affairs, and let us get on with it. And to look at it from the point of view of the people of Pakistan, for God's sake. We want democracy over here. We do not want military rulers. We do not want terrorism. We want peace. We do not want mullahs ruling us either. The majority of this country—unlike what the West believes—they believe that the middle to lower class would not have a problem with maulvis. You just go out in the street, and you ask the people what they would think about maulvis ruling them. People may be religious, but that does not mean that they want maulvis ruling them. And they are sick to their teeth of terrorism. Because they're the ones who are affected!"

❊ ❊ ❊

Islamabad was built as a planned city in the 1960s to replace Karachi as Pakistan's capital. Karachi was and remains the country's commercial hub and port, but it's very far from Pakistan's other major cities and, perhaps more important, it's not in or near the

Punjab. Casual visitors don't much notice Rawalpindi, Islamabad's twin city, and in news reports it tends to be described in passing as a "garrison city" but otherwise largely ignored. But 'Pindi was there first and is home to GHQ, the General Headquarters of the Pakistan Army, and this fact alone goes a long way toward explaining the existence and location of Islamabad. The two cities are at the western edge of the Punjab, nearer to Peshawar than to Lahore. This fact, and the Margala Hills that loom behind Islamabad, and its perpetual incompleteness as its grid of planned sectors is filled in square by square, give Islamabad the air of a frontier town.

In the '90s I enjoyed Islamabad as a refuge from the rest of Pakistan. To arrive there from Lahore or Rawalpindi was to slough off the dust and noise and heat and frustration of lowland Asia. It was an oasis, and the straight streets and cooler climate made a few days there calming and pleasant. In 2003 it was still that way, although the Afghan war had made it crazy for a while. To someone who had known the quiet city during quiet times, to see Western reporters doing TV stand-ups from Islamabad in flak jackets with rugged-looking hills in the background was amusing: The view was from the roof of the Marriott.

"The place was swarming with camera people and reporters," Awais Ahmed Chaudhry, a glum U.S.-educated travel agent and guide whose business had been ruined by the Afghan war, recalled when I met him in 2003. "They used to go all around the city and to Peshawar. And then for the final two-three minutes they would go to the roof of the Marriott, where they could get the government building in the background. The Marriott was full to the brim with journalists. And you could not find a room in the Pearl Continental in Peshawar. You couldn't get a guesthouse in Peshawar that had a room. Journalists were forced to rent houses for six-seven months."

Islamabad wasn't crazy like that when I returned in 2009, but it was bigger, uglier, messier, and a lot less likeable. It was being blighted and crushed by new highway flyovers that seemed worse than unnecessary. There was a big new stadium and a beautiful but depressingly pointless Pakistan Monument that had been, so proudly said the plaque, inaugurated by President Musharraf on March 23, 2007—two weeks after his dismissal of the Chief Justice. There was much more traffic, and the familiar system of square sectors designated by letters in one direction, numbers in the other, somehow seemed a lot less simple and logical than before. The effect was disturbing and disorienting. The transformation seemed too abrupt to have been natural or even careless; some kind of policy had been implemented, or some obstacle had been removed. Not only was Islamabad inevitably becoming more Asian, less tidy; and not only was money being made by cement suppliers and corrupt bureaucrats and property speculators. It was also, I felt, that Islamabad was willing itself to be larger, more notable, more important, and using the crudest of means. It was an ugly and embarrassing thing to see.

"It really is a bigger city than it was fifteen years ago," I said to Pete.

"Well, that's the way it goes," he said. "Look at Seattle."

We had come from Lahore with Tahir, a tall, chubby young man with a sweet personality who worked for an acquaintance of mine named Jawad Iqbal. Jawad was a physician who worked at a hospital in Tacoma, Washington and was pursuing a vision to transform availability of health care in provincial Pakistan, using U.S.-based medical specialists volunteering their time to consult with local doctors via online videoconferencing. I had met Jawad's sister-in-law in Vancouver, she had urged me to seek him out, and he had urged that we visit the small hospital he had just opened in Kharian, a town on the Grand Trunk Road, halfway between Lahore and Islamabad.

"Tahir is a very, very important person for us in Pakistan," Jawad had said. I wasn't sure quite what he meant by this, but I took it on faith as Pete and I found ourselves on the motorway with Tahir from

Lahore to Islamabad. Jawad had taken an active interest in our trip—so active, in fact, that his staff and friends in Pakistan kind of swallowed us whole for a while. In a good way, mostly, though for a couple of weeks we wrestled with superimposed or overlapping agendas. It's not that our agenda and theirs were competing; they just weren't completely identical. In India, Pete and I had grown accustomed to traveling anonymously and on our own recognizance. Now we were guests of Dr. Jawad, as Tahir called him, who monitored our well-being and whereabouts via daily phone calls from Tacoma.

This took some getting used to, though I was grateful for his interest and support. And it helped remind me that in Pakistan, I couldn't expect to be anonymous. This was partly because, after fifteen years of being the guy who kept coming back, I wasn't quite anonymous anymore. But it was more because any white man in Pakistan is conspicuous by definition. This presents obvious dangers, but it also offers opportunities. If you can get past the widespread suspicion that you're a CIA agent, doors will open as a result of your simply showing up and expressing sincere and sympathetic interest. This too presents dangers: of being co-opted or used; of being involved in internal politics that's really none of your business; of being overwhelmed and exhausted by the sheer force of Pakistani hospitality.

In Lahore we had arrived to find that a lot of things had been arranged for us, from accommodation, to a car and driver (Tahir), to interviews, to a film crew of young dudes with whom we shared a crowded van for several days. I was grateful, though I also chafed at the limitations on my freedom of action and decision. Our long days included not only travel and intense conversations, but also forward planning, snap decisions, and ad hoc personnel management. The most maddening part was having to carry a Pakistani cell phone and answer every call, because I didn't have contacts programmed into it or the ability to check voice mail. All of the above was more than I had thought I was signing up to be responsible for, as what

Pakistanis would call the incharge of what was suddenly no longer a simple two-man road trip.

So after two nights in Lahore we had come by car to Islamabad on the modern motorway, the faster of the roads between the two cities. Jawad had helped us find a guest house that was both affordable and secure, and Tahir and his car were available to us to go anywhere in or around Islamabad. One day we went to Rawal Lake, which serves as both a reservoir for Islamabad and a recreational site. I had gone there in 2003 with Zahyd Hamead, an English teacher at the International Islamic University, whom I had met at the Beaconhouse guest house in Lahore. Zahyd was part Turkish, had lived in Iran, England, and Iowa, and took a jaundiced view of Pakistan. He was part outsider, part embittered native son.

The shore that day had been crowded with young men playing loud music and taxi drivers washing their cars in the lake. "I mean, this is diabolical," Zahyd had exclaimed. "Oh, and they've cut down all the bloody trees. Great! And when they do go anywhere there's only two things they can do: stand and listen to jukeboxes in their cars, or do barbecues. This used to be a lovely place. Five years ago, when Zeeba and I and the boys came here, there used to be barely four or five people here. And I brought one of those inflatable rafts from England. We used to go out on the lake."

"I think Islamabad won't be recognizable ten or twenty years from now," I said to him.

"Oh, I think sooner than that," said Zahyd.

"These are all the aimless, jobless youths," I remarked.

"Yeah, and what lies ahead? And they're producing more and more. The worst part of it is, they think this is really cool. This is Pakistan in a nutshell."

Since then the shore of Rawal Lake had been transformed, in a surprising way. A family-friendly marble plaza had been built, complete with walkways, an aviary, landscaping, signs warning of

300-rupee fines for littering or playing cricket on the grass, bouncy castles and slides, and a Krispy Kreme stand. There were guys offering pony rides. Especially given my vivid memories of Zahyd and his mood five years earlier, it was astonishing.

"Rawal Lake new construction," said Tahir.

"Good construction or bad construction?"

"Good construction."

"I don't remember any of this from five years ago," I said.

"All this Musharraf made."

"Musharraf made many good changes in Islamabad?"

"Not only Islamabad. All Pakistan."

"Do you like Musharraf?"

Tahir smiled, and paused, then said: "Yes."

"Zardari?"

"No. *All* Pakistani don't like Zardari. All projects Musharraf. Zardari only ten percent."

The day we were there was March 23, the anniversary of the promulgation in 1940 in Lahore of the Pakistan Resolution. The plaza was crowded with moms and dads and kids, all enjoying their day out.

"Other day not holiday, couples come here," Tahir said. "Like dating." His eyes gleamed with mischief.

"That's great," I said, cautiously.

"In Lahore there is park called Nawaz Sharif Park. Couples go there and ..."

"I understand," I said, noncommittally.

"It is allowed."

"Great."

"In Pakistan everything is allowed!"

"I agree with that. I think that's great!"

"Sorry to say," said Pete, "but if this was in India, it'd be covered with trash."

"And crap," I said.

"Yeah."

From the lake we drove into the Margala Hills toward Murree, one of the hill stations the British built as refuges from the natives and the heat. "This is new road," Tahir told us. "Old road single road. This double. This is Musharraf project," he added, beaming. Tahir beamed a lot.

About halfway up, my phone rang. I had borrowed it from Adnan because I needed a phone and hadn't made any other arrangements, but I really wished I hadn't had to. The more wired the world becomes, the more I cherish the experience I enjoyed in Nepal in the mid-1980s, of being out of touch with the outside world. Little did I know how much I had enjoyed that experience until it was no longer available. Overseas phone calls were prohibitively expensive, and Internet cafes were unheard of. In six months in Kathmandu, I went once to the General Post Office to send a telegram to my parents, for which I paid by the word. Otherwise it was letters written on extra-lightweight folding aerograms, which might or might not arrive. When I trekked to the base of Everest there was truly no way to contact anyone, short of trekking back out. Those were the days.

I answered the phone. It was Yusuf, a friend of Jawad's whom we had met in Lahore. I cringed, because I had tried to dodge Yusuf when he had reached me the day before to announce that he had made an appointment for me with Tasneem Noorani, a former high-level bureaucrat, at "two-thirty sharp" on Thursday. "He was one of the think tanks of Musharraf," Yusuf had informed me. I had nothing against meeting Noorani, but I hadn't asked Yusuf to make the appointment, and I had made other plans for Thursday. When the dreaded ringtone erupted in my pocket again on the road to Murree, I hadn't yet called Noorani because I had misplaced his number, and I cursed the revolution in communications technology that forced me to be reachable even here.

One reason I was diffident about following up Yusuf's contacts was that I didn't know quite what to make of Yusuf. Jawad had described him as a good friend and business associate and had urged me to meet him, which I had done in his office on the fourth floor of a building overlooking Liberty Circle in Lahore. Jawad himself was very presentable in a conventional sort of way, with a well-coiffed head of wavy hair, a tidy little mustache, and a noble bearing whose significance I began to appreciate when I learned in Kharian that he belonged to a leading local family. Yusuf by contrast was a disheveled smoker, with hooded eyes that gave him a haunted air and the mustache of a B-movie bandito. He might well have looked haunted, too, because he was a fount of theories and speculation about what was *really* going on.

As such, he was a Pakistani type. Americans and Pakistanis strikingly share several national traits; both countries are self-conscious settler societies with artificial borders, founded on unattainable abstractions. One of these is disappointed idealism shading into embittered paranoia. Add to that Pakistanis' resentment of the ways they feel they've been used and abused by America since the 1980s, when the Reagan administration enlisted the military regime of General Zia ul Haq to support its use of Islamic extremists—then referred to in the West as freedom fighters—in a proxy war against the Russians in Afghanistan, and paranoia begins to seem understandable. "Pakistan never says no to America," is the way Yusuf summed up the two countries' relationship. Many Pakistanis consider history to have rhymed after 2001, when Musharraf threw in the country's lot with America anew, in the face of Bush administration official Richard Armitage's alleged threat that, if he didn't, Pakistan would be bombed "back to the Stone Age." No wonder people like Yusuf are thin-skinned.

"Pakistan went against your foreign minister, Hillary Clinton," he said, when I asked him about the Long March and Zardari's promise to restore the Chief Justice. "America doesn't want Iftikhar

Chaudhry to come back." He cited the missing persons cases: "He's going to start fingering the local establishment, and the international establishment."

"So you're saying this was a piece of political theater?"

"Definitely. Have you played that game—Conquerer?"

"Do you mean Risk?"

"Yes, Risk. Me and my wife sit and play all night, ten-twelve hours. It's like that. They want to put so much chaos in Pakistan, even if chaos if not there, but through media. If I tell people Casey" —he looked at my business card— "Ethan is a bad boy, if I go to social gatherings and say, 'Avoid him,' this is what they are doing with Pakistan. Now about two days back, you heard, they said we want to do ground attacks on Balochistan as well. What the hell? America does not want China to hold Balochistan." The new port being built with Chinese money at Gwader, west of Karachi in the remote and sparsely-populated province of Balochistan, had the potential to transform international trade, not only for Pakistan but globally. There had been a separatist uprising in Balochistan in the 1970s, and unrest there again in recent years. Yusuf believed the Balochistan Liberation Front was financed by Mossad and RAW, India's intelligence agency, and that U.S. drones attacking Balochistan were intended to counter Chinese influence. "I'm so pissed off at my own media, that every month ten to fifteen Chinese engineers got kidnapped," he said. He wondered darkly at recent talk of "Pukhtunistan," the notional homeland for the Pathan ethnic group that straddles the long, porous border between Pakistan and Afghanistan. "Why the fuck suddenly this name came up?" He was both scornful and fearful of Pakistan's remote and rustic ethnicities, and he quoted Hamid Gul, the former head of Pakistan's Inter-Services Intelligence, on Pathans: "They are at peace when they are at war."

"They smell like anything," added Yusuf. "They don't have shower. They don't clean themselves. But if you ask them do they have hundred dollars, they say, 'Yes, here is hundred dollars.' They have no religion. And Balochi people, we call them basically looters."

"Like Zardari?"

"Ha ha ha! He is basically Balochi."

I took some notes, then just sat there letting Yusuf's bile wash over me. He did give us an interesting piece of information about the March 3 attack on the Sri Lankan cricket team, that I resolved to follow up: "The rocket launcher hit the downstairs shop in my building. The shop is called Bride & Groom Shop. And my servant, who cleans my office, he has seen the whole show. Those U.S. people who came and interviewed from U.S. radio service, they said, 'Are the attackers Taliban or al-Qaeda?' I said, 'Please give me the definition of Taliban and al-Qaeda.'"

Pete and I had left Yusuf's office feeling confused and somehow sullied. It was our first full day in Pakistan, and Pete was a bit shaken. "Part of me wants to interview a guy like that in a really straight way, and just include it in the book," I said. "He's representative of a certain kind of Pakistani mentality. But it's so corrosive."

"Yes it is," said Pete. "But hey, people in the U.S. have that kind of mentality too."

"He thinks it's all just a big plan."

"Thing is, if it is all a big plan, it's a crappy plan."

When Yusuf got worked up, he stuttered. "For G-god's sake," he warned me now on the phone about Tasneem Noorani, "even if you can't meet him, p-please c-call him, and if you cannot reach him, send him a p-proper SMS. He's not any T-tom, Dick, or Harry that you can just say it's all right if I don't meet him." I promised to call Noorani as soon as I had a chance. For now, I pocketed my phone and did my best to forget Yusuf and the intrigues of lowland Pakistan, as we rode up into the hills.

* * *

"Islamabad seems a lot bigger than it used to be," I said to Isa Daudpota, when we saw him that evening back in the city.

"It is," he said. "To my utter disgust."

Isa had invited us to join him on his regular evening walk. "Do you do this every day?" I asked.

"Yes, every day at this time. I've been warned against it."

We told him we had attended a wedding at the Marriott. "It was pretty boring," I confessed.

"Most of them are."

I mentioned that we'd been to the well-appointed new restaurant at Daman-e-Koh, in the Margala Hills above the city.

"I've not been there," said Isa. "Because I'm one of the people who are protesting against that sort of thing."

A single loud explosion stopped us in our tracks. It seemed to come from the other side of the city.

Pete stated the obvious. "That was no car backfire," he said.

"What's over in that direction?" I asked Isa.

"The whole town!" He made a phone call and learned that a suicide bomber had blown himself up outside a police station. Later we learned that a policeman had also died. It was the first bombing in Islamabad since the massive truck bomb attack on the Marriott, six months earlier.

"One thing's for sure," Isa told us. "If that bomb had hit that building, they would be shipping you out."

"They'd have to find us first," said Pete.

"All our friends and relatives will be emailing us," I said.

"Or not," said Pete. "They may not even hear about it."

We walked some more. I asked Isa where he had been when the Marriott was bombed.

"I was actually very near," he said. "There is a very interesting chap called Enrique Penalosa. He's the mayor of Bogota, and he set up this fantastic public transport system. So the Kennedy Foundation had arranged for him to visit Karachi, Lahore, and Islamabad. And he was giving a talk in the Islamabad Hotel—it used to be the Holiday Inn. And that's where we were. After the talk was over we were chatting for about half an hour, and one heard a sound like that, only much louder. So he said, 'It's probably time to make tracks, because you don't want to be in hotels.' So we got the feeling that something is happening nearby, and then the news came that the Marriott had been hit. One of my friends had been there about half an hour before that and had gone out. So many people had very close calls. I knew one girl who was actually where I was, and then she decided to go and join her family for a—that was during Ramzan, I think."

"It was September," I remembered. "It was Ramzan, yeah."

"So she had gone to join her family for a low-cost feast at the Marriott. Maybe they had a special or something. Her car got mucked up; she experienced the whole thing. But luckily she was at the back. The Marriott has this long thing, and then at the back they have the marquee, where they have functions such as this for the larger crowds. So the building took the blast, and she was protected, but scrambling in the dark, etcetera. There's one very well-known journalist who was in there, Imtiaz Alam. He used to write quite a bit. Survived, of course."

"So what was the aftermath like?"

"I saw that place much, much later. I hardly ever go east of here. I did a PhotoShop on the photographs that appeared. I have a page on the Flickr. So I put that up, and there was a lot of interest in that."

"What did you do to the photographs?"

"I just did a PhotoShop, just played around with it. To add my bit to it. It was not my photograph; I acknowledged the source. There was a time, when I worked in that area and I earned more money, that I would go to Marriott for coffee or the occasional meal, when I was working very late. I would stop by there. For a long time it's become unaffordable for me, and now dangerous. And I don't want to get frisked, going to eat. It's demeaning. It's like going for an American visa."

"We had a little taste of that last night," I told him.

"It must be far more now. Before the bomb, it was quite bad."

"You were already being frisked?"

"Yeah. Just too many barriers. And this recent fire, they couldn't get the fire trucks near, because they made the door so narrow the truck couldn't go in. Idiots. So what are you trying to fight? You're trying to hold back the terrorists, and you don't allow the fire brigade to get in. That's what happened."

"Is my memory accurate, that you used to could just walk in the front door?"

"There was a metal detector."

"Yeah, but you came off the street, and there was the front door, and you walked in."

"Yeah. No barriers then."

"Were your daily routines changed at all, in the days after the blast?"

"Not for me, no."

"Because you lived the other direction?"

"Yeah. Even now when I go there, I can't—first of all, there's been this massive so-called development that this idiotic head of municipality came in and put in all kinds of underpasses and overpasses, which of course happened in Lahore too, along the canal. But if it was needed in Lahore, it was definitely not needed here."

"It seems out of scale here," I agreed.

"So I can't make out what's happening there. The first time I went, I just wanted to show a visiting friend from America, a Bangladeshi, some parts of town over there. And we had to backtrack, because it was just too complicated. The roadblocks. And I just said, 'Forget it, let's go back.' And that's when I saw the reestablished Marriott. They'd done the paintwork, and it was amazingly fast. This man

really made it a point to show that he would get back." He was referring to the Marriott's owner, Sadruddin Hashwani.

"Didn't he say that he was going to pay all his employees?"

"Yes. Well, that he must have done."

"Good for him."

"Yeah, he came out looking very good."

"It seemed to me at the time like this was, forgive the cliche, a
9/11-type thing," I said. "That's the way it felt to me. It hit home,
because I've been to the Marriott pretty much every time I've come
to Islamabad. I never stayed there, but I've used the business center
and would have coffee and meet people there. It also just felt like
the symbolism was that it was the equivalent of the World Trade
Center for Islamabad."

"Yes. That and the Red Mosque, I think, are the striking events in
the city." The Red Mosque, or Lal Masjid, was occupied by militants
holding hostages, in a Waco-like standoff that finally ended with an
attack by the army in July 2007. "Red Mosque is another disgusting
whole thing, because the intelligence agency clearly allowed these
guys to build up, to a level where they became a real threat. And had
they not been stupid in hijacking some Chinese women who
worked in a massage parlor, this whole thing could have gone on
longer. Then I think they had some phone calls from Beijing: 'Don't
muck around with our people.' So that's when things happened.
Meanwhile, Musharraf was sitting around doing nothing. Then they
had this massacre."

We were now sitting in Isa's office. He had intrigued me by men-
tioning several articles he had published in the Pakistani press to
mark the 200th anniversary of the birth of Charles Darwin. I asked
him to tell me more.

"Two in *Dawn* and one in *TFT*," he said—the liberal weekly *The
Friday Times*. "Do a Google on my name, with 'evolution' and 'Darwin,' you should get to it. I've always been interested in biology. My

basic training is in electronics and physics, but one has to be interested. In fact, the first article I ever wrote was in the seventies, before the PC, on in vitro fertilization. This was when ..."

"Louise Brown," I said.

"Yes, that's exactly when I wrote it. So I've been interested, so this is a logical thing to do. And I knew people wouldn't write about it."

In an op-ed article headlined "Darwin's year: time to reflect," published in the January 11, 2009 issue of the leading Pakistani daily *Dawn*, Isa had recommended a major new exhibition on Darwin in London and the seven-part PBS series *Evolution*, then recounted his visit four years earlier to the Pakistan Natural History Museum in Islamabad:

I walked to the lowest level. This is where the museum explicitly shows how the evolution of life took place on earth. You enter the moderately sized room with its four walls painted to show quite nicely the story of life. Starting on the right one sees in almost seamless progression the appearance of primitive life forms in water, moving on to fish, reptiles, amphibians, land-based animals, primates and then early humanoids, the hunter-gatherers, finally getting to modern humans. This brings one back to the door where one began the journey. If you stand in the middle and turn around you see the panorama of life before you. A good teacher of biology could keep a class occupied for several hours in this room alone.

One wonders how many teachers in Pakistan would, however, notice the white pillar from floor to roof, over one foot wide, that separates the pictures of the hordes of apes from the hunting humanoids. (Nowhere else in this room are the different life forms shown separated from other groups.) More importantly, will the teacher on noticing this anomaly, point it [out] to the students and discuss it? A clear discussion on this issue alone could lead to a much better understanding of biology (and life generally) than a year of learning facts that fail to unify the subject.

I gathered a number of museum staff nearby to ask their opinion about why the museum chose to separate the apes from the humanoids, given that after Darwin it was generally accepted that humans are primates, i.e. closely related to monkeys and apes. Most remained quiet. One said, in true bureaucratic fashion, that I would need to contact the director who designed the room. Another said that if the connection was shown the museum would be burned down by religious fanatics.

I was chagrined to note that Isa had added:

This phenomenon is not particular to Pakistan or the Muslim world. In America about 55 per cent of adults held a tentative view about evolution for the last decade. A third of adults firmly rejected the theory; only 14 per cent thought of it as 'definitely true.'

"So what's it like to be a globally oriented, pretty secular intellectual in an Islamic country?" I asked him.

"I live on the Net," he said.

"You don't live in Pakistan?"

"Difficult to say. See, I grew up as a single kid, so I'm pretty happy being by myself. I don't seek out company. I don't think I would be necessarily acceptable to too many people. So I don't want to get myself into situations of conflict."

"Meaning you don't want to talk about that?"

"No, I don't interact with too many people. My interaction with humans is largely electronic."

"I've always known that about you," I said. "We were friends for five or six years before we ever met, you and I."

"It's difficult to know how the semi-educated would react to things that are acute in this society," he said. "And my approach to this is that, unless you can change people through dialogue, just expressing one's views to irritate or agitate minds is counterproductive. To be effective, one needs to reach out to younger people who probably still have some neurons intact. So I've largely been working on environmental issues here, to highlight the kind of waste and foolishness in our developmental process. So I came to express it through writing, and I have done one or two TV interviews related to that."

"But you don't seek out confrontation."

"Maybe it's just my temperament."

"What's the significance of Darwin to you? What's significant enough about him that you felt compelled to write these articles?"

"Many have said it, and I'm much less a person than them, to think that he had perhaps the most significant idea ever. Given that we don't teach him too well, probably, in our textbooks—at least the implications of it."

"What did you feel Pakistanis needed to know about him, that you were in a position to say?"

"If the national body doesn't recognize it, that's very significant. The national museum. By putting that white pillar, effectively it talks about humans being special, divine intervention. We are not descended from the apes. Hence pretty much biology's foundational structure doesn't exist. It's just a collection of facts. You have divine intervention—*voila*, you have people. There's no connection. So when I saw it, I thought it was a great story, because nobody had noticed it. And of course staff members said—quite wrongly, I think—that if this were shown as a continuum, people would come and burn the museum. No way. But it's just this latent fear. And they said, 'Well, if you want to know more, go and talk to the director.'"

"Yeah. 'Not my department.'" I mentioned Milan Kundera's account, in *The Unbearable Lightness of Being*, of a photograph in which a Czech Communist Party official is depicted holding the hat of a disgraced fellow official who has been airbrushed out. "The thing that's whitewashed or left out is obviously the most significant thing."

"They always slip up that way," said Isa. "It is very strategic, because that's where the column comes in. Because it's not really a straight wall; there happens to be a column. If I were the museum director, I would say, 'Oh, but it's really the column. We couldn't have drawn over it.' So that could have been the cover-up story, if he wanted to appear rational."

* * *

"McDonald night view very beautiful," said Tahir as we drove past the golden arches in Islamabad's F-10 sector. "Only one McDonald in Islamabad. And one in 'Pindi. After some month McDonald will be in Kharian. They purchase some land."

"You like McDonald's?"

"No."

"I don't either."

"Sometime my friends and I go there, but we don't like. Many people waits you in Kharian," he added.

"Well, I hope we don't disappoint 'em," said Pete.

We were on our way to the office of Developments in Literacy, a nonprofit whose Pakistani-American founder, Fiza Shah, I had met in Pasadena just before the trip. DIL was one of several nonprofits founded and funded by Pakistani expatriates in the United States who seemed to be doing good and necessary work in Pakistan, particularly in health care and education.

If I had a criticism of these groups, it was that they tended to compete with each other for dollars and attention from the same limited pool of Pakistani-American supporters, and that they made too little effort to reach out to the wider American public. Severally they all seemed well-intentioned and competent, but they also seemed too little inclined to cooperate or to acknowledge each other's efforts. They invited and bullied each other into attending fundraisers that were heavy on appeals to patriotism and piety, which was well and good, but I had come to feel that the historical moment cried out for such groups to invite the American public's support and partnership.

Like any immigrant community, Pakistanis in the United States were concerned about and involved with their home country, and their motives were the usual human mix of genuine altruism, guilt, ego, competitiveness, envy, enlightened self-interest, and whatever else. There was nothing unusual in what they did or why, and that in itself was something other Americans needed to know. I made it part of my own quixotic mission to try to help bridge the gulf between Pakistani-Americans who were quietly doing the needful to improve education in Pakistan, but were too timid or myopic to promote their work outside their own ethnic community, and other Americans who kept asking me what could be done to counter religious extremism in Pakistan. The short answer is that, if the state can't or won't provide decent, affordable education to its children, that need will be met either by private groups like the Human Development Foundation, The Citizens Foundation, Greg Mortenson's Central Asia Institute, pop star Shehzad Roy's Zindagi Trust, and DIL, or by *madrassas*.

"DIL started in 1997, with the expat community in the States," executive director Anjana Raza told me in her office. "The key thing was that the group of Pakistanis living in the U.S. wanted to give something back to their country; that's where it starts. It has fundraising chapters in the UK and Canada. Operations are specifically for Pakistan. The focus here has been education, from the beginning. DIL is looking at giving quality education in areas that are under-serviced. We've found that the majority of them are rural, so most of the program is rural. However, in some urban slums, we found that there are very under-served communities, so some of our program is there. We're working currently in all four provinces. We took on some schools which were already existing, but because of various reasons the community or a local group came and said, 'The school is not functioning, can you take over and make it functional?' In other instances, DIL has gone in and started schools from scratch. The model is to work with the community, so these are very much community schools. A very small portion of the program is in government schools."

"There's a do-it-yourself ethos," I said, "that seems to have developed out of the vacuum created by the absence of an effective state school system. There's a lot of resourcefulness among Pakistanis, and DIL seems to be an example of that. There's a paradox or problem, though, in the sense that if private people go in and meet the need, the state has an excuse not to meet the need."

"Of course it's the government's responsibility to provide education to all," answered Lalarukh Raffi, DIL's training director. "Quite a lot of NGOs are working in education. But the purpose is not to build a parallel structure. We try to build schools where there are no schools available. I understand what you're trying to say. But if it's not there, it's something that we can contribute."

"Where the government is engaged in providing services at a huge scale, they don't usually get the time to develop good models or do experimentation, which has to be done at a small scale," added Anjana. "One role of the NGOs is of doing some of that experimental work, taking on certain issues and finding out what is going to work on the ground, then taking that to the government. But second, as Lalarukh is saying, since the government currently is not able to reach every corner, it really is the work of the NGOs to get to those places which the government hasn't gotten to, and to bring the government there. Not just get there, but go there and drag the government there."

"How much does political change affect your ability to work with the state?"

"There are two questions in that," said Anjana. "One is what's happening at the wider political level. DIL is a very local organization, a Pakistani organization. Security situations that put a halt to Save the Children, Oxfam, UNICEF—DIL is not affected by that. On the other hand, local politics affects everyone's work. If we're working in an area, then yes, that local work is affected by local political tensions."

Anjana suggested we visit a DIL school in a village called Guff, outside Rawalpindi. "When you go there you realize how isolated it is, although it's very close to Islamabad," she said. "About an hour and a half's driving distance. And they're completely cut off." Nomadic people passed through Guff, staying three months at a time, and the local people had invited them to bring their children to the DIL-run school. "I found that was a lovely initiative to be taken right there, by the local community," she said.

At eight-thirty in the morning a couple of days later, we got on the road with Salma Sufi, DIL's northern region projects manager, and Ayesha Khurshid, a young PhD candidate in education at the University of Wisconsin. In the car I quizzed Ayesha about Madison, a subject of more than casual interest to me given that it was exactly there, at age seventeen, that I had begun discovering the world outside Greater Milwaukee. That wasn't strictly true, since at sixteen I had gone to Haiti with my father, and I had been to Chicago and Texas and Colorado plenty of times. But still. The town I had grown up in was home then to fewer than ten thousand all-white souls; an hour west by Badger Bus on I-94, the dome of the state capitol came into view and I found myself in a different world. At least that's how it felt. Madison was a city of 200,000 people and, more to the point, of 40,000 students, many of whom were not even from America. To me it was like a faraway land, right there in the middle of America's Dairyland.

"It's nice to work as a TA, but I think many of the students find me a bit strange," Ayesha told me. "I think most of the undergrads come from Wisconsin."

"In what way do they find you strange?"

"They don't say, but I can tell."

I asked how she liked Madison.

"It's very cold, but I like it," she said. "I was working here with a research institute. And my supervisor here knew a professor in Madison, and his work seemed very interesting. I got admission in a couple of other places, in UK and at Columbia, but I decided for Madison because of the professor whose research I was interested in."

"So how long have you been in Madison?"

"Five years. I did my master's, and now I'm doing my PhD."

"Have you been to Milwaukee?"

"Once for Sting's concert, and then once for this Latin music festival, and once just for lunch. Madison is kind of a small place," she explained to Salma, "so sometimes you get bored."

I asked Ayesha about her work. "Actually my dissertation is focused on DIL," she said. "I'm interested, broadly, in how women's education is defined in Pakistan, and how it's implemented. DIL is a women-centered organization. Another aspect I found very interesting is the emphasis on quality education. I think they're doing wonderful work." She was especially impressed with the local teachers she had been interviewing. The way they see the purpose of their work is something very inspiring."

"How do they see the purpose of their work?"

"I think they see themselves as reformers. It's not 'just a job' for them. You see the enthusiasm in the way they teach." All the teachers were women, she added.

"Why all women?"

"I don't think they would be comfortable in the staff rooms with male teachers," said Salma. "And their salaries are not sufficient to support their families. The female teachers also have more patience. Excuse me," she interjected. We were driving through Rawalpindi. "This is the place where Benazir Bhutto was assassinated, Liaquat Bagh, named after Liaquat Ali Khan, our first prime minister."

It was another deja vu moment for me. In 1995 I had stayed at a cheap hotel right here, just across the street from Liaquat Bagh, because I couldn't afford the options that existed then in Islamabad. It was in my windowless room on an upper floor of that hotel that I had suffered for two days with the worst stomach bug I ever caught in Asia, until I mustered the presence of mind to limp downstairs to ask the desk clerk to send a man on a motorbike to a pharmacy. It was in the same hotel that I had gotten stoned with a Danish grad student and two British ex-soldiers who had come to Pakistan to rescue the skinny one's girlfriend, whose relatives had lured her with lies about a dying grandmother to their home village to marry her cousin. The Brits had approached me as I sat minding my own business on the grass at Islamabad's Super Market shopping area, to ask if I knew where they could get some AK-47s. I pointed out that there were only too many gun shops around, but if they walked into one they would be pretty conspicuous. After that evening spent smoking dope together in my room, they had left for the Frontier the next day and I never saw them again.

"Where were you when Benazir was assassinated?" I asked Salma.

"I was very much here in Islamabad, just left the workplace to go home," she said. "And all of a sudden there were riots and tear gas and people shouting, not knowing what was going on. You see, I don't live in Islamabad, I live in the outskirts of Islamabad. And I was asked not to travel."

Before leaving the city, we stopped at a Teacher Empowerment Centre, where young women came for training from as far as an hour outside Rawalpindi.

"But you have to remember that they are all taking public transport," said the master trainer, a small but stout and formidable-looking woman named Misbah Awan. "For us in a car it is one hour. So for them it could be—"

"Two hours?" I suggested.

"Or longer than that." She asked about us.

"I'm a writer," I said.

"From the *New York Times*, I hope?"

"Well ..."

"Because, you see, we are used to writers from the *New York Times*. So they set a high bar."

"Well, I'm at least at that level," I said.

She laughed. "And you're the photographer?"

"Yes," said Pete.

Just like that, she had pegged us as press men. She then gave me what must have been her standard rundown. Indicating the teachers nearby, she said, "They're each given a letter of the alphabet, and they have to show how they would teach it, and they critique each other. So they learn from each other, which I think is more suitable than being imposed upon."

"You mentioned the *New York Times*. Did Nicholas Kristof come here?"

"He did."

"I've met some DIL people in America," I said, "and they're very appreciative of the article he wrote. Have you found that what he wrote has had an impact?"

"Not locally," she said. "It went around by email here, but mostly its impact was in Europe and in the USA itself."

"I suppose it would be useful to fundraising," I suggested.

"Yes. I feel what he wrote was very objective, saying that more aid should go to education. Because some of these students, they can't even afford a five-rupee pencil."

"But there's plenty of money for other things, like airplanes," I suggested.

"Yes. Armored vehicles for every Tom, Dick, and Harry."

Back in the car, Ayesha said: "So, Salma, do you see some significant differences because these schools are semi-urban?"

"They're all community-based," said Salma. "The only difference is that some are nearer the road. We get the same response everywhere."

"But this is where your services are most needed," said Ayesha.

"Is load shedding as bad as it was six months ago?" I asked Salma, using the term for electricity rationing.

"It is bad," she acknowledged. "It's going to get worse."

"The dams are very low, right?"

"Yes. But we have to face it, we have to make do. We have alternatives, generators. But the tough thing is for the schools that are using computers. You should come here when the mustard is blooming, and the wheat is golden. It's very beautiful, in June–July." We were on a smaller road now, driving past fields.

Salma told us about the new school in Guff. "The builders had a difficult time," she said, "because they wanted to have a prefab school, and they had to bring in welders, and they had to bring in a generator, and they couldn't leave it in the village, so they had to bring it out."

"They had to bring the generator out every day?"

"Yes. And they couldn't use the labor from the village, because building a prefab school requires skilled labor, so they had to bring skilled labor from the city."

"Why did they feel it was important to have a prefab school?"

"We wanted to see the economics of it, whether it was worth having a prefab school. We're not completely satisfied." When we got there, we saw part of what Salma meant: Strong winds had torn off pieces of the corrugated roof.

"Since it's not so far from Islamabad and Rawalpindi, I didn't expect there to be no electricity," Ayesha remarked. "And this also seems to be more isolated."

We spent an hour or two at Guff, where we met the beautiful, bright-eyed sisters, Fauzia and Zubia, who ran the school as teachers. I spoke to them briefly, and Ayesha interviewed them at some length in Urdu. "Nobody from outside is going to come in to support this community," they told her. "If we were not educated, we would be doing what everyone else here is doing" —i.e., farming. Their father, an Air

Force officer, had been the first in his family to study past the matric level, and he was actively supportive of his daughters' desire to educate themselves and to teach. When we left, the sisters rode with us to a spot near the larger road, to save time on their long return commute.

"This is a pattern that I'm finding," reflected Ayesha during the long ride back to Islamabad. "That the family is supportive of them, the teachers, getting an education and working. And usually it's men who have to be supportive, especially fathers. For them, making money is not important. They say, 'We learn how to live.' For example, they say, 'Educated people, when they have an argument with somebody, they don't raise their voice.' This is what they mean by education."

* * *

Ghazala was talking on her cell phone when we met her in the lobby of the Islamabad Club. "It's Athar, but he's in Dubai," she said, and handed the phone to me.

"Ethan, I'm sorry that I had to come to Dubai," said Athar.

"I'm really moved and impressed by what you and Ghazala and others have achieved," I told him.

"Well, it's really Ghazala," he said. "She is my inspiration."

We were here for lunch with Ghazala and her mother and her cousin and sister-in-law, Fauzia. Fauzia had been in Karachi earlier in the week when Pete and I arrived in Islamabad, but she was back now. We filled our plates at the buffet and sat down. "There was a queue," Fauzia told me and Pete, "but three different men recognized Ghazala and told her, 'You go first.'"

Ghazala seemed embarrassed by the fuss.

"I guess they think that you led the lawyers' movement, so you should lead the buffet queue," I suggested, and all three women laughed with delight.

"When People's Party is aligning with Maulana Fazalur Rehman, then who is left on the left in Pakistan?" asked Fauzia rhetorically.

"I say there is no left, no right, there is only doing what is right," said Ghazala, sternly.

Of all the Minallahs, Fauzia was the most extroverted and vocal, the most quotable member of a very quotable family. I had come to admire her in 2003, when she took pains to point out to me folk carvings in a cemetery and decorations on the wall of a village mosque. She was an artist and had been a brave political cartoonist for the now-defunct newspaper *The Muslim* in the 1980s, when she was very young, during the Zia dictatorship. She had even published cartoons depicting her own mother, who was a Member of the National Assembly at the time. Her mother was a nice lady and didn't seem to mind. Fauzia had also taken me to visit French Colony, Islamabad's Christian shantytown, where she went often to help and encourage the children in little arts and crafts projects like making Christmas cards.

"I've never seen myself doing big, ambitous things," she had told me then. "I see myself doing small, intimate things." Fauzia may have been modest, but she was anything but shy.

A couple of days after our lunch, Pete and I spent a day tagging along while a filmmaker, Najam Hasan, shot footage of Fauzia at several sites she had written about and photographed in a handsome coffeetable book, *Glimpses into Islamabad's Soul*. In his foreword the late Dr. A.H. Dani, Director of the Taxila Institute of Asian Civilizations at Quaid-i-Azam University, had called the book "a gift to future generations that will remind them not only of the beauty of their natural heritage but also of the historical significance of Islamabad." For visitors like me, as well as for Pakistanis who came to work in government agencies or NGOs, it was easy to see Islamabad only as the new city that happened to be the capital.

Fauzia was an admiring disciple of Dr. Dani. "Until I read his books, I was also thinking that Islamabad had no history, that it was only started in sixties," she said. "But on the other side of the Margala Hills is Taxila, which was a great center for Buddhism. And on this side of the Margala Hills would be the same. So I thought I would go round and photograph some of the places that he had written about. I'm interested in places because of their historical value."

"I know that about you," I said.

"Yah! You wrote in your book about that door that I noticed! This is an old village. You know, before Islamabad was built, this place had villages scattered around the plateau."

In several villages in Fauzia's book were shrines of Sufi *pirs*, saints credited with having brought a benign form of Islam to the region. The Sufis are still widely revered, and their more mystical and ecstatic tradition is considered more indigenous and an antidote to the *wahhabi* extremism brought to Pakistan in recent decades by rich Arabs.

"That was the kind of Islam that the Sufis had developed, so that they could attract people," said Fauzia. "I don't know if the Mughals were able to convert people to Islam. It was these Sufi saints; it was their message. And that's really under threat in northern Pakistan. They blew up this Sufi's mausoleum, Rehman Baba, in Peshawar."

"Like they blew up the Buddhas in Bamiyan," I remembered. I had been in ardently Buddhist Thailand, of all places, when that infamous incident occurred in Afghanistan in March 2001.

"Here in Islamabad they blew up this banyan tree because Buddhists used to go there," she said. "And I got a piece of that tree at my home. I got it and thought I might do something with it."

In *Glimpses into Islamabad's Soul*, Fauzia includes a photo of the magnificent Buddha Tree in the E-7 sector and writes that it was "reduced to a mound of ashes" in 2003 by students at the nearby Madrassah Jamia Fareedia, who also vandalized the small Buddhist temple next to the tree. And she connects the tree's fate to another notorious incident:

> Jamia Fareedia was established by Maulana Abdullah, who was also the cleric at one of the oldest mosques of Islamabad, Lal Masjid

or the Red Mosque. During General Zia's Islamisation in the 80's, there was a spectacular rise in the number of madrassahs in Pakistan. They were being funded by the West and Arab countries and became recruiting grounds for volunteers fighting the Soviet forces in neighboring Afghanistan. Maulana Abdullah was killed in 1990, during sectarian strife, another outcome of Zia's regime. His sons Maulana Abdul Aziz and Maulana Abdul Rasheed Ghazi took over. ... For far too long the two cleric brothers openly challenged the "writ of the state".

The Government did take action against these two brothers in July 2007, but sadly it was too late and too violent. Operation "Sunrise", the military assault on the Lal Masjid, was Islamabad's version of "Shock and Awe". ... It was heart rending to see some of the parents running from pillar to post in search of their missing children. The innocent loss of life on both sides was probably the darkest incident in the history of our quiet and serene Islamabad.

"We get really enraged with these drone attacks because they damage our sovereign-ety," she said to me. "But our sovereign-ety was already damaged by the Saudis, with these madrassas. That was never our way."

Our first stop this day was at a quaint railway station, preserved with colonial-era furniture and vintage cars. On the platform grew beautiful, thick old trees, and goats and children from a settlement across the tracks wandered and played on the machinery. Pete took pictures while the film crew set up to interview Fauzia.

"This is a train station, it's called Golra train station," she said. "It was built by the British in 1886. And we still have the trains coming here. These trees over here, they're probably more than one hundred years old." In her book, Fauzia writes:

> According to Dr. Dani, the modern name of Golra is derived from Goala (cow-herd) and Rai (Raja). I have found many Goaley or milkmen in the villages nearby, such as Sihala, Mehra Beri, Chauntra and Suniari.

"But many of the people around here, they disagree with Dr. Dani," she told me. "They say it comes from *gora*, because the *goras* built the train station."

Najam, the documentary maker, was enjoying the outing. "Basically we are aesthetes," he gushed. "Because we love these old buildings. What I am doing is, I am taking chapters from her book. Because I want to show people that this is our heritage. It is not this terrorism."

"This is very interesting," said Fauzia, indicating a four-panel signboard written mostly in Hindi, erected in the early twentieth century and depicting teacups and teapots. One panel was colored blue and showed three men in different garb, all drinking tea. "You know, the British introduced tea in this area," said Fauzia. "So this is introducing tea to the people. And also, it introduces the benefits of taking tea. See, anyone can have it—Hindu, Muslim, Sikh can have it."

"These are great trees," I remarked.

"This one is banyan," she said. "You see this in a lot of Sufi shrines. And the other one, with the heart-shaped leaves, is called pipal, and that is where Buddha found the great enlightenment."

After a while, the film crew packed up and we drove on. "Now we are going to another village that's called Shah Allah Ditta," Fauzia told us. "This is also a Sufi saint's name. This is all going to be built into, you know, houses. The development is already going on. So now it's good that these people are more aware of their rights than they were forty years ago, when they gave away their ancestral lands for a pittance."

On the way, she railed against the Capital Development Authority's clumsy prettification of a village called Saidpur, where there had been plans to build a restaurant in a Hindu temple.

"I went to the CDA and really yelled at them that, 'How would you like to have a restaurant built in your mosque?' But now that temple has been made into a museum. But people go into it with their shoes.

They have no regard. You have Hindus here, who live in Islamabad, who are Pakistani, but they can't go there. They can go there like any other tourist, but they can't say that 'This is my place.' And between the temple they have opened an ice cream parlor. Now, this ice cream is eighty or seventy rupees per scoop, which only the elite of Islamabad can have. The villagers can't have. So, one, you have destroyed the whole character of that place. It was a simple spiritual place for the villagers. And now all these elite go there for their ice cream. But the children of the village are shooed away by the security guards. I *hate* going there. I used to love that place, because as a child I used to go there for pottery lessons. And now the way they have vulgarized this whole place, you know? I just hate it. And they spent 400 million rupees on I call it plastic surgery and liposuction and hair transplant development. And you know, the problem of the village is the sewerage. When I was a child it was a freshwater stream. And the whole sewerage is running into that freshwater stream. They don't spend money on that, but they spend it on all this makeup. So I don't like that. A lot of people love it: 'Oh, they've done such a beautiful job! Look how beauuu-tiful it is!'"

I told her that we had visited Rawal Lake.

"We have this Environmental Protection Agency," she said. "For three years, they have been asking the CDA to build a filtration plant there, because the whole Diplomatic Enclave, and the Quaid-e-Azam University, their raw sewerage is dumped in the lake. And the lake is not just any lake; that's drinking water for 'Pindi. They would rather spend money on the marble than on that filtration plant. So that is what I hate. There are diarrheal diseases in 'Pindi, children die, because of all this nuisance, this silly spending of money in Pakistan."

"Because the money was spent on the marble."

"And going into somebody's pocket! Come to think of it, Pakistan is one of the most corrupt countries in the world. So if they are saying that this was a 400 million project, how much was spent on the marble and how much went into the pocket of the officer? And there is not enough money to be made in a filtration plant. There's a lot of money to be made in constructing things. The last government was going to build an exclusive resort in the most pristine forest of Murree. That would have meant cutting down hundreds of years-old trees, thousands of trees. Chaudhry Iftikhar"—she reversed the names of the Chief Justice ousted by Musharraf—"stopped that project, because WWF, IUCN, all these NGOs working for environment, they had declared it an environmental disaster. Because most of the rainfall for this part comes from the Murree hills, because of those trees. He stopped it, and when the emergency was declared, Justice Dogar, in his ruling, mentioned that the last Supreme Court was a stumbling block, stopping the development projects. And they cited, for example, New Murree Project. So for one judge it's white, for other one it's black!

"And then there was this Margala Towers. If you see in F-10, that whole building just crumbled like sand during the earthquake." (The big earthquake of October 8, 2005, with its epicenter near Muzaffarabad in the Pakistan-controlled portion of Kashmir, in which more than 80,000 people died.) "They're going to move all that and build a shopping mall. And there were children and people who died in that disaster, because the builder was supposed to use Grade 6 steel, and instead he used Grade 4 steel. And it was a very faulty design. Chaudhry Iftikhar declared him a criminal, for criminal negligence. He went to England, and all the affectees, the Margala Towers victims, they wanted him back to be tried in Pakistan. He didn't come back, and there was a case with the British government, that they should hand him over. And when Dogar came, because of him not only is he a free man, but he's not a criminal anymore. He had three flats in that building, and he got compensation for all three of them. This is shocking! I say that other countries have constitution; we have prostitution of constitution."

"Is Chaudhry Iftikhar going to fix any of this, now that he's back?" "He has to! He has a big, big task in front of him. But it will be very, very difficult, because in this court he is a minority now."

We arrived at Shah Allah Ditta, where amazingly intricate banyan trees cascaded from a steep hillside above a pool fed by a natural spring and caves with ancient Buddhist images. On the other side of these hills was Taxila, the famous archeological site. It was here that I felt most tangibly the significance of the title of Fauzia's book.

"There used to be ten of them, but now there are only two," said Fauzia. "One, and two over there. It's gone under the landsliding. And these are also crumbling."

"It's so many thousands of years old," said Najam with a sigh. "But it's beautiful. We should have had a picnic here. Should I ask him to bring something here? Chicken karahi?"

"Sure," I said.

"Oh, what a lovely place. Basically this place, it's so close to Islamabad, but it's so far."

"Oh, look at that!" cried Fauzia.

On the road nearby, a mountain biker in full skintight biking getup was speeding past us. He must have come from the other side of the hills, from Taxila.

"Hello! Hello!" Najam called. "Hello!" But the biker didn't hear, and then he was gone downhill.

"Was that a *gora*?" I asked, incredulously.

"Yes!" said Fauzia. "For someone who has a passion for cycling, this is really a beautiful place."

She drew our attention to the banyan trees. "This whole thing is one single tree. This big one is the mother. All of these are coming from the big one. And these—"

"Aerial roots?"

"Yes. If you don't cut them they become these." She patted a trunk. "This was once the aerial roots." And she stooped to show us

182

fossils: "Look at this one. This has the full impression of the leaf."
Najam asked me to say something on camera about the caves.
"I wonder what I should say."
"Say something about your book."
"I think I'll talk about my book some other time," I said. "I think one of the tragedies of Pakistan is that people have defaced their history. But I don't want to say it that strongly." What I chose to say was that if we deface or obliterate our history in the name of a religious or political piety, we risk forgetting who we are and where we came from.

"In Swat only two years back, there were stone carvers making Buddhas," said Fauzia.

"Have you ever been to the caves before?" I asked Najam.

"No, this is the first time," he said. "I read Fauzia's book, and I decided to do this. Basically it's awareness, you see. Even I have been living in Islamabad for twenty-five years, and I never knew the caves were here."

Out of habit, I picked up a Mountain Dew wrapper.

"It's all over, you see, these polythene bags and everything," said Fauzia.

"You should send teenagers out here to pick it all up," I suggested.

"Oh, it's a sorry situation, the sanitation in Pakistan."

Pete tried to show me the Buddha images on the cave wall.

"There's a face," he said, "and there's an eye, and there ..."

"Not much left," I said.

"Not much left," he agreed. "But the last sixty years ..."

"Just think what they could have done to preserve them."

"Alls it woulda taken would be to fence it off."

As we returned to the car, Fauzia told us about a rock shelter she had written about in her book. "I was passing by it the other day, and they have blown a piece of it," she said. "Because you know,

there's a lot of construction going on, and it's easy money for them."
A man walked past us uphill, leading a camel laden with vegetables.
"He lives on the other side of the hill," said Fauzia. "Morning
they bring wood, and they go back with stuff for the village. This
will soon be another big housing scheme, like all of Islamabad is."
"At least you're documenting it," I said.
"Yah. Sometimes I wish that I had done it twenty years ago. But
that awareness was not there then, even for me. I took it for granted.
A lot of Islamabadis don't even realize that they're living in this very
healthy environment. And I make it a point, before I get really old
and this osteoporosis and arthritis won't allow me to hike, I go out."
When her sons' school had asked her to lead field trips, she had
readily agreed.
"Because this is really important for them," she said. "Because
this is what we had."

* * *

We returned to Fauzia's house in the afternoon and had a late lunch
and one of those long, maddeningly inconclusive conversations that
I've been having for fifteen years, all about Pakistan's many problems and clouded future. Near the end of it I found myself feeling
distinctly depressed, in a familiar way. I tried to convey points that
to me seemed obvious about my own society, about the growing gap
between rich and poor, the disregard for history, the predatory and
untenable economy. The bigger they are the harder they fall, I
wanted to say. But I didn't say these things, because I knew Pakistanis had a different view of America than I did. "It's like a fairy
tale place, where everything is in order," a young man who had
studied in Texas had once said to me. Who was I to tell him he
shouldn't romanticize my country? Maybe he needed to.
"So, does Fauzia ever get you in trouble with her outspoken-
ness?" I asked Temur, her husband.

Ghazala Minallah

Rawal Lake, Islamabad

A family along the road to Murree

Visiting the Developments in Literacy (DiL) school in
Guff village, outside Rawalpindi

Guff village

Dr. Azizur Rahman Bughio,
former speechwriter to
Benazir Bhutto

Faiysal Ali Khan

Fauzia Minallah at the historic Golra train station

The Buddha caves at Shah Allah Ditta, outside Islamabad

Dr Sattar at the Telemedic hospital, Kharian

The Grand Trunk Road, Kharian

Tahir

The Grand Trunk Road

Dr. Shahnaz Khan at the Human Development Foundation school in Kharol War, outside Lahore

Yusuf Amin

The upper clock stopped running when a rocket-propelled grenade hit the Groom & Bride Shop in Liberty Circle, Lahore, during the attack on the Sri Lankan national cricket team on March 3, 2009. The lower clock shows the correct time.

Ethan Casey with his former Beaconhouse National University
students Adnan and Usman

The Badshahi Mosque, Lahore

Karachi

Karachi

Relaxing in Aurry's village

Three amigos (*tiin dost*): Pete, Essam and Ethan on the last day
of a six-week Pakistan road trip

"No, I disown her," he said with a rueful smile.

"Timmy is like water and I am like fire," said Fauzia. "So we complement each other. If we were both fiery, one of us would definitely have gotten into trouble. He keeps me grounded. During this lawyers' movement, he would say to me, 'Think of your children.'"

"And your poor husband," said Temur.

"So I was not like Ghazala," said Fauzia. "She really put her head in the lion's mouth."

CHAPTER 4

GRAND TRUNK ROAD TRIP

"For the heart, light and prolonged exercise is important, starting for a short period, and gradually working up," Dr. Sattar was saying. "(But before going for exercise, we have to have an exercise tolerance test.) Like brisk walk, swimming, cycling, aerobics. Walking is the easy thing, which we can do everywhere. These should be done empty stomach. Many people here in Pakistan eat dinner, then go for walk. That is very common. But any exercise should be done on empty stomach, or at least two-three hours after eating."

"This is useful for me too," I said.

"How old are you?"

"Forty-three."

"You look younger than that."

"Thanks."

I was impressed by this 56-year-old man, in his wool blazer and tie, hiking like a trouper up four flights to the roof of the hospital. He was jolly and kindly and dedicated, and over several days in Kharian I had come to feel fond of him. One thing that had become clear to me was that he was here, in a nondescript town along the famous Grand Trunk Road,—because he was a patriot and a good human being. We were hiking up to the hospital roof to film him exhorting U.S.-based colleagues in Urdu to put their medical skills and other resources to use for Pakistan's betterment. I had

186

unwittingly launched his disquisition on heart health and exercise by joking, as we climbed: "As a cardiologist, you must know the importance of cardiovascular exercise." To him, it was no joke.

"Any of us, in the forties and after, we should do exercise so that we remain fit," he said earnestly but with a smile. "But heavy exercise after forty-five can be dangerous for the heart, especially if they have not been continually exercising from a young age. We should encourage our children from the very beginning to take part in games. You see most of the people here working in offices, their belly is out." His own colleagues were no better than anyone else. "Most of the doctors, they are giving advice to everybody, but when you ask them honestly, they say they don't exercise. I was very happy to see both of you very fit, very smart. But I see on TV some of these people in America, they are very fat."

"We're fortunate that we live in an area where people are health-conscious," said Pete.

"People here, they don't know the importance of salad," Dr. Sattar complained. "And the way of cooking here is very bad. They put lot of oil, and lot of chiles, and they cook, cook. And the oil is not destroyed by cooking, but the nutrition of the vegetables is reduced. I tell them, 'Your weight is not increasing by the chapatis. Your weight is increasing by this curry you are taking.' And they are also eating lot of meat. I tell them, 'Don't go to a nearby mosque. Go to a faraway mosque. Don't just go to the mosque and go home. If you are traveling by bus, just drop two kilometers before and walk.'"

We had come to Kharian by van after a week in Islamabad, with Tahir and several young guys Jawad had made available to us as a film crew. The van driver was a wild-eyed maniac who used his horn as a weapon, and after a few days with the film crew the van started to feel like a dorm room on wheels. I thought of it as the Scooby-Doo Mobile. On all my previous trips to Pakistan, I had gone from Lahore to Islamabad either by motorway, which was fast and hassle-free, or by train. I had never had the pukka Pakistani experience of traveling the Grand Trunk Road. Built in the sixteenth century by the Pashtun emperor Sher Shah Puri, the GT Road had been improved and extended by both the Mughals and the British, until it stretched from Bangladesh in the east to beyond Peshawar in the west. It had been a major trade route as well as an artery for moving armies. Most of the action in *Kim* takes place along the GT Road, which Kipling called "such a river of life as nowhere else exists in the world." The town of Kharian is right on the road, almost exactly halfway between Islamabad and Lahore.

Kipling would have recognized and appreciated today's Grand Truck Road, although in his day there were no CNG stations. Compressed natural gas is a less expensive alternative to gasoline, and in the five years since I had last been to Pakistan it had become ubiquitous. Many vehicles, including Tahir's car, were set up with a separate nozzle and tank for CNG. You could go much farther on less fuel with CNG, but you had to fill up more often. So, among the many shops and restaurants and buildings along the five-hour stretch of road between Islamabad and Lahore, the most prominent signs were those of CNG stations:

Pearl CNG
   Mart
   Mosque
   Washrooms
Rehan CNG
   Quality & Quantity
   Masjid
   Tuck shop
City CNG
   Mosque
   Tuck Shop

Tyre Shop
Toilet

"Investment we act like the sheep," lamented a man we met in
Kharian. "Where one goes, others go after. For example, you can
see so much CNG station. Now, in winter, we have shortage of gas
because of these."

* * *

The morning after we arrived, I sat down with Dr. Sattar and his colleague Dr. Sufyan, a pleasant young pediatrician with a cheery Char-
lie Brown countenance. "I worked fifteen years for PIMS [Pakistan
Institute of Medical Sciences] in Islamabad in cardiology department,
which is a very good department, equipped with cath lab, nuclear cardiology, echo lab, a 14-bedded CCU, 31-bedded cardiology ward, and
very busy emergency and OPD," said Dr. Sattar. "All over this area,
people referred the cardiac patients to this place. And during this fifteen years I did my post-graduation, diploma in cardiology from
Lahore. Then I went to Saudi Arabia. I joined the Khalid University
Hospital. They took me as a specialist because I had a diploma in cardiology, which is not considered a big diploma. It was a minor
diploma. So they took me as a specialist. But after one and a half
years, my boss promoted me as a consultant. Because I have worked
in a good place, I was very well trained, so he saw my performance
and he took me as a consultant. For three and a half years I worked as
a consultant. After that I came back to Pakistan. And this time I went
to my home place, Sukkur. It is in Sindh, about 400 kilometers from
Karachi. And my people where I worked before, in PIMS, they were
interested to bring me back. But I said no, I have been away from my
homeland for long time, so now I will come and settle my own place.

"I worked there for three years. Meanwhile, my boss from Saudi
Arabia was all the time asking me, 'Please come back and join us.' So

ultimately I agreed, and he sent the visa for me. So I processed the visa and got the visa stamped on my passport, planning to go back to Saudi Arabia. But when I went to Shifa International [Hospital] for medical for my family, there I met my old friends Dr. Shazli and other doctors who were with me in PIMS. They told me, 'Don't go to Saudi Arabia. We need you here. We have a friend in America, Dr. Jawad. He has started a good hospital, and if you work with him you will be very happy, and he will give you almost equally good package also.'

"Then I was double-minded. On one hand I was having good salary, good place, Saudi Arabia, all my family was very happy because they enjoyed a lot there. But on the other hand, I had to leave my country. And Dr. Shazli was giving me a good offer to work in this place, which is a small town, where 'You will be getting good facilities: echo, CT, CCU, and you will help poor patients here.' So I changed my mind. So I came here, visited the place. So I was in doubt whether this hospital will continue, or they will stop after few months and then I will be nowhere. But if I go to Saudi Arabia it is a solid contract; there is no doubt they will continue everything. But here I was in great doubt, initially. It was a big risk. But when I came here I saw, and I talked to Dr. Jawad. When I heard his plans and his dedication about this project, I was convinced. So I joined here. And *inshallah*, God willing, I will continue here."

"How long have you been working here?"

"This is my second month." He laughed. "And still my visa is valid until the 15th. They give three months!"

"In this short span of time, of almost one month, Dr. Sattar has saved almost seven to eight lives," said Dr. Sufyan. "They came here because they know that there is a hospital which is providing the ICU facilities overnight. They came late night, and he stayed with them for four to five hours, the patient became stable, and then he came back to home."

"These seven or eight people were very critical," said Dr. Sattar. "If we would have not worked hard on them, or if we had shifted them to another place, they were not in condition to reach that place. Definitely. Their BP was not recordable, their pulse was very feeble, they were gasping, many other complications. It was very immediate and urgent treatment they were requiring. I don't know why they brought the patient so late. Actually a few of them, they went to local hospitals. They kept them for few hours, and then they found that they were not going to survive. They said, 'Okay, take away this patient from our hospital. Take them to Lahore or Islamabad.' But they came to us. When they came to us we said, 'Okay, patient is serious, but we will try our best, and *inshallah* God will help them.' And we helped, and Dr. Jawad was also in good contact with us from videoconferences."

"What is the value of the videoconferencing?" I asked.

"Great, really," he said. "This is one of the very important things which attracted me to come here. Because all our patients are not only cardiac. They have medical problems also. So I have good experience in cardiology, but medicine and other problems, Dr. Jawad is lot of teaching. I am learning day by day also. With his advices we learn a lot, and we are able to manage other patients also. I remember one lady, she was thirty-five years old. She came pain in leg. So we were thinking maybe she is a diabetic, maybe she had some other problem. So I talked to Dr. Jawad on videoconference. He listened, and he saw the patient. Then he told me, 'Do this B-12 levels.' When we did B-12 levels, they were deficient. We gave her B-12, and she had very remarkable improvement. I would have not thought about this thing, because I am a cardiologist. So this is a good thing for that poor lady."

"Dr. Jawad lives in Tacoma, which is close to where I live in Seattle," I said. "He works in the hospital there. And at night, after his American job, he does videoconferencing with you. But he's only one guy. Is consulting with him sufficient for this hospital's needs, or do you feel that as this hospital grows you may need to have more doctors available in America to do videoconferencing?"

"Yes, of course," said Dr. Sattar.

"He is also preparing a team of doctors," added Dr. Sufyan. "He has already prepared, I think, ten to twelve doctors, of different specialities. They are all American boards, and they are doing job in the America."

"Are they Pakistani?"

"Most of them. A few are Indians, one or two."

"Is this a voluntary thing for them?"

"Yes. They are on voluntary basis."

"We don't have to pay them," added Dr. Sattar.

"What they are getting in America, we cannot pay them," said Dr. Sufyan.

"This is a remarkable thing you're doing," I said.

"This is not an extraordinary thing," said Dr. Sattar. "A patient is critical, this is our responsibility. We have to stay with him, to save his life, till he is out of danger. So this is our routine. When patient is serious we forget sleep, we forget food and everything. Our tentacle is on high, and we are involved with that. And at that time we forget everything: our family, our house, other appointments, finished. Only this patient, till he revives or he dies."

"Alone, without any supportive care or instruments or monitors, we are nowhere," added Dr. Sufyan. "But if we have a good center, where we have central oxygen, or suction machine, or cardiac monitors, then it is easy for a doctor to manage a patient."

"This is a relatively prosperous town?" I asked.

"Yeah, but even the majority, they are very poor people," said Dr. Sattar. "We provide them, according to Dr. Jawad, maximum care without charging them. If patient has money to pay, okay. If they can't pay, don't force them to pay money. He can come next time also without money, no problem."

"Do you feel you've made a career sacrifice, or is this a career opportunity?"

"I was working before in PIMS, and I was getting monthly salary," he said. "In Saudi Arabia, I was getting monthly salary. When I worked in Sukkur, people came with misery and pain and difficulty, then we give them treatment and get money from them. Then I feel, 'This is a very bad job. Patients are coming, they are poor people, they are in pain, and we are asking them to pay us the money.' It was very difficult for me, very painful for me. To survive, I need money. If I don't take money, it is difficult to survive myself. My children, everybody, they need money. So I was praying God, 'Give me some thing that I treat people, but I don't get money from poor people.' Saudi Arabia was a good thing: good money, don't ask people. Here also, I am getting money from this Telemedic hospital. I am not charging directly to the patients, and I know also that these people are not forced to pay lot of money. They are at ease, we are at ease. I am also at the same time having good equipments, similar to what I had in Islamabad and Saudi Arabia."

"Do you enjoy living in Kharian?"

"It is a small place, but it is a neat, clean city," he said. "My family is also here now. My children have joined the school, City School. So they are happy. Islamabad is nearby; they can go and come back."

"Do you get the opportunity to go to the States and see techniques done there as well?" asked Pete.

"If we got a chance, we would definitely go. Because when I was working in PIMS, we were thinking that we were the best. When I went to Saudi Arabia and I saw new things, then I thought, 'Okay, we are not the best.' Advanced machines, good doctors, good teamwork, and we learned a lot. I would suggest all the doctors working in Pakistan, 'Don't stay in one place. Keep on going and seeing what is happening around. Come back, do the same thing here also.'"

"You must be aware that there's a pretty severe health care crisis in America," I said. "Many people don't have insurance, so for many people the cost of health care can be devastating. You're bringing some of the best available medical talent and technology to a provincial town like this, in a Third World country. You're making some of the medical talent that's working in America available to your patients here. And it's affordable for the patients here. This model could work in other countries."

"Yes, this is a need for every place. If this is successful here, I think it should be every fifty kilometers or hundred kilometers. Not only in Pakistan, other countries also."

*　*　*

We stayed three nights in Kharian, one more than planned because, on our second full day there, we learned that all roads into Lahore had been closed after a terrorist attack on a police training school. Lahore was the city I knew best, about which I had written the most, so I had decided to squeeze our time there at both ends for the sake of other priorities. The meetings I had taken care to set up in Lahore were starting to shift and dissolve anyway. Asma Jahangir, the prominent human rights lawyer, had to appear in court in Islamabad and sent apologies through her secretary. The end of Governor's Rule in Punjab had caused a meeting of the Provincial Assembly that conflicted with my appointment with Mohsin Latif, an assembly member and nephew of Nawaz Sharif's wife. Imran Khan was off to London for ten days to see his kids. The newspaper editor Najam Sethi—who was also my publisher in Pakistan—was off to Islamabad for one, two, or three days, characteristically hard to pin down. "Call me a day ahead of time," he said. I thought that was what I had just done, but I shrugged and made a mental note to call him again later in the week. In truth, none of these people was any more important or interesting than the people I was with.

We were hearing that there was a siege of a police station somewhere on the outskirts of Lahore, that nearly 500 people were being held hostage in a police training academy, that twenty-five had been killed and ninety injured. "They've killed a lot of policemen, and the gunmen are still in the building, and there's a hostage situation," my former student Ayela Deen told me by phone. "This city is rather aghast," said Salima Hashmi, the artist and BNU dean who had introduced me to Vidha Saumya in Mumbai. A retired army brigadier I knew was more sanguine: "No, no, there is no problem at all. People are immune to these small things." Anyway, we stayed an extra day in Kharian. "We should have turned on the TV this morning," said Pete. But I was glad we hadn't.

With Tahir and the film crew and a man named Aamer who worked for Jawad as an accountant and facilities manager, we made a day trip out of Kharian to see nearby villages that were prospering from hard currency remittances earned by area residents who had migrated to work in Europe, starting in the 1960s. "You understand wealth of people living here: lot of people have limousine-type cars here," said Aamer. "You can say that if anybody come to Kharian they don't want to go back, because there is lot of chance for things like shops. Did Dr. Jawad tell you what is the origin of people going to Europe? Behind the entire situation is the grandfather of Dr. Jawad. The father of his mother. He pressed people to sell their buffaloes and go there. Dr. Jawad's mother is also very famous lady in this area. She was retired from very good post in Education Department."

We drove past fields of rice and golden wheat. "It is almost ready for cutting," said Aamer. The area was famous for mangoes and a certain kind of orange. Aamer was a born tour guide, a talker. "This is the village of forefather of Dr. Jawad," he narrated. "This is the military firing range." Kharian was the site of Pakistan's largest army cantonment. "Every beautiful and good place is under custody of

Pakistan Army. This is the place where Telemedic came into being some years ago. We will shift again in near future, maybe to Jhelum. Because there is no proper CT scan in Jhelum, but we have to have a CT scan in Kharian." We crossed a bridge over the Jhelum River. "Punjab is famous for five rivers and land of five rivers. But now you can say we have only two rivers. In 1993 the flood came. River came above that bridge. If any country have this much of water, they don't have any energy shortage. You can see we have lot of wheat crop. But still, we have shortage of wheat."

"Why? Do you export it?"

"No. Because some rich people buy millions of bags of wheat, and they store it and sell it when price is high. And—how do you say artificial food for crops?"

"Fertilizer?" suggested Pete.

"Fertilizer. We don't have fertilizer, and this year we will be short of wheat."

"Oh, this is very nice," I said, appreciating the view.

"From road you will see lot of vast area. I think in past this area belong to some river."

The guards at the Rohtas Fort, built in the mid-sixteenth century by the same Sher Shah Suri who had built the Grand Trunk Road, wouldn't allow us to film inside the walls. "I think they are afraid of higher authorities," said Aamer. The ruined fort was impressive, and we stayed so Pete could photograph it at sunset. There was a village inside the fort walls. "This village belongs to Shia people," Aamer told us. "Same people live in Iran. The same caste, you can say. Shia is one of the caste of Islam. This flag belong to them, the black. I came here three-four-five years back. The condition of fort was very bad. But now it is little bit better." Sher Shah had built the fort to block the invasion route between Peshawar and Lahore, after defeating the Mughal emperor Humayun in the Battle of Kanauj, ' to intimidate a local tribe that had refused allegiance to him.

"Waste of money," complained Aamer. "If he do this for the betterment of people, then I can say. But he do this only for his own safety."

* * *

The next morning there was still a high security alert in Lahore. "I think security disturb you, you guys, you foreigners," said Tahir, grinning as if it were funny.

"Are you ready to go to Lahore?" asked Aamer.

"We're not going to Lahore today," I told him. "High security alert."

"I don't think so there is any problem."

"But we want to go to Kashmir anyway."

The Lahore situation allowed us to make a trip to the Line of Control, the de facto border between the Pakistani- and Indian-held portions of the disputed state of Jammu and Kashmir. For much of its length—for example at Kargil, site of an ill-advised Pakistani offensive that precipitated an international crisis in the early summer of 1999—the Line of Control runs at nearly inaccessible altitudes, among some of the most inhospitable Himalayan peaks. Here it was much lower, and you could get there and back on a day trip.

But before we could go, I needed to check my email. There was no Wi-Fi in the hospital, and the only ethernet cable was at a nurse's desk in a room where there was also a bed for patients. It was awkward, and I didn't want to be online, but I had to make forward plans for Lahore and Karachi. Pete and I had been on the road for a month at this point, and the long days and lack of privacy were starting to take a toll. "Hello," said some guy to me just as I was sitting down at the nurse's desk.

"Hi," I replied.

"You are writing a book?"

"Yes."

"About Asia?"

"About Pakistan."

"What do you think about Pakistan?"

"I like Pakistan."

"But most people think Pakistan is a terrorist country."

"But I don't," I assured him.

"Actually, American policy creates problems for us," he said.

"It creates problems for us too."

"American policy creates problems for many countries too, like Iraq, Iran, Afghanistan ..."

"Yes."

I did my best to chat politely and take notes on the conversation at the same time. Then the man went away and Pete came in and asked, impatiently, how long I was going to take. I hadn't even gotten online yet, and we found ourselves snapping at each other.

"Relax," I said. "I need twenty minutes, and that's just tough shit."

"*You* relax."

"I'm not pissed," I assured him.

"I am," he said.

I followed him into the hallway, and we huddled in a corner.

"I'm pissed at you for being pissed," I said.

"It would be all right if I could go up on the roof and take photos," Pete griped. The door to the roof happened to be locked at the time. "But I'm sittin' here with everybody, and it's like I'm a target. Sometimes, I don't know, I just need my space." He had an angular, abrupt way of gesturing with his arms and posture when he was frustrated or annoyed.

Fortunately, my capacity for empathy kicked in. My experience of Asia helped me understand what he must have been enduring while I was stealing a pinch of privacy for myself. And I knew Pete well enough to know how trying it would have been for him. But it was also true that throughout the trip I had been deflecting most of

198

the chitchat by my nice-guy looks and relative gregariousness, and by virtue of being what people in the subcontinent call the incharge. Pete was along for the ride, and he could hide behind his camera.

We got on the road shortly after eleven and drove into brown hills, above a mostly dry river bed. Army trucks passed us, headed toward the Line of Control. "Apple of Kashmir was very, very famous," said Aamer. "But now lot of people have moved from there to the cities. Nobody left to care. I think in summer you will find full of water, due to melting of glaciers. I think glaciers are on LoC." He meant the snow peaks in the distance.

Just after one o'clock we pulled over, because the engine was overheating. We all got out to stretch our legs, and I walked down the road to urinate. Tractors lumbered uphill laden with bricks and dirt, and two men and a boy passed us on a motorbike. Tahir spent several minutes standing in different spots, looking for cell phone coverage. "No service," he said glumly, showing me his phone. "No problem," I said, and everyone laughed.

"There is a town where we will stop," said Aamer as we began moving again. "He will make little bit of repair to the vehicle, then we will check whether we can go to the LoC. If we are allowed, we will go. Much better than here."

The town, named Baba Shadi Shaheed Darbar after a Sufi saint, was a scruffy little string of shops around a bend in the road on a hillside, selling necessities, soda pop, cheap pottery, and chintzy plastic toys. "People came here to sacrifice their animals," explained Aamer. "I think you can smell. I think they are superstitious type of people. People bring their own cattle from outside. Animals are not available here. After sacrification they provide, and they make a meal. People sacrifice animals because they think Allah will be happy, and He will provide them a child. But my favorite place is Wagah border, evening ceremony. Every time I go there, my heart is going very fast."

"Is it Pakistani pride?" asked Pete.

"Yes. Pakistan national are not very much united, but when there is a problem, like after the earthquake, they are."

We ate lunch in the town, then continued uphill toward the Line of Control.

"Life is very much difficult for Pakistanis after change of millenium," said Aamer.

"Yes, I know," I said.

"Not only for Pakistanis, but everywhere!"

I asked Aamer about himself. "I belong to Rawalpindi and Murree," he said. "I have six sisters and one brother. We are eight. One sister died last year. She had breast cancer. Surgery is very painful. All of the hair falls off from your head, even eyebrows." He was 37 years old and had four sons younger than six, including five-month-old twins who woke him up in the middle of the night. And the three-year-old was causing trouble these days, hitting the twins and his older brother.

"Finished, or more?" I asked.

"I didn't plan on these two also," he said with a fatalistic chuckle. "I don't want to use artificial means to block."

We wound around hillsides above valleys planted to rice and wheat, with views across at Indian-held snow peaks, then descended and went along the valley floor to a small settlement, where boys were playing cricket. We were at the Line of Control, or near enough.

My last trip to the LoC had been at the tail-end of the 1999 Kargil hostilities, at the end of a bone-jarring seven-hour jeep ride from Skardu with an army major. We had stayed overnight, I had played ping-pong with the colonel commanding the Pakistani position that exchanged desultory artillery rounds with Indians on the far slope of the steep mountainside, and Major Yahya had shown me the remains of an Indian fighter jet he claimed had strayed into Pakistani territory. That was my idea of the Line of Control. By comparison, this was anti-climactic. Aamer pointed at the hill in front of us and said, "No formal type of line. Just a verbal type of, 'This is yours, this is our.' If Pakistanis are occupied on the up side, then we could go there. But they are on the down side, so we will waste our time."

"This is Indian hill," said Tahir.

I remembered several days I had spent in the far north of Thailand in early 2001 with my journalist friend Tony Davis, a wiry, bearded, rugged type whose father had served in the British Army. Tony had chosen journalism as the next best thing for himself, because his father had warned him that, with the Empire winding down, there was less adventure to be had in a military career. After we visited a Thai Army camp near the Burmese border, where our visit must have been the most interesting thing to have happened to the soldiers in a while, Tony had remarked: "Soldiering is probably the profession with the most time spent sitting around with nothing to do. But journalism—or at least our kind of journalism—is a close second." The Thai-Burma border is long and ambiguous; many of the "hill tribe" people on both sides of it are stateless, and many hills are not clearly known to be in either country. You learn things from standing there, reflecting that that hill is in Burma, whereas this hill is in Thailand, that you can't learn from reading a map. In the real world, the border is somewhere between these soldiers and those soldiers. As Tony said to me one evening over beers on the roof of our hotel in Mae Sai, "There's no substitute for the sniff on the ground."

On the drive back, Aamer defaulted to talking about cricket. "But nowadays because of some situations, like IPL, ICL, we have a shortage of good batsmen," he said. These were the innovative and ambitious Indian Premier League and Indian Cricket League. The Pakistan Cricket Board was Pakistani cricket fans' favorite boogie man. "I think main source of this problem is incompetence at higher level of PCB," said Aamer. "Pakistan team can perform good, if we put fully under control of Imran Khan. I don't think so we have *any* international standard batsman, after Mohammed Yusuf."

"You mean Yusuf Yohana?"

"Yes, Yusuf Yohana."

Yusuf Yohana had been the only Christian on the Pakistan national cricket team. When I attended a one-day match between Pakistan and South Africa at Gaddafi Stadium in September 2003, the young village teacher who befriended me had called him "the backbone of the Pakistan team" and "the first Christian to gain so much fame in Pakistan." Since then Yusuf had converted to Islam, reportedly because he had been given to understand that if he didn't, he stood no chance of being made team captain.

"Mohammed Yusuf is a singles hitter, right?" I asked Aamer. "Not fours and sixes."

"According to the situation," he said. "But traditionally, yes. Complete cricketer. Shoaib Akhtar was my college fellow."

"Rawalpindi Express," I said, using the fast bowler's nickname. I had seen Shoaib Akhtar bowl that same day in Lahore, and he was exciting and fun to watch. He bowled the way he looked: like a wild man, with arms akimbo and stringy hair flying all over the place. His checkered personal history reinforced the impression of an undisciplined personality; he had been suspended from play for everything from curfew violations to performance-enhancing drugs to ball tampering to treatment for genital warts.

"Maybe he is a good cricketer," said Aamer. "But he does not have a good character."

At the National Cricket Academy next to Gaddafi Stadium in Lahore, Pete and I had spoken with the academy's chief coach, Aaqib Javed, and senior general manager Ali Zia about the March 3 attack on the Sri Lankan team and the refusal of some teams to tour Pakistan even before that incident, and about the Indian team's famous 2004 tour of Pakistan. "I think that was one of the best times for this country," Aaqib Javed had said. He had recently met an Australian cricket delegation in Dubai. "They said, 'Are you happy living there? It seems like very difficult to survive there,'" he said. "I think people only read the headlines, and the biggest headline has always been attacks and problems. I think if you go around, if you really look at the whole Pakistan, life is I think almost normal. So I said, 'This is my country, and how can I think of leaving and settling down somewhere else?' And one thing you must mention: Sri Lanka. They won the '96 World Cup in Pakistan, even in Lahore. And after they won, Ranatunga, the captain of that Sri Lankan team, said, 'The way we have got support from the local Lahoris, even it's more than Colombo.' That was the biggest statement. When they won, they rode through this Liberty area. And thousands of people came out from their homes to cheer them."

"They didn't want Australia to win," joked Ali Zia.

Aaqib Javed had told a story about his Dubai trip. "That visa was sponsored by the Sharjah Cricket Club. And that guy looked at me and said, 'Are you a cricketer?' I said, 'Yes.' And there was a guy behind me. He said, 'Come with me.' And I had just a handbag, slightly bigger than this. And he checked each and every thing. And he said, 'Okay, come with me.' He said, 'Take off your shoes, socks, trousers, shirt.' One of our players was caught in Dubai with some illegal drugs. And after that incident I just felt that, 'The thing we used to feel proud of, it's become a shame.' I'm going again on the second, so it could be the same story." He smiled. "So I'm ready, as a Pakistani, to take off my trousers."

I related some of this to Aamer, but he was less interested in geopolitical ramifications than in cricket per se. He was enthusiastically appreciative of Aaqib Javed. "I think we should take him as a bowler coach," he told me with feeling. "Because he work *very* hard to become a good bowler. In his time were Wasim Akram, Waqar Yunus, players who were greater than he was. But he worked *so* hard. Imran Khan also said he wants Aaqib Javed as a bowler coach. He say Wasim and Waqar are God-gifted, but Aaqib Javed work *so* hard."

We passed through a village called Ladian. Aamer pointed and said: "This is the tomb of Raja Aziz Bhatti. He died in the 1965 war against India. He received the biggest award in Pakistan, called Nishan-e-Haider. You can say symbol of courage. If you put his name in search, you will find his story."

"Was he Army?"

"Yes, Army."

"How was he killed?"

He laughed. "When I was in school I used to know all the stories of these national heroes. But now I can no longer remember. A lot of water has gone through the bridge, you can say." Maybe reflecting on just how much water, he added: "Next year if you come, maybe there will be peace in Swat. But I am optimistic. I don't think there is much hope."

"You mean you're pessimistic," I suggested.

"You can say."

* * *

"Yusuf says first you check in at Gymkhana, then you do other things," Tahir informed me as we arrived in Lahore, late the next afternoon.

"That's Yusuf's idea," I said, carefully. "I have a different idea. I'm worried about our tickets to Karachi, and I'm worried about the bank."

A week in Islamabad and several days in the Scooby-Doo Mobile with the film crew had left me and Pete feeling crowded and overloaded. It's true that if you don't want your style to be cramped you shouldn't go to Pakistan, but I badly needed to be back in control of my own movements and decisions. Our train tickets to Karachi were our tickets to that freedom, and I needed to make it to the big branch of Askari Bank on Main Boulevard before the end of the business day. It turned out that many thousands of rupees had accumulated in my account there. The account was a vestige of my semester teaching at Beaconhouse National University, when I had opened it to receive direct deposits of my salary. I had kept the account open to take payments for columns I wrote for two Pakistani newspapers, but I had never really expected to retrieve the money. In Islamabad I had shown my passport at an Askari Bank branch and, to my surprise, had been told my account number and exact balance. But to withdraw funds I needed a new checkbook, and I could get that only at the branch where I had opened the account. I wanted some of those rupees, because I didn't want to miss the chance to buy a couple of suits while we were still in Pakistan. We no longer had enough time for me to get them tailor-made, but I was hoping to find a couple at good prices off the rack in Karachi.

So I was insistent about going to the bank and the train station before checking in at the Gymkhana guest house, where Yusuf was generously putting us up. Arriving late in the afternoon meant crawling through traffic and dragging half a dozen other people around Lahore in the van, but we accomplished both errands. The day ended with about eight of us, including three bellhops whose help we hadn't asked for, carrying bits and pieces of Pete's and my luggage into a room at the Gymkhana. I churlishly refused to tip the bellboys—I wasn't carrying any small cash anyway—and when everyone had finally left, I called room service and asked for a whiskey and soda. Alcohol is illegal in Pakistan, but that's not the same thing as unavailable, and it had been suggested to me that here I could get anything I might want. Right now, what I wanted was a whiskey and soda.

The bellhop didn't understand the part about soda, so I asked for whiskey and ice instead. He returned a few minutes later with a full bottle of Black Label and a big bowl of ice cubes.

"Only full bottle available," he said.

So I asked for a beer instead.

"Can?"

"Bottle."

"Can."

"Okay, can."

"Cash payment."

"Never mind," I said. Getting a drink in this country was more trouble than it was worth.

What we did get were a couple of disappointing sandwiches with soggy fries. We ate them as we cherished our hard-won little bubble of privacy, feeling drained by too many demands taking the form of solicitude. "It's like I can't even carry my own frickin' bag!" said Pete. "I was never meant to be rich and famous. It'd drive me nuts." I recounted to him the plot of *The Dispossessed*, the Ursula Le Guin novel I had reread in India. The protagonist, Shevek, is a brilliant young physicist on Annares, a bleak planet-sized moon of Urras, from which anarchist revolutionaries called Odonians were banished by mutual agreement 150 years ago. Since then contact between the two planets has been minimal and essentially colonial, although that awkward fact goes largely unmentioned on Annares. Shevek makes the controversial personal decision to visit Urras, because he craves the company and needs the challenge of intellectual peers, and because he has an inchoate feeling that the two planets are really, after all, one society and that he should do something to help them reconcile. But he's naive and, on Urras, out of his depth, and he fails to understand the ways he's being used and manipulated.

There were times when I felt like Shevek. For me, the mystery was not why Pakistan should be dysfunctional and rife with intrigue, but why I felt compelled to inject myself repeatedly into the miasma of its perpetual national drama. I was the guy who kept coming back; I had an open, friendly, Midwestern demeanor and a genuine interest and sympathy; my friend Dennis in Seattle said he imagined me strolling through Pakistan with marquee lights on my forehead flashing the words NICE GUY! NICE GUY! Pakistanis asked me all the time, often with a tinge of incredulity, how and why I had become interested in their country. I offered them various semi-satisfactory short answers, but the real answer is that to begin to understand my own motivation requires writing at least two books.

"I'll write about this," I told Pete, "and how weird it's been, and then I'll allude to *The Dispossessed*, which'll be great because I'll have been alluding to it earlier in the book. And then I'll point out how it's actually a metaphor for—"

At that moment the lights went out.

"—for my whole experience of this country over the past fifteen years."

Pete fumbled in his pack and brought out his flashlight, which was a special kind that stood up in a little stand and shed light across the room like a candle.

"Yep, that's the perfect flashlight," he said with satisfaction. After a pause he added: "Imagine me and three Malagasies, and Clarissa, walkin' down this here ridge, and the wind's blowin', and the grass is up to here, and—" He savored the memory. "And that flashlight was our only light."

Pete and I lived in the city that was home to the REI flagship store. For this trip he had brought along a sleeping pad, a first aid kit, and a special fast-drying towel that folded up really small. In all my travels, I had never carried any of those things. He had made a special trip to Costco to buy instant oatmeal, granola bars, and bags of peanuts, cashews, and almonds in bulk. And he was a bit of a know-it-all about matters microbiological. "You shouldn't rinse your toothbrush in that water," he told me one morning.

"Yeah, but it'll dry out before I use it next," I objected.

"No." He frowned and shook his head. "It's a bad idea."

And he had brought his special flashlight. He wasn't a nut about it, but he was definitely the type.

After a couple of minutes the generator kicked in and the lights came back on.

"Well, one thing I can say is that this trip has been anything but boring," said Pete. "It's been an education. I can say that as well. A little disheartening."

"How disheartening?"

"I don't know. Just all these people, they just can't get a decent government. You gotta wonder where all that money the U.S. has been givin' to 'em, to Musharraf and such, where it's goin'. And you see the monument, and that park at the lake—"

"Imagine the Taliban picnicking at Rawal Lake," I said.

"Yeah," said Pete. "No more blow-up castles. No more music."

✻ ✻ ✻

"They're building a circular road around Lahore, so people don't have to go into the city to get around," said Shahnaz to us over her shoulder from the front seat.

"That's a great idea," I said. "They should have done it fifty years ago."

"Actually, they've been planning it for a long time. But governments change, and then these projects go sideways." We were crawling through Lahore traffic again, the next morning. "Shahbaz Sharif is doing a lot of construction on the roads, so it's causing a lot of congestion."

Shahnaz Khan was a family-practice physician in Zephyrhills, Florida, between Tampa and Orlando. She and her cardiologist husband had lived since 1983 in the same house in Lake City, where they had raised two daughters. I had been their guest there in 2007, when Shahnaz invited me to speak at a Human Development Foundation fundraiser in Tampa, and she had shown off her garden to me.

Shahnaz was currently chair of HDF's board. She was diminutive but intrepid, and I had come to think of her as a model of Pakistani-American leadership and involvement. She had started as a pediatrician but "frankly got bored," so had switched to family practice. "To me it's the most interesting, because of where I am," she said. "Most of the people were sixty-five or above. The area has really grown—tripled or four times. The demographics have changed."

"How do patients relate to you as a Pakistani?" I asked.

"I have no problem, really no problem at all. Even after 9/11 and all of this negative publicity. A lot of my patients ask and say, 'How is your mother?'"

"They know you."

"Yeah. It becomes personal. They know my mother lives alone, so they're always asking about her. They knew when my father passed away. They actually tell me they think of me when they listen to the news. In fact, a lot of them probably didn't know I was from Pakistan before 9/11, or didn't even care. They say, 'Be careful, Dr. Khan. Come back safely. Don't get lost, don't get hurt.' It's a good feeling, a lot of goodwill. A mother and daughter came to me, and they told me that they have this circle of prayer. And I don't know how churches work, that's my ignorance. But they told me that whoever gets put on the circle of prayer gets prayed for."

I asked for her thoughts on the American health care crisis.

"What I'm seeing now is a reflection of the economy," she said. "A lot of people losing their jobs, in the past one year. How people are coping with that is, they're postponing anything that is not an emergency. People are shopping around for cheaper sources for medication. If they don't have the money to pay the premium, what are they going to do? The past year or so, this big change has occurred. I had a patient whose wife came to me and said her husband was really depressed. He was a builder, and he had built five houses to sell, and he couldn't sell them."

We were on our way to an HDF-run school at Kharol War, outside Lahore. Our being here at the same time was a coincidence, and I had seized the chance to spend a day with her. Shahnaz visited HDF sites every time she came to Pakistan. Often she would fly into Quetta, the capital of remote Balochistan province, drive six hours to an HDF location, then drive another five hours to Dera Ismael Khan, a crossroads city near Waziristan, the region getting bombed by unmanned U.S. drone aircraft. Dera was where she had grown up.

"It's a small, sleepy town," she told me. "People were minding their own business, don't want to get in any trouble, to the point of being lazy, frankly. Since all this happened, a lot of people have migrated into Dera Ismail Khan. My father, I told you he was in the army. So he built a house in cantonment. And cantonment used to be open. That cantonment is right next to the river, and people used to go out and walk by the river. And now they have bunkers, and it's very difficult for people from the city to go there. My mother lives there and now, we have friends, and it's really hard for them even to visit her. Now we hear about this suicide bomber in Dera Ismail Khan. That was something that was never even in the dreams of people. In spite of that, women still go to shop. In some ways it has changed; in some ways people just get on with their lives." The flood of displaced people from Waziristan fleeing the drone attacks was disrupting life in Dera. "They don't have any permanent places to live, and they have a different language, different culture," she said.

I had seen Shahnaz the previous summer in Washington, DC at the annual convention of APPNA, the Pakistani doctors' organization in the United States. Entering the lobby of the Marriott Wardman Park off Connecticut Avenue during those five days was like stepping onto a *Star Trek* holodeck programmed as a temporary mini-province of Pakistan. Everybody who was anybody came to APPNA to see and be seen, to scout prospective marriages for their children, to cut business deals, to browse in the bazaar for dresses and jewelry and Islamic books. APPNA was not only a professional convention but the biggest annual social gathering for Pakistani doctors who toiled severally the rest of the year on the coal face of the health care system in places like Little Rock and Nashville and Omaha. APPNA was a big deal.

On the last morning of the convention in DC, Shahnaz and I had reconnoitered by cell phone and sat together in the loud and crowded lobby for a hurried catch-up. She had told me then about Dera: that it was a frontier town where provinces and ethnicities met and mingled, that it was suffering because of the influx of refugees from Waziristan. She urged me to visit Dera if possible, and her own example of traveling there overland from Quetta motivated me to try. But when I asked whether white Americans showing up with video equipment was feasible and safe, she had demurred. These days Pakistani friends urged me to think carefully even before visiting Peshawar, a major city where, in calmer times, I had gone alone with no support or protection. So in the end we had not added Dera to an already ambitious itinerary, but I had sought out people who could tell me about the situation there.

A friend of a friend named Faiysal Ali Khan, a young businessman who ran the DHL franchise in Islamabad, had echoed Shahnaz. "Dera Ismail Khan is a gateway into the Punjab," he had told me. "A gateway from Afghanistan. Traditionally it's been a town where we've had Hindu traders, a Christian community. It's been a sort of multicultural rural metropolis. People have always been very tolerant. It's been a trade-focused town, around the banks of the River Indus. Today, it's a victim of everything that's wrong in this country."

I asked him about the mindset of people there. "They are in a territory that doesn't have a status, so you don't know whether it's going to be here or there," he had said. "They tell us for the last sixty-two years that we're supposed to guard this border with Afghanistan, and we get nothing in return. We are supposed to make our own way with whatever we have in that territory, and we get a slap on the wrist if we come down to a settled area. The reason that the tribes loot and plunder and do all the rest of it is that there's nothing over there. What are you supposed to do? It's not as though there's nice, irrigated lands. They're bare mountains. And you're almost like in a cage. There's been a systematic deconstruction, stripping of the tribal system over the last 150 years. I don't think this is something that started with Pakistan. This started with the British. They started deconstructing the system, because it goes against central authority. Any central authority would do the same."

The refugees, he said, "have had a huge, huge impact on our culture, our society, our people. All these things got disturbed. They brought in the guns, the narcotics, all the illicit trade. Not that I'm saying that they're bad or anything. They're refugees; what are they supposed to do? So the Afghan thing obviously has affected us a lot. This jihad thing moreso—this organized jihad against communism has had a huge impact on us. The fact that there were networks of madrassas set up across this area, where young kids were taken in. Kids from Afghanistan came, who were orphaned or whatever. Imagine a young child whose mother is raped, home is destroyed, everything he knows is finished, he's picked up from there, plonked into this compound, and for the next fifteen years he never sees a woman in his life, he's fed all this propaganda, he's sodomized and abused, beaten, etcetera, tied in chains reading a book he doesn't understand, no education, nothing, and then you arm him and everything, and then you release him. I mean, just think about it. Forget about religion or anything. And you release hundreds and thousands of them. Can you imagine?"

I asked him about the loyalties of the general public in Waziristan. "On one side, the drone strikes are happening," he said. "On the other side, Pakistan Army is also bombing you. Americans also bombing you. International community in NATO, ISAF;

they're also bombing you. Everyone is bombing. They're bombing, bombing, killing innocent people, everything. Why should we have any feeling towards any of these? So the Taliban at least are fighting them, so they're doing the right thing. So we should also be with them. In the end, what are the Taliban saying? The basic tenets of this whole civilization war with al Qaeda and all is what he says, Osama. It's something that even I wouldn't disagree with, to be honest. He says that the Palestine-Israeli situation should be resolved. He says foreign troops should go out of all Middle East countries and we should run our own affairs, they shouldn't be here. These kingdoms and all should be finished, because they're agents of the West. The public is getting nothing; these few people are getting rich, and everybody else is suffering."

"All of that makes a lot of sense," I said, "and even I wouldn't disagree with that. But Osama bin Laden picked a fight with America by blowing up the World Trade Center."

"I'm trying to communicate to you sentiments of people," Faiysal said, "since they don't have a chance. They say, 'Okay, so these three and a half thousand or whatever innocents died. So how many thousands of us have been dying, innocents? And no one cares.'"

"One of the challenges I face is how to get across to Americans the humanity of these people who happen to be Muslims," I said.

"People here don't know the human side of America," he replied.

Faiysal and Shahnaz were both articulate and affluent people, easy enough to find and interview. In Karachi the next week, I was fortunate enough to interview a 15-year-old boy from Waziristan, who told me through a translator: "Most of these drone attacks kill innocent people. They ask our government to tell the people that all of the people who are killed are foreigners. But that is not the case. Most of them are innocent people. Every person has now become a victim of the U.S., from these drone attacks. What the U.S. is doing by these drone attacks is creating more problems for themselves, rather than solving problems. Every person now that did not want to carry weapons, now wants to carry a weapon, because his children have died in these U.S. attacks. They're just making it worse for themselves."

* * *

"The schools that we have are two different kinds," Shahnaz was telling us in the car. "One is non-formal schools, which are often just one room and a teacher and kids of all different ages. When we see that the number of kids has grown so they can't be accommodated in one room, we make it a formal school and try to separate the grades. Where we're going is a formal school."

I had done my bit at several HDF fundraisers over the past couple of years, and this was my first chance to see the group's work on the ground in Pakistan. The school was an L-shaped concrete building surrounded by fields, with a gate and walls enclosing a small courtyard. Until it opened in 2003, there had been no school in this area. There were 200 students in this school and 400 in the area, including non-formal schools. There was also a health center, skill training for women and men—men trained to be welders, plumbers, and electricians—and an adult literacy program. HDF practiced what it called an "integrated development model" addressing health and poverty as well as education and featuring tube wells, local roads, tree planting, and promotion of health care awareness. "We organize people into a village development organization," said Shahnaz. "They get registered with the local government as Citizens' Community Boards. The land is always donated by the local people."

"How much does a school cost to build?" asked Pete.

"We started with an estimate of like thirty thousand," said Shahnaz.

"Rupees?" I asked.

"No, dollars. I wish! And then came the earthquake, and the building codes all changed. So I think it ended up like eighty thousand. They all contributed to build these washrooms."

"And if they add a second story, how will that be financed?"

"We'll have to find donors. To be honest, it's mostly Pakistani-Americans. They feel almost obligated."

"What would you say is the average income of their parents?" asked Pete.

"Seven, eight thousand," answered Adnan Saleem, an HDF staff member from the Lahore office. "Ten thousand."

"Rupees a month," said Shahnaz. "Actually, that's not bad." The Pakistani rupee was trading at the time at about eighty to the dollar.

"I assume most of them are farmers," Pete said.

"Actually, some of them are laborers in the city," said Shahnaz.

"How many kids are there in a family?"

"Seven to eight," said Adnan.

"They've just finished taking their exam," Shahnaz told us. The school was on vacation, but the kids had come today especially for our visit. Each classroom visit was a little occasion, with polite words with the teachers and boys and girls asking and answering questions. In one classroom Shahnaz looked with concern at a boy's eyebrow, which she thought might have a fungus infection. I stood aside and watched, while Pete moved around taking pictures.

"What do the girls think when they see someone like you?" I asked Shahnaz.

"Even in places like Balochistan, they say they want to be doctors and pilots and things like that, and we try to encourage them," she said.

"You're an example to them."

"We hope that it's a good example!"

Shahnaz quizzed the girls about their aspirations. They wanted to be things like engineers, teachers, and painters. "She wants to go in the army, maybe be a doctor in the army," said Shahnaz, indicating one girl. "They all want to be doctors. A lot of teachers, when they start, they're actually still studying themselves. Sometimes HDF helps them, sometimes they do it on their own."

We went to a nearby village, where Shahnaz met with a small group of "lady health workers," local women whose children were or had been at the HDF school. "The closest college is like twenty kilometers from here, so they all say they want a college here," she told us.

"Is that realistic?"

"We haven't done it yet, so I don't know," she said. "Rather than building a college here, we can arrange their transportation. The parents want that the school should go up to 12th grade. For the exams, when they take the government school exam in fifth grade and eighth grade, they can't take it here. So that's a transportation issue."

"It's also a road issue, isn't it?"

"Yes, and it's also an expense issue. But you would be surprised—most of the people do want their kids to learn. It's just that they're not comfortable with their kids going so far away. They want everything to be brought to them!"

The health center included a small lab that did basic testing, including pregnancy tests. "Hepatitis B is a big problem here," Shahnaz told us. "It's something new, hepatitis B vaccination of all the newborns. The problem comes when you can't be sure that they're actually doing it."

The lady health workers went house to house, covering 250 houses in a month, checking pregnant mothers and weighing children. An HDF "unit" consisted of a thousand households. "So in four months they cover all the households. That's how we oversee what's happening. The lady health workers have a three-month course. They prefer to have a married woman from this area, because otherwise they'll train and then leave, and then you have a brain drain." Only ten percent of women were literate. "That creates another challenge, because if you don't have educated women, then you have trouble getting teachers. And if you can't get teachers locally, you have to get them in the city, and then that becomes a transportation issue."

Health costs were nominal to patients: five rupees basic charge, ten for a one-day prescription, fifteen for two days. "It's more than modest. She's been the longest here for five years," Shahnaz said, indicating a woman. "When she used to go, people thought she was coming in for family planning. But gradually people feel more comfortable. People used to hesitate to share their problems. Now they feel more at ease. A big problem here is the facilities for using the bathroom. People used to go in the fields. Now most of them have installed latrines." Domestic animals were another problem. "Now people are trying to separate them into a separate little area. There's arsenic in the drinking water. And boiling water is a big problem. And of course the bottled water is out of reach. And another problem is the goiter, because of iodine deficiency. That's a big problem in Pakistan; they keep the drinking water and the drains together."

At the adult literacy center there were fifteen students, all young women. "These are girls who had never been to school," said Shahnaz. "They have done their five months now. They learn basic reading, writing, and math. I think now they are able to read a newspaper." They studied six days a week, two hours a day for six months, then took the fifth-grade government exam. "They don't want to get married now. They want to continue their studies. I'm not surprised. She has a business, like a beauty parlor, at home. So she has to take days off from school. They have beauticians here mostly during weddings and stuff. But if they don't know how to do it properly, they can transmit skin problems. So they're planning on having some trainings for that."

Lahore was one of eight HDF "regions" around the country. Back in the car, on the way to the regional office, I asked if HDF did microcredit. Not in Lahore, said Shahnaz, "but in pretty much all the other regions." Each office employed a health manager, an education manager, and staff in charge of economic development, which included training and credit. HDF always did projects in partnership with local communities. HDF would put in capital, and the community contributed labor, skills, and land. "The essence of HDF is how we interact with the community," said Shahnaz. "We don't just go in; we make sure that they want us there. The school fees are determined by the community, because they know what their giving capacity is. They are always expected to contribute something." Half of the medical fees was used to replenish medicines, and the other half went in the bank for future use. School fees went straight into the bank. "What the community puts in actually goes back into the community itself."

"Shahnaz, does politics ever disrupt HDF's work?" I asked.

"Not really. In Karachi once, when Benazir came and there was a big bomb blast. It becomes an issue of transportation, for HDF staff to show up at work. But otherwise, no, it doesn't affect us much. Any political upheaval that disrupts life and creates transportation problems, that is what impacts the staff."

"What about when the administration of a province changes?"

"We don't really have anything to do with the government. The only time is when we facilitate connections between the community and the local government. And even local governments are pretty far removed from the center. So when this movement of the lawyers happened, it really didn't have any impact out here. In the villages, life goes on as usual."

The visit took longer than planned, which meant we risked failing to liaise with the Scooby-Doo film crew to shoot me mouthing platitudes in front of the Minar-e-Pakistan monument, which I didn't mind. We rode to Shahnaz's sister's house, in a big new subdivision past the airport, and sat down to a late lunch.

"The house next to it is mine, I built it," Shahnaz told us. "But it's not furnished yet. I built it for my mother, because she doesn't want to live with my sister, but she doesn't want to live apart either." The gated colony was still under construction, with big new houses springing up next to empty lots. "It reminds me of Florida," said Shahnaz. "The land is being taken over by all these subdivisions. My younger daughter is into conservation. And we see all these deer on the roads in Florida, because their habitat is basically being taken over by human beings. And when she was younger, she used to say, 'Why don't you buy all this land and just keep it for all the animals?'" She smiled at the memory.

* * *

Yusuf was moaning about load shedding: "This light problem never happened until 2007. Especially in the month of December and January, when you don't have the light, and you don't have a fucking heating system. Because in my house is full of marble."

We were back in Yusuf's office to thank him for putting us up at the Gymkhana guest house, and to interview Syed Arsalan Ahmed, the 17-year-old "peon boy" who cleaned the office, about what he had witnessed out the fourth-floor window on March 3, the day of the attack on the Sri Lankan cricket team. Maybe because I felt grateful for his hospitality, maybe because we had become acclimated to Pakistan, I was feeling more comfortable with Yusuf now.

"They were cleaning the office, himself and the sweeper," Yusuf translated. "He came at about eight o'clock, sweeper was ten past eight in the morning, and they were doing the whole thing, and suddenly when the rocket launcher hit the Bride & Groom, they thought initially that was an earthquake. The whole building was in shock. Then when firing started, they just came up to that window and they saw the whole thing. Six people coming from Gaddafi Stadium side, that side. There's a building called Big City Tower.

"From there they appeared, six people, and two of them stayed on the bus in which the Sri Lankan team was there, and they were fully loaded, they had got the bags on their shoulders and the Sten guns on their hands, and then they divided in three respective teams. So two people went straight to the boulevard side, two people went towards the Liberty side, and two were on the ground. The people who were on the ground, in the middle of the roundabout, they were firing for half an hour continuously."

"Those were the two that we saw on TV?"

"TV. And he saw a sergeant, they saw that they shoot him just lying on the street, and the fourth policeman was being shot in the back of the police van. Then, after half an hour, two just ran away towards the boulevard side, two ran towards the Liberty side, and two ran towards the Al-Fatah Departmental Store side. Al-Fatah is just near the UCH hospital, on the left side of the roundabout. The backside of the Shell petrol pump in Liberty Market. The people who were firing for half an hour, they went to Al-Fatah side. He said they were not afraid of anything. They were so cool and calm. They were just thinking that nobody was gonna shoot them. They were so cool and calm, they were firing for half an hour."

"That's strange."

"Strange. There must be a security lapse, definitely. There was a security lapse. At that time there was a Governor Rule. And before Governor Rule, they had been intimated that this incident might be gonna happen. And they are supposed to provide them a president's security, which is VVIP security, which means at least twenty-one altogether. The ambulances, the rescue teams, and plus other twenty-one patrol vehicles of the police were supposed to be with the bus. And there were only two patrol vehicles of police. That's it. That's very strange."

"I agree," I said.

"And now Shahbaz Sharif, as soon as he took the charge three days back as Chief Minister, he initiated an inquiry against those police officers, and the management at that time, why they did not take that action. And according to the newspapers, those three superintendents of police who were supposed to be with the Sri Lankan team, they were at their homes and they were sleeping. And that's why—not now, but probably very soon, within the span of one month—I think they will get suspended. Shahbaz Sharif is not going to leave them alone. He is going to take action against them. They were sleeping, and they were supposed to be there with the Sri Lankan team."

"This gets up onto a political level," I said, partly to goad him.

"People are busy there," he acknowledged. "But still, these things go on everywhere. But the security should be provided."

"I think the security lapse has a political dimension," I persisted.

"You cannot ignore that fact. But still I am saying, whatever happens, the performers, especially the cricket team, or any foreigner who is here as our guest, we are supposed to provide them a full security. And full security had been provided to them when they came to Lahore for two one-day consecutive matches. They have been given a proper VVIP security, at the time of Shahbaz Sharif. I think it's a security lapse, but it's also pre-planned."

"You don't mind saying that?"

"I think 80 percent people think like that. But nobody has the balls to say."

"Do you have any idea who pre-planned it? That's speculation, but ..."

"It's not speculation. Mumbai attacks—I'm not saying I'm against Indians or whatever. I think every nation should be at peace. I've got my daughter and my kids, I don't want these bomb blasts; I don't want these attacks, for God's sake. Look: Police training institute, about three days back in Lahore, the incident happened. India has forty consulate general offices in Afghanistan. Why? Suddenly, within the span of four years. They do not even border with Afghanistan. So now they are coming into Punjab. And Punjab's most important area is Lahore. For last three months you have seen that they are doing things in Lahore, unfortunately. And we don't want it. Now your president, Mr. Obama, he said, 'We think that some al Qaeda people are settling in Quetta or somewhere in Balochistan, we have to follow them.' Follow them, it's—I have to say my words very politely—it's just an excuse to invade into Pakistan."

"So you don't give Obama credit for being better than Bush?"

"Well, he is doing the same thing Bush was doing. It's always the think tanks of USA who actually runs the whole world. It's not Obama, or any other president of USA."

"What do you think about the big thing that Obama announced about a week ago, about the new aid to Pakistan?"

"Look, it's the same old story. You are giving me a hundred dollars, and you expect me to do your work."

He returned to his peon's account. "When he came to that window, he saw for like one minute these people firing on the bus. Then bus driver drives very fast. Then he saw the bus; bus was moving towards Gaddafi Stadium. So it was the driver who, with his bravery, took the bus away from the firing. And just about 500 yards back was the Pakistani team bus. They had been asked to stop. And they divert their bus on local roads and took them back to the hotel."

"Is it possible still to see damage on the Groom & Bride Shop?"

"No, I think they already repaired the shop. But if you want I can take you down there, and you can take the snaps."

We went downstairs and outside and in the front door of the shop, where Yusuf introduced us to the proprietor, Tariq Bashir, and his son Sajeel. In 2003–04, when I had lived in Lahore and frequented Liberty Market, the Groom & Bride Shop had been a landmark for me. I had never been inside it, but its sign was prominent and, somehow, iconic. I had felt then that I was at the end of something: of a phase of history, maybe, or of my own Pakistani adventure. That feeling had been part of what spurred me to write *Alive and Well in Pakistan*; I thought of it as a tying up of loose ends, a summation, a settling of accounts that would allow me to move on to other books, other adventures, other countries. In the ensuing five years I had made decisions and decisions had been made for me, and I had moved forward, only to return full circle. I should have known that history wouldn't stand still, that in Pakistan loose ends are never tied up.

"By grace of God we are safe here," Tariq Bashir told us. He was a rotund little man with a friendly mien. "Maybe if rocket come in here, damage shop. Jesus save with his hand his own people. From which country?"

"America," I said.

"This is Christian shop. We are Catholics."

He showed us the pillar the rocket-propelled grenade had hit, which had effectively shielded the front counter and the shop as a whole, and the pockmarks from shrapnel on the concrete front step. The shell had landed on the counter, he said. "Also pieces of grenade here," he added, and rummaged in the drawers behind the counter to show us.

"I think maybe if it didn't hit the pillar ..." I said.

"Then lot of loss," he agreed.

"Pakistani people are not bad," said Sajeel, his son. "They are polite people. They like peace. And we don't know who are those people who are behind the attacks, who are disturbing the country, who are disturbing the economy."

"How has your business been since the attack?" asked Pete.

"It's been coming down and down because of the attacks. No foreigners are coming in. And local people are not coming out of their homes."

"Specially the congested areas," injected Yusuf.

We browsed and chatted for some minutes, and I bought several neckties. Father and son were clearly rather proud, in a strange and touching way, to have experienced the attack. The clock on the wall behind the counter had stopped working and still showed the time of the attack, 8:41 a.m. On the wall beneath the clock was a hand-written sign in Urdu:

Liberty cricket team attack
03-03-09
08-41 morning time

Beneath that was a new clock showing the correct time.

"Police investigation teams come and they say, 'Give us this watch,'" said Tariq Bashir, firmly and proudly. "No no no. We keep it here."

* * *

In the back of my mind throughout the trip had been the prospect of a sentimental reunion with my former students from Beaconhouse National University and my teaching colleague, Taimur-ul-Hassan. Adnan Latif had been the most devoted, to the point of meeting Pete and me at the border, but others had stayed in touch too, and as a group they represented a happy cluster of memories for me. I had exchanged emails and Facebook messages with most of them in recent weeks, and I had planned ahead to try to ensure that a get-together stayed on our ever-shifting itinerary. I knew bits and pieces of their recent lives: Adnan was pursuing his ambitions in journalism and politics; Usman had joined a PR firm. Amit, the bright but high-maintenance Indian boy, had followed through on his plan to attend journalism school in the United States. Several of the girls were now married, and Zainab and Neelum already had babies. Sadaf was living in Kenya. Ayela Deen, the class leader, had left BNU but then returned as an instructor.

I imagined a restaurant dinner like the one my students had thrown for me just before my departure in February 2004, where we would have relaxed and caught up thoroughly. This notional dinner would have happened either soon after Pete and I first arrived in Pakistan, before we went to Islamabad, or now, as we came back through Lahore. In real life, each time we were in Lahore we turned out to be en route to somewhere else. This was partly by design, because I knew it was all too easy in Lahore to enmesh oneself in a web of appointments and commitments, and to avoid that we stayed on the move. And we had ended up staying an extra day each in Islamabad and, because of the attack on the Lahore police academy, in Kharian. I had Facebooked and spoken several times with Ayela, and she had said she would arrange something as soon as we got to Lahore. I knew that wouldn't work, and I was right; the dinner never happened. Several students came to BNU one afternoon when Pete and I couldn't make it; and now, on our last full day in Lahore, when we had just enough energy and time to walk across Zafar Ali Road from the Gymkhana to the university, they couldn't make it.

The reunion that wasn't seemed somehow fitting, though: It had been overtaken by events. I would see my students again, *inshallah*. I certainly would return again to Pakistan, and when I did I would have more time, *inshallah*. This time, I was happy at least to see Ayela and Taimur briefly.

Ayela seemed happy and fulfilled as a respected instructor at what was now an established and growing university. Taimur was effusive but distracted, and after the niceties he had to excuse himself to handle a minor crisis somewhere else in the building. Dr. Mehdi Hassan, a senior professor and member of the Human Rights Commission of Pakistan whom I had known only slightly, came in and sat at Taimur's desk and lectured, as professors will, about this, that, and the other while I fought the urge to nod off. It wasn't only that he was droning on; after five weeks of long, overfull days and overland travel, Pete and I were exhausted.

"... all these people who are writing about Pakistan," he was saying after about an hour, "the young intellectuals, and some not-so-young intellectuals, settled outside Pakistan, their knowledge about Pakistan is superficial."

"Mohsin Hamid?" I said to be provocative, naming the celebrated young author of the novels *Moth Smoke* and *The Reluctant Fundamentalist.*

"Mohsin Hamid is the brother of our teacher, Zebunnisa Hamid, and son of my old colleague at Punjab University." I took this as his polite way of saying he wasn't going to rise to that bait. "Then there was a very senior intellectual, he died two-three years ago, very famous, Eqbal Ahmed. He lived for sixteen-seventeen years, all the time of Zia-ul-Haq and Ayub Khan, outside Pakistan. And when Benazir came to power, he came back into Pakistan and started talking about Pakistan and what is happening in Pakistan. And there are so many other intellectuals like that. Some of my old colleagues from Punjab University, they migrated to America during Zia's time, and they are teaching at various American universities, and very critical of Pakistani conditions. I tell them, whenever they visit, that 'You have no right to criticize Pakistan, because you are not aware of what is happening inside Pakistan, and how do people survive these conditions, specially eleven years of Zia-ul-Haq.' You have to live through those times to realize what happened with the people of Pakistan. ...

"... our presidents are in the habit of writing books," he was saying another ten minutes or so later. "Ayub Khan also wrote a book, *Friends Not Masters.* Musharraf wrote a book. Benazir wrote a book, *Daughter of the East.*"

"I want to read *Daughter of the East.* I haven't read it," said Ayela. "I spoke to Sir Taimur," she added to me. "He's stuck; he won't be coming back." Dr. Mehdi excused himself and left the room.

"That's too bad," I said. "I'll try to reach him by phone."

"You've never met Zebunnisa?" said Ayela. "She teaches reporting and magazine journalism. She came in a year after you."

"No. I've met Mohsin a couple times."

Just then Dr. Mehdi returned from the hallway with a young woman. Pete and I introduced ourselves.

"I've heard about you from your old students," she said with a smile.

"Ethan's met your brother," said Ayela.

"Actually first here, at a *mehndi* in Lahore," I told Zebunnisa. "Mrs. Navid Shahzad's son's wedding." That was around the time *Moth Smoke* was becoming a byword for the dissolute youth of Pakistan's urban elite. "And when he came on his book tour he came to Seattle, where I live."

"That's right, he was in Seattle."

"We did a little interview with him," I told her. My friend Laila Kazmi and I had interviewed him before his reading, in the room next to the coffee shop below the Elliott Bay Book Company. I had found him thoughtful, literate, and polished, and I liked his Graham Greene-like penchant for involving himself in the global conversation about Pakistan by writing for newspapers and popular magazines. "I admire that he does as much journalism as he does," I said to Zebunnisa.

"Yeah, I think he's actually been doing a lot more of that than writing recently."

"He said, 'I'm a seven-year book guy.' That he writes a book every seven years."

She laughed. "I was teasing him the other day. I said, 'How many years has it been?' He said, 'Well, I should come up with an idea. It's two years now since the last one.' He's coming here this weekend."

"Well, I'll just miss him. That's too bad."

"Yeah, they're coming for a week. His wife's brother's wedding. So where-all have you been so far?"

I told her.

"Wow. You must be exhausted."

"We are. You know about the book I wrote, *Alive and Well in Pakistan*? I'm writing a new book that's a sequel to that."

"Actually, you know where I read that book?" she said suddenly. "At my brother's. He has a copy of it. He actually told me to read it. I was visiting him one summer, and I read it there. It was great for me because I was reading about all these people, BNU. It was a strange experience, teaching here and reading about it. I really enjoyed it."

"It's like a little slice of BNU."

"Exactly. You almost feel like it's a secret joke or something."

Serendipitously meeting an attractive woman who not only had read my book, but had enjoyed it for specific reasons that she took the trouble to explain, and who happened to be the sister of a Booker Prize-shortlisted novelist, was a balm for my failure to reconnect with my students. Every writer envisions—at least, I envision—such readers out there somewhere, and occasionally one bumps into one of them. More poignant, as we said our good-byes and walked across the sewage canal back to the Gymkhana, was something both Ayela and Taimur had said: that I should consider returning to BNU for another semester, or even a year or two. The notion was intriguing and even made some sense. The thing about being a member of a sentient species is that you're aware of the lives you don't and can't live, as well as the one you do. I tried to fit it mentally into my life and plans. It almost fit, but not quite. The difference, this time, was that my life elsewhere was happy.

But I took with me and cherished something Ayela had said: "You were good for us."

CHAPTER 5

DIFFERENT WORLDS

"Which country you are from?" asked the burly man in our train compartment. He was sixty or so and wore a loose-fitting shalwar kameez.

"America," I told him.

"I also am from America," he said. "I am Green Card holder. I live in Florida. Palm Beach. Which state do you live in?"

"Seattle," I said.

"Washington," said Pete.

"Florida is a great state," said the man.

"I agree," I said. And I meant it. As sleazy and tawdry as I knew it to be, I was fond of Florida. I had happy memories of times spent in Miami with my cousin Cindy and her family, during a period when my life was in disarray. And the blatant sleaziness of the state's economy and politics made it more interesting than most of the rest of America.

"Except when there is rain," said the man.

"And hurricanes," I suggested. In September 2004 I had flown out of Fort Lauderdale to Colorado Springs via Dallas, leaving Cindy and her family to fend for themselves, a day ahead of a big hurricane. Other than that, the nearest I had come to a Florida hurricane was the Carl Hiaasen novel *Stormy Weather*.

"Yes, and hurricanes. Three hurricanes at one time, three years back. Many people moved out after that. Property used to be very high, before that. Now you can buy a house for not so much."

That was the extent of the conversation with our berthmate. He seemed affable and talkative, but that was the problem. Pete had nudged me to chat with him, but I just didn't have it in me.

* * *

Adnan Latif's younger brother had driven us to the station in Lahore, while Adnan reminisced again about his trip to India. "In India everything is good except politics," he said.

"What do you mean?"

"The people are good, hospitable. But I don't think so the politicians and some other pure religious parties, they are not good. The trip was excellent. We welcome where we go."

"What was the most interesting thing you saw?"

"Our VIP moment. We came on Friendship Bus. Two police cars were in front, and two were in back, conducting us. It was a really remembering and interesting thing. Before border and after border. Both side. And one other thing was Verendra Public School, in Delhi. It's like Beaconhouse here in Pakistan, something like that. They invited us for goodwill trip. They were very hospitable. Many gifts—diaries, ballpoints, and other stuff like stationery. And in front of one student group Ayela said, 'He's the film star from Pakistan.'"

"About you?"

"Yes. And the children surrounded me and said, 'Give me your autograph, give me your autograph.' That was when I became famous. Even their peons and other school staff came for my autograph. Without doing any movie, I become the big star. In India the rickshaw people was very clever. At night Sir Taimur and I coming back from Nizamuddin shrine. He went round and round and round.

Sir Taimur's BP was increasing. He say, 'Adnan, ask him, where he want to go?' I say, 'Don't worry, calm down.' It was about one and half in morning, at night. It was very foggy night. And in the end he took eighty rupees rather than fifty. They are very clever."

"Yeah, you gotta watch out for them," said Pete.

"So did you bring your brother so he could drive, so he wouldn't scare us so much?" I asked Adnan.

"He is safe driver," Adnan assured me.

"You are not agree?" asked the brother with a grin.

"I agree," I said. "You are a good driver. Better than Adnan."

We ran late because I wanted to show Pete the Badshahi mosque.

"This also from Mughal era," Adnan said, as Pete photographed the magnificent mosque from the balcony of the nearby Cooco's Den restaurant. "And Taj Mahal from Mughal era. India publicize well, you see?"

"First time Karachi?" his brother asked me.

"No, third time Karachi."

"Lahore people better or Karachi?"

"That's not fair. Okay, Lahore people better."

"Yes!"

"*All* Pakistani people better," said Adnan. "Except some. Not much—some. Oh-oh-oh!" he cried out. We were crawling through late-afternoon traffic.

"Are we worried about traffic now?" I asked him.

"This is true Lahore." He looked worried.

We had had to abandon Adnan and his father's Pajero and pick our way through stalled traffic the last half-mile or so to the station. "One thing I told you," he said as he hugged us and waved us off. "This place isn't safe. Pickpockers, other bad peoples. If we were in airport, this place is safe."

The platforms were crowded, and our train was delayed. We found a spot by the wall to squat in relative comfort, and Pete minded our bags while I crossed the tracks to get boxed meals at the station diner.

I had last been in this station not to catch a train but to see one off, with Adnan and two other students at seven in the morning on January 15, 2004. The train was the Samjhota Express to Delhi, and it was being relaunched with fanfare and hoopla. "And you know what *samjhota* means?" Medium-sized Usman had asked me.

"No, tell me."

"Agreement," said Big Usman.

"It is an agreement," agreed Medium-sized Usman. "But like an agreement between husband and wife whose relations are not good."

I had sent my students onto the train with the assignment to report whatever stories they heard from passengers going to India, and the outing had tickled and energized Adnan. "Sir, I spent very nice time with Japanese boy!" he exclaimed after the train pulled out and we regathered on the platform. "He is coming from Japan on world tour. When I ask him about Vietnam, he said America is doing very wrong. And when I ask him about Israel, he said one side Muslim right, one side Israel right. Oh, and sir—he has no religion! When I asked him what was his religion, he said, 'I have no religion.'"

"What did you say to him?"

"I say, 'Oh, it's good! One of my teachers has also no religion!'"

Later, in the lobby—the same lobby Pete and I had just elbowed our way through—we had helped ourselves to tea and little sandwiches, and Adnan had said: "I think this is good job."

"Journalism?"

"Yes. You learn things, meet people, see some sort of new things."

That was a happy memory: happier than the thought of trains arriving here filled with corpses during the summer of 1947.

* * *

"Reminds me of Southern California," said Pete the next morning, staring out the train window at the bleak brown landscape of rural Sindh.

"Looks like home?"

"Yeah, looks like home. Except for the occasional camel."

I had been to Karachi twice before, too briefly. My visits to Pakistan had always revolved around the Lahore-Islamabad- Peshawar axis, and getting to Karachi took a special effort. This was strange and unfortunate because, at 15 million or more people, it was by far Pakistan's largest city and one of the world's largest. It was the country's port and commercial hub and had been the capital until the construction of Islamabad in the 1960s. Lahore is Lahore, say smug Punjabis like Adnan, and Lahore is the capital of the province and ethnic group that dominate Pakistan. Islamabad is the political capital. But Karachi is, so to speak, the capital of the rest of the country; it's where you end up if the winds of history blow you into Pakistan and you have nowhere else to go. Dr. Sattar in Kharian had told me a joke: that when Muslim refugees crossed the new border from India in 1947, Lahoris pointed toward Karachi and said, "Pakistan is that way." This was an allusion to the longstanding and sometimes explosive tension in Karachi between ethnic Sindhis like Dr. Sattar—the people who were there in the first place—and Urdu-speaking *mohajirs* or immigrants, who flooded into the city after independence. "We've never caught up," Zaka Shafiq, a young man I met on this trip, told me. "Karachi went from 300,000 to a million in a few weeks in 1947, and it's been growing ever since."

I had first come here in March 1995, in the midst of the sectarian and ethnic bloodletting that was then engulfing Karachi. It was sectarian in the sense of Sunni vs. Shia, but it was mostly ethnic in pitting the better-educated *mohajirs* whose parents' mother tongue, Urdu, had been made Pakistan's national language by fiat, against native Sindhis, in a city with too few jobs to go around. Zulfiqar Ali

233

Bhutto, himself a Sindhi, had instituted quotas for government jobs and university placements that favored Sindhis and made Sindhi the province's official language; in response the MQM, or Mohajir National Movement, had arisen under Altaf Hussein, a London-based demagogue who was described to me as "almost Hitlerian" in the charisma he exerted over crowds. The MQM was considered fascistic and had been held responsible for Karachi's violence and lawlessness, but now it held the office of mayor and was, I found to my surprise, appreciated by some for keeping a lid on things and running the city more or less competently.

But as of 1995 the Afghan war of the 1980s had flooded Karachi with secondhand American and Russian weapons; the army had tried and failed to occupy the city and had withdrawn, humiliated; and some 1,500 people had been killed in just over a year. I was in Pakistan that first time because of a high-profile court case involving trumped-up blasphemy charges against Pakistani Christians, including a 14-year-old boy, in Lahore. I was getting on-the-job training in making a living as a journo in Asia: If it didn't push Western buttons by involving white people or at least Christians, it wasn't likely to pass the WHOGAS test. At least the paper that was my bread and butter at the time, the *South China Morning Post*, was based in Asia and took coverage of Kashmir and Pakistan from me thanks to its readership among Indians and Pakistanis in Hong Kong. But what occasioned my first trip to Karachi were the deaths of two Americans.

The *SCMP*'s foreign editor reached me by phone at my hotel in Rawalpindi to tell me that two employees of the U.S. Consulate in Karachi had been killed in an attack on a consulate van during their morning commute. The incident made Karachi briefly international news, including above the fold in *USA Today*. I made some half-hearted argument for the current interest of other, Islamabad-based stories, but the editor pointed out that if I went to Karachi he could take stories from me and pay me, whereas if I didn't he couldn't. So I went, notwithstanding that the real reason for my hesitation was fear for my own safety.

The train from Rawalpindi to Karachi took 33 hours and went through rural Sindh province, an area I knew then only as a big blank space on the map. We were on the same route now. I spent most of that first journey nursing my fear in my upper berth, and I rudely refused a man's offer of an orange when his family broke open their provisions for dinner. The train arrived in Karachi after dark, and I had had to find my way by auto rickshaw to a district of substandard hotels with bad plumbing, because I knew no one in the enormous city.

This time I had introductions from a group called Future Leaders of Pakistan, whom Pete and I had met in Islamabad. "All over Pakistan, and specially in our generation, you see a sense of pessimism about the entire country," chapter head Atif Siddique had told us during the evening we spent with a dozen young men and women. "This is bad, that is bad, the political situation is so bad. Everybody is so bad, right? All this negativity. This organization has started to question me as a person: 'Okay, if everything is negative, what are you going to do about it?' FLP is a completely non-political thing, but we gather groups of youngsters and try to give them roles where they can establish themselves as leaders. There's a thing called Dialogue on Leadership. We do that on an annual basis in different cities. The winners of the competition are asked to design a social project that they can actually implement. And we hold a dialogue between mainstream professionals and experts and the person who designed the project, and if FLP thinks that a project is good and feasible, then FLP takes on that project and executes it." There was also an Entrepreneurs' Club. "It's very ambitious," said Atif. "It connects FLP entrepreneurs to each other so they can help each other out, and it works on entrepreneurship development. The average person who's graduating here does not see entrepreneurship as an option. There's a spark in a lot of young people, but when they get institutionalized, they lose everything. They lose the spark, they lose the spirit, and they get pessimistic. We want to challenge that."

I felt Pakistan's political and civic life had lost a generation, because of the Zia regime's suppression of student politics in the 1980s and the myopia and selfishness of the country's leaders since then. "We've just come out of this twenty-year period where there are two main civilian political parties," I told the group. "And then you had the military regime. So you had Benazir-Nawaz, Benazir-Nawaz, Musharraf, and now what we've got now."

"There's no word for it!" someone said, to general laughter.

"Political organizations in Pakistan have the demographics all wrong, in terms of their strategy," said Atif. "Sixty-six percent of the Pakistani population is under thirty. None of the political organizations are actually focusing on the youth, and what the youth want, and what the youth can do."

"The only parties that are going after that youth vote are the religious parties and the ethnic-based parties," said someone else.

"I'm working closely with the two main parties right now," said Atif. "They do realize that they need to focus on the youth, but there's a huge gap between what they're saying and what the youth is thinking. Added to that, there's no internal democracy within the parties. I think a revolution is due. It's actually far overdue. It's a matter of waking up the youth."

Atif and his FLP friends in Islamabad had arranged for us to be hosted at the Sindh government guest house in central Karachi near the Sheraton, courtesy of the provincial Minister of Information, Shazia Marri MPA. When you tell Pakistanis you've been to Pakistan or to a particular city, they ask who you know there. It's an unsubtle way of gauging your alignments, sympathies, and influences. And in

Pakistan connections are hard currency, so Pakistanis want to know whether their connections might trump yours, whether they might be able to help or influence you. So when I say that Shazia Marri hosted us in Karachi, it might mean something political. Or it might mean only that, at the time I needed accommodation in Karachi, she and her family and network were the ones who came through for me.

She sent a car to take us from the station to the guest house, and in the evening her younger brother Aurangzeb met us in the Sheraton lobby. Aurry was a cheerful and well-upholstered young chap, and an actively thoughtful host. I was arriving in Karachi feeling under-prepared and confused, but then again that's how I always feel in Pakistan. Whenever I feel I'm starting to get a handle on things, I'm overtaken by events. I've learned to hold on for the ride, take things and people as they come, experience it all as anecdotal narrative rather than trying too hard to square circles or make sense. Aurry and his friend Essam took us for dinner at the Boat Basin, where there was a strip of outdoor restaurants similar to Lahore's famous Food Street.

"Pakistan has more brain drain than any other country," complained Aurry when we sat down. "And it's really a sorry sight. And if we don't do something about that, who will?"

"But there are some people who don't want too many people to think with their brains," I said.

"Those are people who like capitalism," said Essam. "Most of the things that you see on TV, that is propaganda. It's not as bad as they show. And that is because that is how they win and we lose. Whatever they fear, that is what they implement here."

"Who's they?"

"Anybody who supports capitalism. Capitalism is a man-made system," he clarified. Essam was very actively involved in his father's business and savvy about the national and global economies, so I wondered at this. But he seemed to be groping toward a distinction between Western capitalism and business run on principles he could appreciate and endorse as Islamic.

On the way back from dinner, Essam showed me a text message joke on his phone: "65 yrs back, a nation was looking for a piece of land. And now a piece of land is looking for a nation." And Aurry played Sindhi folk music for us on the car CD player. "In this song he's singing about this girl that he loved," he translated. "But now she's marrying someone else, and he's saying that all I can do is pray for you. Sindhi music is different. It has a lot of acoustic beats. And the vocals are very loud."

Essam offered to show us the chicken farm he ran for his father outside Karachi. "Have you had breakfast?" he asked when he picked us up early the next morning. "I'm hoping you haven't."

"We haven't had breakfast yet," I said.

"Good. We'll stop at Dunkin' Donuts."

"I gather they must have coffee at Dunkin' Donuts?" Coffee wasn't easy to come by in Pakistan, or anywhere in Asia for that matter. In private homes and even hotels, one usually had to make do with tea or Nescafe.

"They do. Have you had Krispy Kreme donuts?"

"I have." Whenever anyone mentioned Krispy Kreme I thought of my friend Lenny Miller, who had written, in his book about his adventures as a black team owner in NASCAR, that the driver for an opposing team sponsored by Krispy Kreme looked like he had had his fair share of donuts.

"I had Krispy Kreme donuts in Dubai, and I thought they were way better than Dunkin' Donuts," said Essam.

I asked what he thought of Dubai. I had never been outside of the airport there, and I kept hearing all sorts of stories.

"The concept behind Dubai is very nice," he said. "It's like a meeting place for everybody. So I believe it should have a correction from the bearish situation now."

Essam's farm was a good hour's drive out of the city center, so we had plenty of time to play the Pakistani parlor game of fixing the country in theory. "Education is part of the solution in Pakistan, and it's part of the problem," said Essam. "Because the people who are educated are the ones who are causing corruption."

"Mr. Ten Percent," I said.

"But it's not just him. Everybody in the country wants to be Mr. Ten Percent. It's just that he got the opportunity, and that's what bothers them. So the key is to educate the rest. That's why the media is playing a really important role: It's educating people."

The transformation of the Pakistani media was one of the most astonishing and encouraging stories of the Musharraf era. In 1999, the year Musharraf overthrew Nawaz Sharif—who had picked a fight with the country's largest media group—state-run and little-watched PTV was still the only news channel on television. Now there were many, and they were independent and assertive and widely watched not only in Pakistan but worldwide. They also were crucially supportive to the lawyers' movement. "The media was amazing," Ghazala Minallah had told me in Islamabad. "Because you see, they were also targeted. And whenever they were targeted, we'd be out on the streets with them also, in their support. And they believed in this cause, because an independent judiciary means that no one can mess with the media."

When I interviewed Azhar Abbas, managing director of Karachi-based Geo News, the most popular and influential of the new independent channels, I asked him whether Musharraf deserved credit for the flowering of free media that happened during his rule. "I would give a lot of credit to Musharraf, actually," he replied. "It's always easy to say that, you know, we struggled for it, and we achieved this. Probably even I will be making a speech at a journalists' trade union, I would say that also. But to be perfectly honest, yes we have struggled a lot, but Musharraf made a conscious decision. And Musharraf freed the media not just because he believed in freedom of the press, but also he felt that for the agenda that he was carrying, to liberalize Pakistan a little, it was very important to actually free the media."

Musharraf, Ghazala had said, "was so full of himself that he never believed that it would turn against him. They shut down all the channels in the beginning of the emergency. Then the sellers of these dishes were having a whale of a time. At ten times the price, they were selling them! When they shut down the channels, they shut them down just because of some specific programs and some specific hosts, anchors on those programs. All of those anchors started having their shows in public. This was outside the Press Club, near Aapbara [in Islamabad]. It was a wonderful idea; they used to have it on a daily basis. And all the people who used to sit at home watching them came out!"

"The media in the last year or year and a half was very critical of Musharraf," Azhar Abbas agreed. "But then Musharraf also lost the plot. Why was he there, the last year or so? He should have quit at that point. He was just dragging his feet unnecessarily. But yes, it was Musharraf. And I think I have not seen a leader with such tolerance. Musharraf was not that vindictive, as compared to some of our political leaders. He actually allowed a lot of criticism of himself. He absorbed so much. I've seen him fuming during interviews, and after the interview he was just like normal. We interviewed Benazir Bhutto once, and she got furious and she just threw off the mike. On camera! There have been so many instances where Nawaz Sharif and others have also said that, 'No, I'm not going to answer this question.' Musharraf never said that. So you have to give him that credit."

"Most of the Pakistani channels are news channels," Essam was complaining to me now. "They hardly have any entertainment. So people have to go out to get entertainment."

"Why don't the channels have entertainment?"

"The news channels, they have a lot of criticism, and the criticism is their entertainment. There are a few drama channels. But they don't make you laugh. It's so depressing." There were some "Oprah-type shows" and cooking shows, he said. "Pakistani ladies love to cook. That's what makes them a complete lady."

We wanted to make a long day trip or, if possible, an overnight trip out of Karachi, but our time was limited. "If you had time on you, we would go to Balochistan," said Essam. "We would go to Gwader seaport, and we would see the Hingol National Park where you can see deer, and there are volcanoes that glow in the dark. There are Hindus that live there, and they put the remains of their deceased in the volcanoes, and there's a lot of phosphorous in the ashes, and they glow, especially when there's a full moon."

We had to settle for visiting his chicken farm. "Pakistan's second-largest industry is the poultry industry," said Essam. "First largest is the textile industry. Poultry supplies two percent of the GNP of Pakistan, and there's a rough estimate that it contributes ten to twelve percent towards the employment of Pakistan. Karachi's land is very expensive. You cannot do business here until and unless you have a lot of money. Or you have to take land on rent." His family held a 30-year lease on the land, and a group of poultry farmers were negotiating with the government to convert the lease. They wanted to take advantage of the excellent location near the port and the superhighway to build a bonded warehouse.

"Do you have concerns about things like avian flu?" Pete asked him.

"Yes, we take preventive measures. We give vaccines to our birds."

"Is this part of why you want to get out of chicken farming?"

"No, it's a very profitable business. We've been in the business for forty years. Higher the risk, higher the reward. We're in an oligopolistic situation now." They had 400,000 birds, seventy percent of which laid eggs on any given day. "You see these warehouses? They're all new. They're for rice. Pakistan's biggest rice mill is over there."

Essam reflected on the situation of business people while he drove us around. "This is a country where people keep a very low profile," he said. "There's a list that came on Yahoo that had the one hundred richest men in the world. And there were people from countries around the world on the list, but no Pakistanis. And someone who was Pakistani wrote a letter saying, 'Why are there no Pakistanis on the list?' And I would not be surprised if there were Pakistanis in the top ten of that list, but they don't disclose their wealth. It's not white money; it's all in the parallel economy. People here are extremely courteous. And the more richer you get, the bigger heart you have. These are my farm lands. These are carrots. The government never built this bridge. So the industrialists got together and said, 'Let's build the bridge.' Karachi is an industrial city, but the industries, they are making their own energy. Because we have energy crisis here in Pakistan." Passing a group of dump trucks—"dumpers," he called them—he said: "A truck like this would cost around six million rupees. That's around $80,000. And you would get your costs back in about a year and a half."

The bailing out of the banks in the United States led me to ask Essam about Islamic finance and banking in Pakistan. "Islamic banking is actually more popular in the UK than it is here, because Islamic banking never posed a threat to the West," he said. "What is a threat is the Islamic economic system, because it totally opposes the capitalist system. Now the stock market of Pakistan has stopped margin financing. It's called *badla* here. Now you have to buy on delivery basis. That's called spot buying. Margin financing is why the Pakistan stock market has suffered more than any other. But for four years consecutively, this market was the best-performing stock market of the world.

242

Pakistani stock market has stopped all financial instruments, like future markets and swaps and margin financing. That's why it's recovering at a better pace than any other market. None of the Pakistani banks have come even to the verge of bankruptcy. Because they don't just give loans easily. You have to have something in your hands to get loans. And mortgage-backed financing is very difficult in Pakistan. And this is why one of our biggest banks, MCB—that's Muslim Commercial Bank—was bought by a Malaysian company. They see that there's lots of potential in the country."

We returned across the city the fast way, on the new elevated freeway. There was little traffic on the freeway, and we actually stopped and got out of the car to take pictures. "This bridge was built over the sewage," Essam told us. "So the land was free. People just wanted to live somewhere, so they built their houses." He pointed toward the ocean and said: "Sea is one of the beaches. The sand is like clay, and it really sticks to your feet. That's where everybody comes." We could see some birds circling in the distance. "Seagulls?" I said.

"They're not seagulls."

"Hawks," said Pete.

"There's a dead dog over there," said Essam. "That's why."

＊ ＊ ＊

"You will be able to meet all kinds of people," Mahera had told me on the phone. "It's another part of Karachi that even people living here don't get to see. Waterfront development is like a big issue in Karachi. The fisherfolk communities have been protesting against the authorities."

Mahera Omer was a documentary filmmaker and a friend of Tahereh Sheerazie, a woman I had met in Southern California. Tahereh and her husband had put me up on a visit there, and she had recommended Mahera as someone who could show us around out-of-the-way Karachi neighborhoods. The two women had walked around Karachi together. "Everywhere we went, we met so many interesting people. And they all have stories, sad stories," Mahera said. Tahereh was a walker; she had hiked from Pakistan into China to attend a wedding, and she had urged me to bring my hiking shoes to Pasadena. I figured anyone she put me in touch with was likely to be similarly interesting.

It was another early morning for us. Mahera picked us up outside the guest house in an SUV with her mother and aunt. "These two haven't been to the island themselves, even though they live here," she said.

"Well, I'm glad to be the occasion for you to see it," I said.

"We are tourists in our own country, thanks to you," said the aunt.

"I had to drag them out of bed," Mahera said. "Because with all the weddings going on, they're staying up till six in the morning. So last night I made them go to sleep at four."

The women were from that class of Pakistani society where everyone knows everyone else. When I asked for some reason whether she had heard of Ahmed Rashid, author of the widely read books *Taliban* and *Descent into Chaos*, Mahera replied, "He's my uncle."

"Small world," said Pete with a smile.

"Everybody is connected here," said Mahera.

"Unfortunately our city is very filthy and dirty," said her mother.

"Well, it's a huge city," I remarked.

All three women wore jaunty hats against the sun. We parked on the waterfront and stepped into a small boat.

"Those are the navy boats," said Mahera. "There's a guy who sits at the top of the lighthouse with a notepad and binoculars. And his job is to note the number of every ship that comes in. And with his binoculars he can see everything. One guy told us that foreigners have to register. And another guy told me that they don't. So I said let's go quickly."

The boat dropped us on a small island where a fishing community lived. As we wound through a narrow alley on the island, we saw a toothless old woman dishing out food in tiny bowls to several eager small children.

"You see the female doing business?" Mahera's mother asked me.

"She just cooks the food and brings it out?"

"Yes. That should be the spirit!"

"This is a fortune-teller," said the aunt. "You give him some money, he puts it on a picture and tells your fortune. These are the small entrepreneurs of Pakistan."

"The way I look at it, it's quite pathetic the way our government has criminally neglected our country," the mother tut-tutted. She pointed out some unremarkable-looking shacks with roofs made of red tile. "All the red-roofed buildings are pre-Partition." Sure enough, individual tiles were marked with dates: 1936, 1865. "They sell all these then. I wish there were a society to preserve these. It's too late now." In the water below us floated little rafts made from scraps of styrofoam gathered together in a net.

We stepped into a local family's home: a single wooden room on stilts, over the water.

"Do they have any problems when there are storms?" asked Pete.

"Yeah, the villages that are closer to the sea are on stilts," said Mahera. "And once in a while they do get washed away. It's not that rough here in the monsoon, because these are the backwaters, and the mangroves. It's so polluted now, but at one point they could catch fish here. Out of this window exactly, they would hang a fishing line and catch fish."

"Where do they get their drinking water?"

"After forty years they got drinking water. It was a community effort, and now they have pipes. But before that they had to cart water in on boats."

"How long has he been fishing?" Pete asked.

"Thirty years. Since generations." The island was called Baba Island, and its community was about three hundred years old. Its current population was about 10,000.

"How is the fishing these days?"

"The season has just started."

"How about last year's season?"

"About twenty years ago or so, they would go just one nautical mile and catch. Now they have to go forty nautical miles, one hundred nautical miles. These boats, they go out two hundred nautical miles, and they stay out ten days." It took six or seven hours to get that far out. "To get to deep sea which is about six hundred feet, it takes them twenty-four hours to get out. Most of the smaller boats here catch the small fish, which is known as garbage fish, because it's fed to the poultry. They also take the young. There are a lot of illegal nets. The other fisherman we interviewed said the foreign trawlers take most of the fish."

At the school, Mahera's mother quizzed the *nazim* or mayor. "Ever since they got piped water, that's when they started coming to school," Mahera told us. "He's saying they believe in girls coming to school. Most of these conversations between Pakistanis tend to be about 'Why is this place such a mess?' That's why there's no sense of community here. People just feel different from each other."

"Is she interrogating him?"

"She's saying, 'Why don't you get a bin and gather all the garbage?'"

From the island we got in another boat for a tour of the nearby mangrove forest and a floating picnic. "These mangroves are chopped illegally." She gave us a mangrove leaf to taste; it was salty. "If you feed these leaves to a cow, the milk will be salty," she said.

"That's all you get," said her mother. "That's your lunch."

Actually, we were well stocked: Skittles, M & Ms, Snickers, gum, soda pop, coffee and tea, omelette rolls, and biryani in Tupperware. "Biryani's my favorite dish," said Mahera. "And it's good cold also."

As we floated around, we saw evidence that the mangroves had been cut. When we saw other boats, the women asked the men on them whether they were cutting the mangroves. "Same question: 'Do you cut wood?'" Mahera translated. "No, we catch crabs.' They're Bengali. A lot of Bangladeshis go on the fishing boats. Crabs from here go to Thailand, Singapore, Japan. In Japan, catching of crabs is banned for forty years."

"So they get crabs here instead?"

"Yeah. From here Pakistani prawns and fish are sent to Dubai. And in Dubai they're stamped 'Made in Dubai' and sent to Europe. Because EU has banned Pakistani prawns, because of pollution."

I asked if the Bengalis had come here before 1971, when Bangladesh broke away from Pakistan after a bloody war with India. "A lot of them have come since, I believe, because the Pakistan rupee was stronger," she said. "But they're not issued ID cards. There are many without cards. They're here illegally. But they were born here."

"You see, they came to Pakistan to work as domestic help," said her mother. "People are lazy to get their ID cards. And they are afraid."

"They all applied, but some got them and some didn't," added Mahera. "He says if they roam around in the city beyond their areas, the police always catch them and harass them. They are born here, but the authorities say you are Bangladeshi, you are not Pakistani. Their parents came."

"But the children didn't go back?"

"They cannot, because they don't have ID cards."

A local man from the fishing village had come with us in the boat. "He says when he was young, the huts that we could see from the top, he couldn't see those huts because the trees were so tall," Mahera told us. "Now they're just little bushes. Chemical waste, industrial waste, it's all coming here. It'll take five years at least for something to start growing. In the winter a lot of migratory birds come here. So this is full of birds in the winter. So we're destroying their habitat."

"Plastic bag is a big reason of pollution," said the man.

"They go fishing, and they dig up from the bottom, and they bring up plastic bags," said Mahera.

"I think the worst thing that was ever invented was the plastic bag," said Pete.

We lingered on the water and talked, while Pete photographed the mangroves and the birds. This was Pete's Pakistan, his element. "Wow, that is a great shot," marveled Mahera's mother after he fired off a rapid-fire series of exposures. "The camera got all excited."

Pete smiled. "The person behind the camera." He pointed at some hawks. "There's a whole bunch in that tree right there."

"They've lived in Karachi all their lives, and this is the first time they've come here," Mahera said to me again about her mother and aunt, as if she were the one who should be grateful to us.

"Isn't it a big irony that in our schools we learn about River Thames, about geography of Germany?" said her aunt.

"They made us draw maps of Australia," remembered her mother.

I was curious about Mahera's work. In addition to her obvious passion for documentary filmmaking, she was an animal-rights activist. With her friend Maheen Zia she had founded the Pakistan Animal Welfare Society (PAWS)—"to create a more just and equitable relationship between humans and animals in Pakistan," as its website declares.

"Some relatives came from Canada for a wedding," she said, "and I ordered some books from Amazon, and I asked them to bring them for the PAWS library. Because the young vets here don't get good books. I'm going to write to every vet school in America and Canada, maybe Australia, and ask them to donate one book. I can't keep buying books myself, or I'll go broke."

"I'll make sure to get this into my book," I offered.

"I have to take time out to do the PAWS stuff. I'm supposed to rescue a donkey this week, but I have this Sunday deadline for my rough cut."

"So do you consider yourself more of an activist or an artist?"

"I guess what I can do is just a tool, to make people more aware of certain things. But I also enjoy the medium itself. I studied like biology, and I always wanted to be a vet. I ended up not going to veterinary school, but just majored in biology. So because I couldn't be a vet, I want to open up a good veterinary hospital, and employ other vets."

"So your dog thing is a continuation of your longstanding interest?" She wanted to make a documentary about Karachi street dogs. This was not unproblematic given the distaste, at best, that most Muslims feel toward dogs.

"Yeah. That's something I want to start doing. I'm really passionate about that. I want it to be about stray dog management. We have a lot of stray dogs in the city. The media is always reporting about rabies, and they sensationalize about rabies. And the result is always, 'Kill the dogs, kill the dogs.' It's usually on the people's complaints that the nazim gets all this poison, and they kill the dogs, and they publish photos in the papers. Urdu papers. They don't publish in the English papers, because I think they know that people will go nuts. Killing dogs is not an effective way to deal with the problem. Killing them is a quick fix. We want to implement something that actually works. That's controversial also. I want there to be a debate. Dogs are very much part of our urban ecology, and it's part of population biology. We don't have an animal welfare association in this city, like many cities in India do. So my documentary will be about the miserable life of our poor street dogs. And some nice things also."

The popular TV host Faisal Qureshi had invited her and Maheen on his show. "Very few people are brave enough to take this step, to talk about such things in the media," she said. "Because they consider it a non-issue. Except when it comes to rabies, and then people go ballistic. We got a lot of hate calls."

"Did you get positive calls too?"

"One positive call. A veterinarian from Peshawar. But others were like, 'People are dying, there are drone attacks, why are you talking about dogs?' Those are the stories that we want to tell, but politics keep going on. Nobody is interested in the environment, or wildlife, or other creatures that are miserable. These are the things that we want to fix. It's supposed to be a media boom, with more than eighty channels. But us poor documentary filmmakers—nobody is interested in documentaries."

Given that, I wondered how she made her living.

"If a foreign channel comes and wants to film about the Taliban, or visit a madrassa, then that's a day shoot, and that's good," she said.

"Are they only interested in Taliban and madrassas?"

"Yes, that's all they're interested in. The only things I see about Pakistan are just Taliban stuff. Which is annoying. They'll go to India and do the human-interest stories. When the lawyers' rally happened here, all the foreign channels were here. And they hire a lot of the local camera people, like me. And others went, but my family went ballistic, so I refused. Teams from abroad will come, and they will want to hire local filmmakers, because they themselves can't come here because it's not safe, or their channels won't let them. Then they send you out to do their work."

"What do they send you to do?"

"They're like, 'Go and film a rally.' But even male cameramen sometimes won't go, because their mothers fear for them. They don't want to come back dead. They love rallies, refugee camps, madrassas. You film one madrassa, you've filmed them all. You interview one maulvi, you've interviewed them all. They're all crazy."

Related to the dog problem was the garbage problem, and that was another subject Mahera wanted to tackle on film. "We need to fix the garbage situation, and the poor dog situation. If you want to catch a stray dog, you need a cage," she added.

"How do you catch them?"

She smiled. "With great difficulty. A lot of the stuff I make ends up being about shit, quite literally. I'm just concerned about what a dirty city it is. Twenty million people, we don't have any treatment plants. People don't even know about the garbage, what happens to it. I like to shoot with a small group, because I also shoot myself. And for an assistant I often take my servant along."

"Does he enjoy it?"

"Yeah, because he gets out of the house. So usually there are three of us, plus the driver. And usually also some local people. Sometimes the call is for five o'clock, which means they have to get to my house at five. So sometimes we'd get tired and we'd say come and sit in the car. And munchies. Munchies are very important. Sometimes my mother gets upset because I take the servant, and housework doesn't get done. But I'd rather take him than hire someone. Because it's really hard to get good workers."

"That's the whole logistical side of filmmaking, I guess," I said.

"Yeah, yeah. And that's fun too. I always get my cook to cook the food; it's always home-cooked food."

"So you're like a quartermaster."

"Yeah. Filmmaking is just a little bit of it."

Tahereh Sheerazie, our mutual friend in Pasadena, had urged me to ask her about an incident that had happened to the two of them one morning when they were out exploring Karachi. "We were in Punjab Colony, which is next to Defence Housing Authority," Mahera told me. "It's next to Sunset Boulevard, which is one of the main arteries. Sunset Boulevard stinks, because of these garbage trucks. And the trucks are open, and they're dripping with crap. So you really have to plug your nose. So one morning in search of the bread factory, Tahereh and I stumbled upon Punjab Colony. And we would go with my dog, Chelsea."

"And Chelsea is intrepid and doesn't mind going out on the street?" I asked. Pet dogs on the street were not a common sight in Pakistan.

"Chelsea is a springer spaniel, and even though she's a small dog, she loves her walks, and she loves discovering our neighborhood. And our goal was to have breakfast with strangers, to get to know our neighbors better. So we asked everyone on the way, 'Where is the bread factory?' We went through the Punjab Colony neighborhood. There was this car over there, with two cats sitting on the roof. And we're like, 'That's a nice shot.' So we whip out our cameras. And Tahereh's got the camera, and she's taking a picture of these cats on the car.

"And suddenly from behind us, this maulvi pops up. And he's like, 'What are you doing?' And we turn around, and we say, 'Excuse me, who are you?' And he says, 'I am university recognized!' In English—he's talking in English. And we are replying in Urdu. And he says, 'Do you have an NOC?'" A no objection certificate. "And we're like, 'No. We need an NOC to take pictures of cats?' He says, 'I have been to Rome, I have been to Paris, and they wouldn't let me take pictures there.' He was being really weird. He said, 'You can't take pictures here, because I couldn't take pictures abroad.' He said, 'You keep your freedoms to yourself.' We said, 'We are Pakistani also. We live here. We live across the boulevard.' They think of you as foreign. He was speaking in English. His English was sort of okay, and we were replying him in Urdu. But for some reason he felt very threatened."

"Why do you think he felt threatened?"

"Because I think people from different communities or different areas feel that they're very different from each other. Maybe they don't know each other; that's why they feel threatened. We do live in different worlds. There's no sense of community. So he feels he's Pakistani; I feel I'm Pakistani. We're all Pakistanis, but we still don't connect. What's going to bring us together, I don't know. Because we were two women and one guy. We did have a Canadian with us, a white Canadian journalist. Maybe because we also had a dog with us. So they think, 'Oh, these dog-walking people in Defence.' And then he realized that he was talking to women, and he said, 'I'm not talking to you,' and he disappeared inside a house.

"So then we reached the bread factory, and the bread factory people were very nice." It was a certain kind of crisp bread, "the bread that poor people eat. You won't find it in posh areas. Even in my neighborhood you won't find it, except at this one particular place. The Parsee people eat this bread. So these people let us inside the bread factory, and they even let the dog inside. It was a very dirty, skanky kind of place. Very dark, greasy. There was bread everywhere."

The bread had failed to expunge the bad taste in her mouth left by her encounter with the maulvi. "How am I supposed to love my neighborhood if my neighbor is being such an idiot?" she said. "I went all the way to his neighborhood to find bread, which was being supplied in my neighborhood. How can there be any understanding if we don't accept each other? We're like, 'We're never going back there again.' You know you're not very welcome."

* * *

We returned to shore late in the afternoon, and that evening we had a commitment at an event put on outdoors (but behind walls) at the Arts Council. The Shanaakht Festival was a project of a group called the Citizens Archive of Pakistan, which was also undertaking a much-needed oral history project capturing the country's history, particularly the crucial and increasingly remote moment of Partition, through interviews, photographs, and memorabilia that would otherwise have been lost. Before coming to Karachi I had asked the journalist Beena Sarwar if there were any venues where I might be able to give a talk. Beena had been a friend for a decade, through many projects and transitions in my career and hers. For a while she had been op-ed page editor of the English daily *The News*, where she took me on as a columnist. I solicited and included her essay "The Hijacking of Pakistan" in a collection I published after the World Trade Center attack. "Television viewers in the USA, fed on images of fierce, bearded men chanting 'death to America,' may also find it surprising that ordinary Pakistanis don't hate Americans," she had written in late 2001. "The roots of the anti-Americanism are not envy, as President Bush has suggested, but resentment of U.S. policies abroad, of which the American public is largely unaware." She had been a Nieman Fellow at Harvard University, where she had invited me to be a panelist at a seminar she convened on democracy and human rights in Pakistan. We had also met in London, in Seattle just after I arrived there, and previously in Karachi, where she had invited me home for dinner with her parents. I saw Beena as an exemplar of Pakistan's perpetually besieged but energetic and talented liberal elite, and she was a great person to know, because she knew everybody. It was Beena who had first introduced me to Isa Daudpota, for example. Through her friend Sabeen Mahmud, who was involved with The Second Floor, a coffee house committed to "intellectual poverty alleviation," Beena had arranged for me to speak in T2F's space at the Shanaakht Festival.

I was in the middle of my talk and, frankly, it wasn't going all that well—my exhaustion was taking a toll on my coherence and enthusiasm—when I began hearing a ruckus from somewhere behind the audience. I was standing in an open tent in the courtyard of the Arts Council, not far from one of the entrances through the wall to the street. Nearby tents hosted other events and exhibits. Before my talk I had sat in briefly on a panel discussion with one of Pakistan's early cricket heroes and purchased a Citizens Archive coffee mug, but I had not had time to visit any of the other tents. My audience of 75 or so people was turned toward me, so what they could hear was my amplified voice. What I could hear was the shouting coming from behind them. Distracted, I stepped away from the microphone to try to see beyond the audience, and it's then that I remember the crowd running toward me from the far corner of the courtyard.

The next thing I remember is a young woman saying, "Come with me, please. Please leave everything and come with me. He's a guard with guns. Please go with him." Turning to the guard, she said: "We have the responsibility."

"Come this way," he said to me.

I lost a few moments unplugging my laptop and grabbing my notebook because, riot or no riot, I wasn't going to leave them behind. Then the guard hustled us toward a door while the crowd milled and surged around us. Then Sabeen was with us, explaining breathlessly: "There's an exhibition over here, an art exhibition, and I think it's pretty stupid, but they've done a poster called 'A Stiff Competition,' and—it was a caricature—but it showed Benazir sitting on Musharraf's lap. And so it was the PPP that came in pitching a fit. And I really don't think people should push boundaries like that, because now I think the festival is ruined on its first day. Because this is going to be in the papers." The Pakistan People's Party was the party of Benazir Bhutto and her husband, Asif Ali Zardari, who was now Pakistan's president. I never saw the poster, and from descriptions I heard it was never clear whether it was Musharraf's or Zia ul Haq's lap Benazir had been depicted sitting on but, either way, what was clear was that it had caused offense.

"Guys, I think we should leave," said Beena. "Come with me. My car's outside."

"Was it something you said?" Pete joked to me. "Hmm. It's kind of unfortunate. I wanted to look at some of the artwork."

But it was decided that it wasn't yet safe for us to try to leave, so instead we were spirited into a low room, where a guy with a ponytail stood watch by the door. I sat there, reflecting on the fact that the door was the only way in or out of the room, until Pete had the presence of mind to turn off the light so we couldn't be seen through the windows. There was another door in the back of the room, but it led to a storeroom with a low dormer roof, which our new friend checked out with a cigarette lighter.

"Excuse me," he said. "If the next time public hyper, you go in here."

"Thank you," I said. I wasn't sure I liked the idea, though.

"Now it is okay. Next time. I am here, *inshallah*. It is my duty."

The ruckus was continuing right outside, well within earshot. Eventually, someone decided that, even if the coast wasn't clear, the moment was more propitious, and we were spirited back outside. Sabeen was there, talking on her cell phone. "*Aachchaa*," she was saying. Good. "We're taking them out through the other gate."

A small lady of a certain age took my hand and led us toward the rear of the compound. "When you started speaking," she said in a kindly tone, "I realized that I had met you at Beaconhouse guesthouse."

"I had good times there," I said.

"Step lightly, dear," she said to Pete. "Please come."

The lady took us to her car outside the compound on the street. Then it was decided that we would go in Beena's car instead, and we walked along the sidewalk, glancing sidelong at the cars and trucks passing us on the road.

"They're saying, 'Hand her over to us so we can lynch her,'" said Sabeen, referring to the young woman who had made the poster. "People have been irreverent before, but it's become such a difficult country now."

"The problem is, artists are so disconnected from the public," said Beena. "This is probably the first time they were exhibiting their work. I was afraid at first that these were people who were favoring Zia ul Haq. In which case they would probably have started firing by now. But they did grab a security guard's gun. I didn't want to leave without you guys."

"We appreciate it," said Pete.

"This is the sort of thing you associate with Jamaat-i-Islami or the MQM. But Benazir's dead now."

Beena's mother, whom I knew as a distinguished retired educator, was with us. "And they should have had more security," she said.

"Is there any chance that these are not PPP people?" I asked.

"N-no," said Beena. "Because the guy I was talking to … But he wasn't in the central group. So yes, there is a chance. And the scary part is that they were asking for the artist to be delivered to them. And somebody said, 'I don't care if she's a woman. She should have thought of that when she made the picture.'"

"Two wrongs don't make a right," said Beena's mother. "Somebody said to me, 'Bhaji, why don't you go?' I said no, because we have guests. And he said, 'Ladies?' And I said, 'No, men.' And he said, 'They can take care of themselves.' And I said, 'No.' And I didn't say any more than that."

We were safe now, in Beena's car on the way to her house, where we talked until she drove us back to our guesthouse, on her way to help draft a statement for the press about the incident. Pete and Beena had both seen a car drive past, flying the PPP party flag and carrying a man who was glaring angrily at us. "I was a little concerned at that moment, but anyways," said Pete.

"We were really vulnerable when we were in that room," I said.

"Yeah, well, yeah," he agreed.

* * *

"Sorry to get so into politics so early in the morning," I said to Aurry Marri and his pals in the van, on the way to the village.

"No, it's all good," said Essam. "We're used to it."

Essam and another young man named Abdullah were with us. It was our last full day in Pakistan, and we were making the most of it by accepting Aurry's invitation to make a day trip to his family's village in the rural interior of Sindh province. We had picked up a copy of *The News* on the way out of town and, sure enough, there was the story on the front page, above the fold:

PPP workers disrupt Shanakht festival
By Asadullah

KARACHI: Armed persons stormed the Arts Council, ransacking the Shanakht Festival 2009, which had begun on Wednesday afternoon. Eyewitnesses claimed that the armed men opened fire and threatened to kill the organisers for their alleged "political blasphemy" in the artistic realm.

It all started perfectly well for the second edition of the four-day festival organised by the Citizens Archives of Pakistan (CAP), but the sunset descended like doom. ... According to organisers, armed men scaled the walls of the Arts Council and were highly enraged over a painting. "Initially they objected to the painting and we agreed to pull it down, however they resorted to firing," said Sanam Meher, one of the organisers. "We had to run for cover as they started ransacking the exhibition area and displaced paintings and the TV." ...

Provincial Information Minister Shazia Marri, who visited the crime scene, deplored the incident. ... Meanwhile, in a late-night statement, the Citizens Archives of Pakistan said: "One part of this very large festival was to invite contributions in any form from Pakistanis. One of the contributions has offended some persons. Thus we sincerely apologise and have removed it. Our intention was to celebrate a rich history and create harmony and peace. We hope that tomorrow, the city of Karachi will support the festival and will come together to celebrate our country, our history, and our identity."

According to Aurry, his sister had "chewed out" the festival organizers and was not at all pleased.

Today's road trip was a microcosm of the journey as a whole: all too rushed and superficial, yet it was what we were in a position to do. I had never visited rural Sindh before, and Aurry's invitation gave me the opportunity to do that. We were asking too much of ourselves in terms of attention and mental, physical, and emotional stamina, getting on the road at six a.m. after having been caught in a minor riot the night before, and we wouldn't get back to Karachi until late tonight. But this was what we had been doing for six weeks; it was why we were here. There would be leisure later to absorb and articulate it all, to give the trip a measure of narrative coherence. It was time now for the trip to be over. Pete had a job he had to get back to, and I had a life back in what GIs in Vietnam used to call the world; I could begin to write only after I had stepped away from the fire hose of direct experience that was Pakistan. Tomorrow we would be on an airplane. But today, we were still on the road.

The village was three or four hours away, on a crowded highway stretching into the interior, past factories and colorful Pakistani trucks shipping goods and produce to and from the Punjab and Lahore. The landscape was flat and unlovely and blighted with dust and concrete, Aurry's driver was as reckless as Jawad Iqbal's had been along the Grand Trunk Road, and it was still awfully early in the morning.

"We want American scholars to do justice to us," Abdullah was saying. "Pakistanis laugh when you attack us with drones, and then your senators talk about establishing a relationship with the people of Pakistan and not with the government." Abdullah was just nineteen, several years younger than Aurry and Essam, but he held his own in conversation. He was thin and wispily bearded, extremely well-read and literary (he recommended Nadine Gordimer's novel *The Pickup* and gave me a book of poems), intense and thoughtful and earnest and thin-skinned. We had met him a few days earlier at Aurry's house, where he had grilled me about my intentions and about America. I liked him a lot.

"This is the first time in the history of Pakistan that the army is going against the U.S.," said Essam. "I don't know why, but they just don't want to meet anybody from the U.S." Ambassador Richard Holbrooke and Admiral Mike Mullen were in Pakistan trying to have meetings, and ISI chief Ahmed Shuja Pasha was rumored to have refused to meet with them. "Yesterday people had a lot of issues with Holbrooke saying that India has to become the leader in the fight against terror. Because they say we are the ones who have suffered, we are the ones who have sacrificed the most. That's it. That's the end of the relationship." He turned to Abdullah: "I have serious issues with the master-slave thing that you said. Because there are two kinds of people who are the most sensitive: the most powerful, and the most weak. I am not in favor of the army or of military coups. But I would like to know what have been the developments in these democratic—*so-called* democratic—governments."

I let the conversation wash over me as we hurtled down the highway. On our right loomed the enormous Lucky Cement factory, like something from a Pink Floyd album cover. "It's the biggest cement company in Pakistan," said Essam in a tone of admiration.

"It's like a goddamn town in there, it's so big," said Aurry.

They caught me scribbling in my notebook. "Ethan! Are we going to find our names in your new book?" asked Aurry in a playful tone.

"Wait and see," I said.

"Let me write a foreword for it," said Abdullah.

"We're waiting to become famous at the hands of Ethan Casey," said Aurry.

I was finding myself more interested than I had ever been before in Benazir Bhutto, and Aurry and his friends gave me a little laboratory for seeing her from angles that hadn't been available to me before. Most of my previous Pakistani experience had been in the Punjab, where Benazir's bitter rival Nawaz Sharif and his brother Shahbaz ruled the roost, and my perspective on Benazir had been shaded by my having first visited Pakistan in 1995, during her second disappointing stint as prime minister and years after the charm and novelty of her righteous return as Z.A. Bhutto's daughter, come to avenge her family and nation for the depredations of the evil dictator Zia, had worn off. In 2003 my impeccably liberal Beaconhouse National University colleague Taimur-ul-Hassan had treated me to the following rant:

> Emotions were high because we had been through hell in Zia's days, and we thought Benazir Bhutto might be able to change things. She is so arrogant. She doesn't take any counsel. She thinks she is a wisdom unto herself. She could have opted to sit in opposition and wait her time [after the 1988 election], but she chose to compromise with the establishment. So where do we stand? Where do people like us stand, who thought she would take on the establishment? She cannot say anything to people of Pakistan. People of Pakistan brought that woman twice to power. People of Pakistan owe nothing to Benazir Bhutto. She turned out to be a weak woman, in fact. A weak, emotional woman. At least she could have organized the Pakistan People's Party at the grassroots level. There was not a party office in Lahore, when she was in power. Zardari is in fact Baloch. Zardaris are people who used to do business with these camels. [Zulfiqar Ali] Bhutto's picture is still in my wallet. But this woman is dishonest, corrupt, revengeful, reactionary, and incompetent. She may be a good opposition leader, but she cannot run a good government. If you talk about merit, I think Musharraf has served the interests of secular classes more than she did. She really disappointed us. She took that dream away from us.

By then Musharraf was in power, Benazir was back in exile—largely self-inflicted this time, as a result of the widespread corruption allegations against her and, especially, her husband—and she seemed a spent force. But always in the back of my mind was what Najam Sethi, the editor of *The Friday Times*, had said when I asked him if she could ever return to power: "Stranger things have happened." Pakistan was, after all, a country where strange things happened every day. "For somebody who has had the taste of power," Ghazala Minallah had told me in 2003, "for her to live in a flat in central London must be suffocating. She's far too ambitious ever to give up politics. The problem is that every time they come into power, the whole of their time is spent obliging their syco-phants and taking revenge on their enemies. And I can't imagine it would be any different next time."

But these were Punjabi perspectives on Benazir. The Bhuttos were Sindhis, and Sindh was the stronghold of the Pakistan People's Party. The Marris were ethnically Baloch but had been in Sindh for several hundred years, and Shazia Marri was an elected Member of the Provincial Assembly from rural Sindh. Benazir was seen very differently here.

In Islamabad we had met Isa Daudpota's friend Dr. Azizur Rahman Bughio, an old man who, after his retirement from the civil service, had been one of Benazir's speechwriters during her time in office. Like Isa and like Benazir, Dr. Bughio was Sindhi. "She always spoke in human terms, like her father," he told me. "Never talking of interests of the influential people, but of the interests of the lower people, of the commoners, of the poor peo-ple who were suffering at the hands of bureaucracy and ministers. And she used to, like her father, tell them to serve the people hon-estly, sincerely. 'They are the people; they can really one day make you or mar you. The power lies with them.' She was in many ways like her father. Till her death. You can see, she got the same mar-tyrdom as her father got. She lived like her father and died like her father.

"She was very bold like her father, courageous. People advised her not to come now: 'You remain outside.' But she didn't accept their advice. She said, 'No. I will go back, I will live among my people, serve them. Since we have fought for restoration of democracy, which now I can see will be coming *inshallah*, so elections will be held, and how can I remain outside at this stage? No.' So she came, and she met her martyrdom here in Rawalpindi. That was really a tragedy. A tragedy not for her family only and for the people of Sindh, but for the entire nation. Because she was sincere, and she had come this time with greater force and hope to serve them better."

"She seemed to be carrying all the hopes of the nation," I acknowledged.

"Really," he said. "And the people also had great faith in her. They were convinced, during that period when she was outside, that it was only she who could serve the people's interests, and who could effectively face the world. Because she could speak also. She could speak not only the language of the Europe and Western countries, but she could argue with them. As you know, she was very popular among the Western countries."

So, although I had always looked askance at her populist pretensions and at the free pass she got from the West, her return from exile and, even more, her death compelled new perspectives on the role she had played and might have played.

"I think she had become bigger than her father," Aurry was saying now.

"Do you think she grew while in exile?" I asked.

"Yes, I do."

"Yes, definitely she had grown," agreed Essam. "Because, you see, if you are away from your people, you have been away from your husband for so many years, you have seen your country in turmoil, you have seen your country disintegrate—it makes you mature to a certain extent, that so many years you have nothing to do but plan out what you're going to do next."

"She was using her global outreach to get back into the system," said Abdullah. "People here believe that [Z.A.] Bhutto died for antagonizing America. She died for apparently the opposite reason. That's what confuses me. What confuses me is that there were rumors of a deal, when Bibi was coming in. I don't know if there was or there was not. Condoleezza Rice was said to be the parent of that deal. I don't know. In the end, Bibi might have changed her opinion, as she did of Musharraf as well. She was very antagonistic towards Musharraf in the end."

"I agree," said Essam. "There must be a deal. But I make of this deal that they set up a trap for the rabbit, and the rabbit fell in the trap, and now she's with us no more."

"She used to roam around in England," said Aurry. "She used to walk around in England with her kids. She used to go to McDonald's, she used to go for walks. No one can do anything to her over there. They brought her to a place where she can be killed. And she was dead the day she came."

"But you know what she also was in England?" I said. "I think she was profoundly bored."

"She was!" he agreed. "Because this is where she found everything. This is where she belonged. Did you see the 18th October proceedings? Were you able to watch them on TV?"

"No."

"There was an ocean of people. And, you know, if you were in her place, you would have been the most proudest person on earth. 'This is where I belong, and I don't know what I was doing for so many years.'"

"She was the embodiment of—something," I suggested.

"And many people believe that People's Party has won because they got sympathy votes. I believe that if Bibi was alive, People's

Party would have swept even more. Because she was not going for her own constituency. She was not going for her own elections. She was working for every single member of her party. She was making trips, nonstop trips, from NWFP to Balochistan, Punjab, Sindh. She was making nonstop trips. You could see that even people who had been against her for so many years, this time around, I've heard them say, 'We see a changed leader.' And now those same people who were once against her, I've heard them say, 'If Bibi would have been here, the country would not be in such a bad state.' Even people who had been terribly against her."

"Yes, I agree with that as well," said Abdullah.

"She was so proactive," said Aurry. "She could just brisk through something and give you a whole summary of it within minutes. She was so proactive. You would email to her, you would receive a reply within two minutes, three minutes, four minutes. She was so proactive. She used to have a bad back, because she had to check out her email for hours."

"She was very young when she first came in," I observed.

"She was always in America's good books, right?" said Abdullah. "As compared to Nawaz. Nawaz was the bad guy. Nawaz is the guy who provided the world with an atomic Pakistan. And Bibi's the guy who, in a joint address to Congress, said in '89 I believe, 'We neither have, nor do we intend to make, nuclear weapons.' Bibi's that guy. That is why I disagree with her on policy. But had she been the prime minister today, it would have been a lot better."

"What about the relationship between her and Zardari?"

"It was a healthy husband-and-wife relationship," said Aurry.

"Let's not tell them the conspiracy theory," said Abdullah.

"I believe from what I've seen, the pictures that I've seen, whenever I've seen them together, I want to see a healthy relationship," asserted Aurry.

"Now it's said that, within the party, Zardari has a different team," said Abdullah. "I'm not saying there's anything wrong with it. Zardari has a different team, and Bibi had a different inner circle. Because party is ruled by trust. One thing that rules a party, that supersedes all other things, is trust. You have to be surrounded by people you can trust when the time comes."

"Relationships usually work on two things," said Essam. "Either understanding, or either love. If you don't have both things, there's absolutely no way that a relationship can be a healthy relationship. And in this case there was definitely no love, and I wouldn't be the only person saying that. When it comes to understanding ..."

"There are a lot of people who were close to them who believe that they had a very healthy relationship," said Abdullah.

"It's a silly argument," said Essam.

"Let's get on a different subject," I suggested.

"I do believe that she had become bigger than her father, because she had become more of a global figure," said Aurry. "I believe that she had outgrown her father."

"That may be a feminist's point of view," said Abdullah with a laugh.

"I believe that in the global world, and in the global situation in modern times, the exposure that she had gotten, she had become more prominent than her father," Aurry repeated. "For example, your friend wouldn't have called you up and told you that Zulfiqar Ali Bhutto had been hanged, but your friend called you up and said she had been killed."

"Maybe that's a good thing, maybe that's not a good thing," said Abdullah. "There is no doubt that Shahid Zulfiqar Ali Bhutto was a far, far bigger, and a greater, leader for the Pakistani nation. Because he's a person that actually represented the people of Pakistan, exactly the way they were."

"I'm not saying ..." Aurry tried to interject.

"I am just arguing the fact that he was a greater leader than his daughter. He was the teacher of his daughter."

"I'm not saying that she was a better leader than Zulfiqar Ali Bhutto," said Aurry. "I'm not saying that she was a better decision-maker than Zulfiqar Ali Bhutto. She had become more global; she had become more known."

"I don't know if that's a good thing," said Abdullah.

"I believe her name was bringing up more impact than her father's name."

"It's because of the timeline," said Essam. "I believe there was more media coverage in this time. If you go back, and you see the speech that Bhutto made ..."

"At the UN Security Council," said Abdullah.

"The speech is remarkable," said Essam.

"In seventy-one," said Abdullah. "Seventy-two or seventy-one."

"After the fall of Dhaka," said Essam.

"And he tore down that paper, the resolution," said Abdullah.

"I've seen coverages of it," said Essam, "And if you showed it a billion times, I'd watch it again and again. And he said that, 'Yesterday, my eleven-year-old son'—he was talking about Murtaza Bhutto—'my eleven-year-old son called me and said, "Father, we do not want to see you back here in Pakistan."' And everybody was silent at that point, at the UN Security Council. "If you are going to bring this paper back, then we do not want to see you back."'

"Wow," I said.

"And he's like, 'For four days that I've been here, you haven't secured any agreement. You've left us in a state where we would say, "Do what you like. Do what you like. Do whatever you like, or do whatever you want to do, and we'll see what you can do. Had you taken us to this position a lot earlier, we might have been party to what you were saying. But you never treated us well."' He was remarkable. The way he used to talk, the way he used to carry himself, he was a true leader. He was a person who was representing the people."

"You seem very sad," I said to all three of them. "You seem like you've really been affected by her, and by her death."

"I spoke to Shazia," said Aurry, "and she was like, 'Aurry, what will happen now?'"

"I really couldn't believe it," said Abdullah. "I was at a friend's house, and I had to spend the night at my friend's house, because of the riots. I seriously couldn't believe it the whole night."

"My sister Anny was talking on the phone with someone who was there, and there was suddenly a blast," Aurry continued. "And she said, 'What happened?' He said, 'Oh, there's a blast over here.' And she said, 'Bibi?' He's like, 'Well, she's okay.' He's like, 'There goes another blast. Now people are gonna say she's got this blast done, like everyone is saying she got the 18th October blast done.' That's what people were saying: 'She did the 18th October blast herself, so that she could get a vote of sympathy.' That's what most of the people said. Eighty to ninety percent of the people said that, that she has done it herself."

"That high a percentage?"

The others objected. "I would not agree," said Abdullah. "I would not agree."

They started shouting over each other.

"Aurry ..."

"You don't agree now, but if I would have spoken to you on 18th October, I'm sure you would have said ..."

"Aurry, I, Aurry, I ..."

"A lot of people said that! A lot, a lot ..."

"My mother used to say that, but I always ..."

"And I said this in their face, that she was not a party to that. And that's what Anny said. Anny said, 'There goes another bomb blast, and that's what people are gonna say, that she had this bomb blast done, and she's saved, and she's killed so many people, and look what she's done, and this and that and blah and blah.' Thirty minutes later she got a phone call. They said, 'Bibi's gone.' And five minutes later it was on the news."

"You know what bothers me?" said Essam. "And I think it bothers Bibi's kids as much as it bothers us. Perhaps even more than that, of course. Their father, the president, comes out and says, 'We know who killed Benazir Bhutto.' And if he does know that who killed Benazir Bhutto, then why not tell it to everybody? Why not put them to trial?"

"Zardari says this?"

"Yes! He came on the national television, and he said that, 'We know that who are the murderers. We know who killed Bibi.' If you do know who killed Bibi, then why don't you state your case? And this is the major disagreement that he's facing with his kids at this moment."

"With his kids?"

"Yes, at this very moment in time. Because his kids demanded, 'If you do know, why don't you tell us? Why don't you put them in trial? You are the head of state. You have a lot of powers. It's not very difficult to find out.'"

"Ron Susskind, I believe, wrote in his book that Musharraf told her on the telephone, 'Your security depends upon your relationship with me,'" said Abdullah.

"Bibi herself gave five names, right?" said Essam. "Those five names are suspects. At least what you can do is get them to talk about themselves, you know? Just hear their point of view. This is all what we are asking. There is nothing that has been followed up."

"Shit!" I cried abruptly, as the van driver slammed on the brakes. They all laughed nervously.

"It's okay, nothing, don't worry," Aurry assured me. "You're in safe hands. Don't worry."

"Well, that's nice of you to say," I said.

"But these bumps and these things come often. But *inshallah* nothing will happen. You're in safe hands, *mashallah*. Thank God."

"Thanks, Aurry."

"Ha ha ha. He has a habit of hitting brakes like this. Even if the car is like a hundred to two hundred meters away, he'll hit the brakes."

"But this time it wasn't," Essam pointed out. "I knew that I was safe, because I was all the way back."

"I think the car stopped," said Abdullah, meaning the car in front of us.

"But what about the people?" I asked.

"That's what I was concerned about."

"I mean the people who were there on the road. The people standing there."

"Yes, yes."

"*Mashallah* we all survived," I said. "Anyway, I've spent so much time in Punjab in the past, and I haven't been down here much at all before. So things can become very Lahore-centric. People tell me things like 'Lahore is the heart of Pakistan, Punjab is where everything that matters happens.' This is very much the attitude that a lot of people express up there."

"You need to understand that when People's Party comes into place, it's sort of backing for feudal lords," said Essam. "Whereas, when the leaders from the Punjab side come in, it's a backing for the industrialists. And it's the industrialists that make the country. It's the businessmen."

"And the chaudhrys," objected Abdullah. "The chaudhrys are the feudals of Punjab."

"I hope you guys are not tired," said Aurry, "because we're just about to reach, in the next thirty minutes."

"I'm not tired, but I am hungry," said Essam.

"Well, you have a Sindhi feast waiting for you," said Aurry. "Fried potatoes, fried okra, eggs, and paratha. You'll really like the house. My mom has given it a nice Sindhi touch. It's really Sindhi-ish on the inside."

We turned off the big highway and stopped at a roadside stand for what Aurry billed as special Sindhi sherbet. "This cools you from the inside," he said. "It's good to beat the heat."

I went to pee between the banana trees behind the stand.

"It's dangerous between the bananas," Essam warned me. "There are snakes."

"For real?"

"For real."

"Maybe there are terrorists too."

"No, there aren't."

Aurry's driver escorted me to the edge of the banana field. When I came out, he was waiting with a pitcher of water so I could wash my hands.

"My drive is good," he said as he poured. "Please don't upset."

As we drove on, the road was crowded and we had to go slowly because we were unable to pass. "The real reason it's difficult to get through is that the horn is not working," said Aurry. "So he cannot honk. So it becomes a bit difficult. Now the bumpy road starts. A bit of a bumpy road to the village." He called ahead to order omelettes made to our specifications. "My sister is going to do something to repair this road, because you can see that when the water rises up, it damages the road."

"Does the water go all the way over the road in the rainy season?" I asked.

"Sometimes."

"So your sister is the MPA for this area?"

"She's the MPA for this area, along with four or five other MPAs. But she's the most powerful because she's a minister right now. This is Bari Ammar High School. Bari Ammar was my grandmother, and my dad had it built on her name."

A billboard with Shazia's picture loomed above us as we entered the village, which was called Berani.

"I haven't told anyone that we're coming," said Aurry. "Because if I had told people that we were coming, there would have been a big rush." We drove in the gate into the house's courtyard and sat down inside the house. "The electricity is gone. It'll be back in a while."

"This is nice," said Essam. "Away from technology."

"We have technology," said Aurry a little defensively. "There's just no electricity at the moment."

The long day, and thus our action-packed six-week road trip, wound down uneventfully, not with a bang but with a lingering lunch and a bit of sightseeing. Aurry was a gracious, thoughtful host. He staged a cockfight for us, invited us to fire an AK-47 and an antique rifle, and gave each of us a length of printed cloth and a Sindhi *topi*. We went into the village and walked around the market. We got back in the van and drove to an impressively vast, bleak, silent expanse of flattened brick ruins. Amid the sea of crushed bricks stood part of one single-story structure, perhaps a temple or mosque. Idly climbing this, Abdullah slipped. "If it were America, I'd sue 'em," he joked.

"Maybe somebody should do *azaans* here," said Essam. The call to prayer. "That would be awesome!"

Pete took photos of the mosque and the well and all the bricks and the camels standing around nearby. "I just wish they had a story to go with it," said Abdullah.

"We'll put all these pictures on the Facebook," said Essam. "And I'll tag you."

"This had been attacked by many emperors," said Aurry.

"Maybe that explains the mosque," suggested Abdullah.

"Because Muslims were always a minority in this area," said Aurry. "I'll give you the exact name of this place, and you can look it up on the Internet. Because they don't tell you the exact story, they just tell you parts and parts and parts, what they know."

I willed myself to record dialogue in my notebook, but the sun and the lack of rest were sapping my will, and I lacked the mental stamina anymore to catch more than snatches. And I became self-conscious when Abdullah suggested that I was observing them like an anthropologist. He was right; I was. But, I wanted to object, I've been observing Pete in the same way for six weeks.

"I believe in a god," I overheard Pete say to Essam or Abdullah. "I'm not an atheist. I choose not to believe in any specific one. I was raised Catholic."

And I overheard Abdullah say to Pete: "You can always work on your photos later on PhotoShop."

"Uh, I don't do that," said Pete. "That's not legit."

"Ah, you are a great believer in pure art."

"Yeah."

"He does not believe in Benazir sitting with Zia ul Haq," said Essam.

"Oh, it's easy to take photos here," said Pete, "'cause there's just so much goin' on. There's so much life here."

ONLINE RESOURCES, FURTHER READING, ACKNOWLEDGMENTS

Talk about being overtaken by events: As I write these acknowledgments, the earthquake in Haiti has compelled me to start work on another book, not to mention having rendered rather startling the first paragraph of this one. The quake confirms the wisdom of acting rather than hesitating, and of documenting events and stories, because you never know—especially these days—how suddenly or drastically the context might change.

The blog is a wonderful invention that, when handled right, can turn a book from a static document into what any book should be: one voice in a dynamic, ongoing conversation. I invite you to follow my blog at **www.aliveandwellinpakistan.com**, where I try to write a new entry once a week, sharing stories that didn't make it into my books and reporting on my conversations with Pakistanis and others in my travels around North America. There's also a "Pete's Pakistan" feature highlighting Pete Sabo's photographs in glorious color, and an online store where you can support my work by purchasing *Alive and Well in Pakistan* and *Overtaken By Events*, by sponsoring copies to be given to schools and libraries, and by pre-purchasing the book on Haiti that I'm writing for spring 2011 publication, which will prominently feature the Pakistani-American community's response to Haiti's earthquake. The store also offers a selection of Pete's photos as 5.5″ × 4″ magnets featured in my No Fridge Left Behind program, whose goal is to put a nice picture of Pakistan on every refrigerator and metal filing cabinet in America. The website also includes my professional bio and travel and speaking schedule. If you'd like me to speak to your group, contact me through the website or email **ethan@ethancasey.com**.

I intend this book and its predecessor to be at once edifying and entertaining, on the spoonful-of-sugar principle. They're stories: subjective, contingent, suggestive, whimsical, anecdotal ("merely anecdotal," as a haughty scholar once taunted me), anything but definitive. If, as I hope, you feel moved to do the work of informing yourself more thoroughly about Pakistan, I recommend two books very highly: Ahmed Rashid's authoritative *Descent into Chaos: The United States and the Failure of Nation Building in Pakistan, Afghanistan, and Central Asia* (2008), and *Pakistan: Eye of the Storm* by veteran BBC correspondent Owen Bennett Jones. The substantially updated 2009 third edition of Bennett Jones includes a thorough account of the Musharraf era; the first edition (2003) features a fascinating blow-by-blow narration of the October 1999 coup that brought Musharraf to power. If you can get your hands on it, Emma Duncan's *Breaking the Curfew: A Political Journey through Pakistan* (1989) does for an earlier period something like what I've tried to do in my two books. I should add, although it's off-topic, that my friend Edith Mirante's *Burmese Looking Glass* (1992) is not only a classic of modern Asian travel writing but a model for me.

I've put off writing these acknowledgments until the last moment, paralyzed by the fear of omitting someone. Now that I'm out of time, I'm taking the easy way out by omitting everyone but a few. Jafer and Arshya Hasnain egged me on at just the right moment, on a cold day in Chicago in December 2008. Fawad Butt of Zeus Capital Advisers (**www.zeuscapitaladvisers.com**) has been my confidant, ally, public speaking and business partner, and above all friend through many permutations, since the day we met in November 2007. I cherish the adventures Fawad and I have shared in Washington,

San Jose, Denver, Pittsburgh, Toronto, and Fort Worth, and above all in the Dudes' Room in Chicago, though not yet in Pakistan. I look forward, *inshallah*, to many more. Pete Sabo (**www.petesabophotography.com**) was equally crucial and, in a way, this entire book is a tribute to him. There's little I could say about Pete that I haven't already said, except to emphasize that he has always been there when it counted. (As I write this, Pete is in Haiti.) And Jawad Iqbal was crucially hospitable and encouraging.

My parents, Judith and Dayle Casey, and my brother Aaron, are wonderful human beings who have always believed in me and my work. So are the rest of my family: Paul and Cindy Haralson, Kelly and Carolyn and Jeanene Rominger, Art and Elaine and Steve and Alison Haywood. Jenny's love and companionship have seen me through many dark nights of the soul, and we've enjoyed many adventures together, too. I find it impossible, anymore, to imagine journeying through life without such a buddy and best friend. Stefan is like a son to me; in a way, this book is written for him.

No ballplayer ever gets on base in a vacuum—what would be the point? My editor, Sharon Green, has been a rock of patience, good taste, thoughtful advice, availability, and encouragement. Page designer Barbara Swanson, printer Scott Morris, website guru Imran Arshad, conscripted proofreader Kate Myers, and cover designer Jason Kopec all were a pleasure to work with, to put it mildly. The fact that I intend to hire them all again for my Haiti book says it all. You should hire them, too. Their contact information is on this book's copyright page. I'm also grateful for the moral and intellectual support of Priti Ramamurthy, Jameel Ahmad, Sunila Kale, Julia Major, Christian Novetzke, Keith Snodgrass, and other colleagues at the South Asia Center at the Henry M. Jackson School of International Studies at the University of Washington, where I'm pursuing a master's degree and finally learning to speak, read and write Urdu.

Millions of readers and supporters know Greg Mortenson's Central Asia Institute (**www.ikat.org**), but not even he can do everything that needs doing in Pakistan. I urge readers for whom this book might have been a first introduction to the admirable nonprofits founded and funded by the resourceful U.S.-based Pakistani expatriate community to get to know them better. They include the Association of Physicians of Pakistani Descent of North America (**www.appna.org**), The Citizens Foundation (**www.tcfusa.org**), Developments in Literacy (**www.dil.org**), the Human Development Foundation (**www.hdf.com**), Impak: Pakistan Service Corps (**www.impak.org**), and Zindagi Trust (**www.zindagitrust.org**). If we really do care more about combatting terrorism than about scaring and titillating ourselves, we should support these groups that are quietly—too quietly; they need to be better known and more widely supported—bringing education, health care, and hope to Pakistan's large and young population. I'm setting aside 20% of the proceeds from this book's sales into a special fund to support them.

Finally, please read the joint statement published on January 13, 2010 by me and Todd Shea of CDRS Pakistan (**www.cdrspakistan.org**):

How Pakistanis Can Help Haiti—and Why
www.aliveandwellinpakistan.com/helphaiti/

And click on Todd's name at the top of that page to learn about his work in Pakistan from Adam Ellick's excellent *New York Times* article and video.

Ethan Casey
Seattle
February 18, 2010

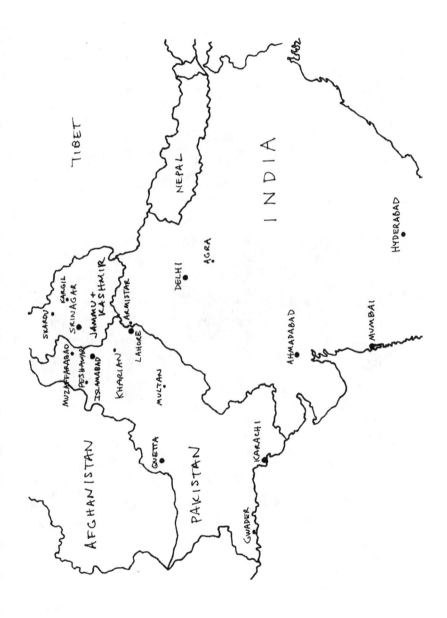

279